As I Knew Him

AS I KNEW HIM

My Dad, Rod Serling

ANNE SERLING

CITADEL PRESS
Kensington Publishing Corp.
www.kensingtonbooks.com

CITADEL PRESS BOOKS are published by

Kensington Publishing Corp.
119 West 40th Street
New York, NY 10018

Portions of chapters 1 and 36–42 first appeared in Salon, a Web site located at http://www.salon.com.

All Kensington titles, imprints, and distributed lines are available at special quantity discounts for bulk purchases for sales promotions, premiums, fund-raising, educational, or institutional use. Special book excerpts or customized printings can also be created to fit specific needs. For details, write or phone the office of the Kensington special sales manager: Kensington Publishing Corp., 119 West 40th Street, New York, NY 10018, attn: Special Sales Department; phone 1-800-221-2647.

CITADEL PRESS and the Citadel logo are Reg. U. S. Pat. & TM Off.

First printing: May 2013

10 9 8 7 6 5 4 3 2 1

Printed in the United States of America

CIP data is available.

ISBN-13: 978-0-8065-3615-6
ISBN-10: 0-8065-3615-2

First electronic edition: May 2013

ISBN-13: 978-0-8065-3616-3
ISBN-10: 0-8065-3616-0

This book is dedicated to my father.
Each and every day, you are still here.

"You're traveling through another dimension,
a dimension not only of sight and sound but of mind;
a journey into a wondrous land whose boundaries are that
of imagination. That's the signpost up ahead—your next
stop, The Twilight Zone!"

—ROD SERLING

MOST PEOPLE KNOW my father through *The Twilight Zone*. Some can quote a portion of the introduction and many can hum the mesmerizing music. They are familiar with the man in the dark suit standing against a dramatically lit set, intoning cautionary observations about human beings, fate, or the universe.

My father could command an audience with his presence and his insights. He could also scare the hell out of viewers—many can still recall specific scenes and recite bits of chilling or poignant dialogue from favorite *Twilight Zones*:

"It's a cookbook!"

"Room for one more, honey."

"We never left the earth! That's why nobody tracked us. We just crashed back into it!"

"This is Maple Street on a late Saturday afternoon, in the last calm and reflective moment—before the monsters came."

And so many more.

But the man I knew, my dad, was not the one the public

saw. Not this black and white image walking slowly across an MGM sound stage, cigarette in hand, speaking in a tight, clipped voice, introducing that week's episode; not the Angry Young Man of the Golden Age of TV; not the writing professor, the documentary narrator, or the commercial pitchman, and *certainly* not the dark and tortured soul some have suggested.

In *Twilight Zone* reruns, I search for my father in the man on the screen, but I can't always find him there. Instead, he appears in unexpected ways. Memory summoned by a certain light, a color, a smell—and I see him again on the porch of our old red lakeside cottage, where I danced on the steps as a child. He will emerge, come back to life, just like the old snapshot in the album, just like the day the shutter clicked and the picture froze. There he is, playing the stone game, holding it tucked into one hand behind his back. I am one of the children there, his youngest daughter. I see us in our summer shorts, barefoot, all lined up in rows, my sister, our friends, our tiny, sunburned shoulders touching, guessing which hand holds the stone, moving down a step, closer, closer to my father who waits to shake the winner's hand.

I think of his *Twilight Zone* episode: "A Stop at Willoughby," a simple, serene time imagined through a train window. A day just like this.

On a summer afternoon the wind blows hot, humid air, and for just a fraction of a moment, my father, all of us, are there.

Chapter 1

THE LAST TIME I saw my father, it was 1975. He was lying in a hospital bed in a room with bright—too bright—green and yellow walls, inappropriate colors intended to console the sick, the dying. As he slept, curled beneath a sheet, I watched him breathe, willing him to, his face still tan against that pillow so white. And as I sat looking at him, I thought of how, when I was small, I would awaken in my room beside the flowered wallpaper and listen for his footsteps down the hall, comfortable in their familiarity, secure in the insular world of my childhood, knowing without question or doubt that when I followed those sounds, I would always find him.

When he first got sick, I wiped his forehead dry until he became too ill and I could do nothing. "Pops," he said, calling me one of my many nicknames, "don't you worry. I'm going to be just fine." And I looked at him then and nodded because I couldn't find the words.

My father died there, three days later, on the eighth floor of Strong Memorial Hospital in Rochester, New York.

He was just fifty years old, I barely twenty.

I was so blinded by the loss. Terrified by each day that took me further from the last that I had seen him. Incapacitated by the idea of a life without him, my world grew impossibly small and inaccessible. I did not know how to grieve, to accept, to move on. I shut down. I detached. I fell apart.

I replayed those last days of the hospital—the waiting, the doctors in their silent shoes, the unimaginable words—in excruciating, explosive detail as if in the revisiting, the outcome could be changed in some way.

Walking aimlessly outside, I was stunned by the normalcy of those obscenely bright summer skies. I knew it was useless, but I would whisper, "Dad, if you can hear me, make the leaf move. Or the bird; make that bird fly now," and I would wait. I needed something tangible, some acknowledgment that he could hear me. Some sign that I was not losing my mind.

All of the years that I mourned my father and all of the "magical thinking" that I engaged in could not bring him back. But that didn't stop my trying. In those first weeks I sat alone in his office chair reaching for pens he had held, papers he had touched. I looked at his photographs, imagining him talking to me. I panicked when I thought it might be possible I could very soon forget the way he smiled, or the sound of his laugh and the way his voice trailed up the stairs calling me Pops or Miss Grumple or Nanny. I was so afraid that I would lose him, lose him incrementally, lose him for good.

But grief is a strange thing. After it slams you, it has nowhere else to go. This understanding can take years, can take its toll, can excise you off the planet. And it did for me. I finally started seeing a therapist after the insistent prodding of friends. It took more than a year, but there I sat with Dr. Feinstein, week after week, in a room with shelves of books and no sunlight.

He told me, "You need to visit your father's grave." He said it quietly but emphatically. My mother, my friends were all telling me the same thing: "You need closure." I felt ambushed from all sides. I was not doing well. Although I had just graduated from college, I was depressed. I had panic attacks and the start of agoraphobia. I was overwhelmed by this sadness that was acute and all-consuming and sometimes left me gasping for air. A year passed, then another. June, July, August. Suddenly summers were gone. Fall filled the air in a barrage of color and then succumbed to November skies. It was gray and windy and cold, and I still hadn't done what I needed to do. I could not go to my father's grave.

I found the simplest memory could cause the greatest ache. In one, my father—wearing blue shorts, no shirt—is carrying a small green plate with a corned beef sandwich he has just made; in his other hand, a Coke. He is going outside to eat his lunch in the sun. Thinking the sliding doors are open, he walks right into them and yells, "God damn it!"

He is not hurt. When he sees me, he laughs. "I'm okay," he says, and we are both laughing. On our hands and knees, we clean up the mess with paper towels and pick up the pieces of sandwich. He has a small purple mark on his forehead that within weeks will disappear.

A sticker remains on those glass doors still. It is faded and peeled in one corner but warns when the doors are closed. And sometimes, if I stand there at just around noon on a summer day, I can see the soda spilling across the wood floor, the soaked corned beef on rye, and the green plate tipped in my father's hand. I can see him turning, tanned, and smiling in the sunlight. I can hear my father laughing in the empty room.

Chapter 2

ON AN EARLY WINTER morning a few years after graduating from college, I drive from Ithaca back to the cottage. It, and the newer house my parents built next door, has been closed for winter. My tracks in the snow will be the only ones except for rabbits, squirrels, maybe a deer. I get out of the car, search in my pocket for the key, push open the door to the house, and turn on the light, grateful that the electricity has not been turned off and that there is still a little warmth.

Nothing really changes here, and my father's presence, even in the stillness, is powerful. A shadow can so easily be transformed, his voice imagined, and for just a moment I envision him there. I hear the familiar sound of his footsteps on the stairs, but of course I see nothing—only the empty steps in the faint morning light.

Although I should be, I am clearly no further along in this grieving process. I haven't found a teaching position, and so I sub in elementary schools when I can and tutor. It isn't lost on me, though, or those around me, that I'm on auto pilot, not fully present, not really engaged, at all.

As I walk from room to room I find the quiet unbearable and so in the kitchen, I switch on the radio—my mother's station, the last one played—classical. The music breaks the silence, but it feels jarring, droning, and I quickly turn it off and walk into another room.

In a closet I find what I have come for. My father's box of old letters, his 511th Airborne booklet, other memorabilia, and the family photo albums, a myriad of colored covers, each one marked with a specific year. I sit on the floor, the books and letters and other items spread before me, and I open the first album; Dad on the boat saluting behind the wheel; playing poker with his friend Dick; swimming with my sister and me in the lake; Dad rolling around with the dogs on the lawn. Another album, then another, a slide show of images flashing too quickly, on and on, until the pictures stop on a half-filled page because weeks later my father was gone.

I get up and stand at the window, watching as a bird feeder, empty for years, swings precariously. I look at the vanishing light and the falling snow, and I am surprised so much time has passed.

Kneeling again on the floor, I begin stacking the albums, carefully refolding the letters and other items and placing them into the box. I see I have forgotten to put my dad's old yearbook in. I open the cover and find him quickly. His brown eyes looking back at mine.

I return the book and close the top, ready to set it back on the closet shelf. But I worry about the dampness and the passage of time, the erosion of what remains, and quickly decide this time I will not leave it behind. I will take the box with me. These things cannot be lost.

I stay a moment more in the silent room, the empty house, knowing that I'll have to keep doing this. I will have to keep looking. That in order to go forward, I will have to go back

because even all this time after his death, his absence feels unmanageable, implausible still.

At the landing I reach again in my pocket for the key and
lock the door behind me. It has begun to snow heavier and I
can barely see my tracks.

Starting the car, the wipers battle the falling snow and a
blast of air hits me as I turn down the gravel drive and begin
back...

Chapter 3

DURING THE SCHOOL YEAR, we live in a large Tudor house in Pacific Palisades, California, on the west side of Los Angeles. But every summer we fly to our cottage in upstate New York, built by my mother's grandfather and great-grandfather where, with the exception of the years my sister Jodi and I were born, my mother has come every summer of her life.

We pack up our two dogs, our two cats, give them their prescribed sedatives, and put our three pet rats in their tiny yellow fabric-covered travel cages in preparation for the long flight. We always arrive at night, crunching down the gravel drive, the suitcases piled up in back and the dogs leaning out the window, like a Norman Rockwell painting. June, fireflies in flight, glowing in and out of darkness, my dad whistling and then all of us calling in a singsong voice, "We're here! We're here!" There is no greater thrill than this first arrival, with all of summer, a lifetime, just ahead; my father as ecstatic as my mother, my sister, and I when we see the little red house.

The cottage has three tiny bedrooms with sliding wooden

doors and one bathroom with only a toilet and sink. We bathe in the lake or in a small shower in the trailer across the lawn where my great-grandmother stays in the summer months.

One day my dad will tell me how he was once washing in the lake when a boat approached. "Pops, I was standing there in my birthday suit, and I heard the boat coming closer and closer. I made a mad dash and crouched under the dock so that I wouldn't be seen."

At the cottage, we dry our clothes outside on a line and my mother hands me pins from a small blue and white cloth bag so that I can hang my own. I am a little chubby in those early years. My hair is curly like my dad's, and my mother makes me get it cut in the summer, which I hate. I am also short for my age and sometimes have to stand on my toes to reach the clothesline.

We talk a little as we work. "Did you know," my mother says, reaching into the bag, "this is the same clothespin bag we used when I was a little girl?" She helps me pin up my wet bathing suit. "Maybe you'll keep it for your kids."

Our days in the summer relieve my dad of his life in Los Angeles, show business, and the madness and pace of the city. Still, he struggles to balance the two ways of life, and I watch him running in and out of the house to answer the ringing phone, jarring against the quiet voices from the lake below, the hum of the cicadas—all of the summer sounds.

Even at the cottage he is continuously writing and creating. But for a while, at least, he takes himself out of the passing lane. He turns the phone down and lies in the hammock, reading there every afternoon, pushing himself back and forth with a stick he found on the beach, his glasses sliding down his nose while he dozes. When I am six or so, I dance around him, playing, balancing pebbles on his toes, challenging the sleeping, snoring giant to awaken and chase me away.

My sister, Jodi, three years older than I am, often plays a few feet away. Her long, brown hair is tied back as she gallops two toy palomino horses, making them whinny as they round a tree. She is obsessed with horses, even then.

And my mother, in the distance, arms full of freshly picked orange day lilies, walks across the porch and then into the cottage.

For a while there are just the sounds of the screen door closing as my mother carries the flowers inside, my father continues his rhythmic snore, my sister talks to her horses, and a boat motors slowly along the shoreline of the lake below.

The afternoons are spent with a family that lives five minutes away. The Delavans. There are four girls—readymade instant friends. We are together almost every summer day. Ann is Jodi's age and Debbie just one year older than I am. Edie is a year younger and Cathy four years younger. Debbie, Edie, and I are all reading the Laura Ingalls' books, and together we set up a house in the woods with boards for mattresses and colorful old sheets and blankets to cover them. We furnish the "house" with chairs and tables we find in their barn or our attic. We even have an old spinning wheel and a red-checkered tablecloth for the kitchen table. In dresses of our grandmothers', stored in a dress-up trunk, we spend hours cleaning and sweeping that dirt floor. The trees provide a canopy from the heat, and every day we are there singing and playing in the woods in our old-fashioned, too large dresses that we tie at the waist to hold up. Jodi and her friend Ann—before boys become their main interests and tormenting us is less exciting—often spy on us from a small tree house several yards away. They once find a dead fish that they stick in one of our pots when we're not there. We all scream at the discovery, and they try to muffle their wild laughter where they sit watching us from above.

When it rains or threatens to, we make a mad dash down the path talking to each other in character all the while,

"Laura, you get the sheets! Mary, hurry!" and we quickly put the blankets and tablecloth and anything else not waterproof under cover.

Throughout these early summers we eat chocolate ice cream cones, my dad reads stacks of *Mad* magazine and plays hide-and-seek with us. He plants roses and even corn, and keeps a diary of the garden's progress. "Bunny," he tells me, "look, it won't be long now until we're having corn on the cob."

Everyone in my family has nicknames; even the animals. Rarely is anyone called by his or her proper name. My mother calls my dad "Elyan," after his Hebrew name Rowelyan Ben Shmuel. He calls her C.B. for Carolyn Bunny, and Jodi is Jo-Ball or Steve (one day she will marry a Steve). I call my father "Roddy Rabbit" or "Stuart Little." He even signs notes to me: "Love, S. Little." He calls me Miss Grumple, or simply Grumple, Bunny, Little Raisin (he was Roddy Raisin), Small Rabbit, and both Momma and Pops.

There is something timeless and joyful and tranquil about being at this old, red house built so many decades before and where, in photos on a wall, generations of relatives gaze out at us from another time in their heavy, old-fashioned clothing,

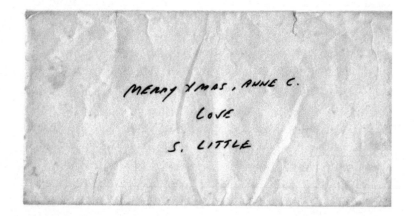

sitting on the same porch we do with the lake in the distance. It is this simple peace that we miss the moment the cottage is boarded up for the season and we fly back to California.

My father loves it here, skipping rocks along the shoreline and swimming in the cool, clear lake. He loves the summer storms that blacken the sky, that are both exhilarating and alarming and seem to roll in from nowhere. He lies out in the warm sun, walks on the beach, and pulls us aquaplaning behind the boat. He and my mother have drinks on the porch, and my dad cooks on the grill. My sister and I and our friends stage dog shows and make-believe horse shows. We brush the dogs until their coats shine and then practice for hours, finally presenting the performances on the lawn after dinner. Jodi is the designated announcer. "The show is ready to begin," she says in a deep, dramatic voice, and she turns and signals for us to start circling around the "ring." We lure the dogs with biscuits, but there is generally a struggle as they often fail to cooperate (unlike in rehearsals when they listened). With the added attention and excitement, they charge up the porch steps to escape us and greet our parents. We have to pull them back, whispering loudly, "No Maggie!" "Come Michael!" and we lead them back to the "ring," the biscuits crumbled in our hands. Once we have them in control again and doing their routines, our parents applaud, and one or the other of them gives out the ribbons we have carefully cut out and colored for the winners.

Sometimes our parents and the Delavans go out for dinner and we have a babysitter for the six of us. One early summer evening while the babysitter is busy with Cathy, the youngest, the rest of us decide to dress up our Irish setter, Michael, in my dad's T-shirt and underpants. The minute we get outside, Michael lifts his leg . . . in those underpants. We are all giggling until Michael spots a squirrel and takes a run for it down the path, leaving the underpants, and us, behind.

Michael doesn't stop. He keeps running. Past the other cottages, past families sitting on the beach or on their docks—

the four or five of us kids chasing him, calling him, trying to
sound stern behind our laughter, *"Michael!"* excusing ourselves as we run weaving between the families, everyone
smiling and pointing at that red dog racing miles ahead in my
father's white shirt.

Early in the morning, my dad sits with his blue porcelain cup
filled with black coffee and two scoops of sugar and leans
back in the wicker chair, his feet on the porch rail, listening as
fish jump in the lake below.

He loves the visits from friends; his childhood friend Julius
"Julie" Golden and wife, Rhoda, come every summer from
Long Island and stay a week in July. One year, Julie brings an
old photograph of their Boy Scout troop that he has enlarged. I see them unrolling it on the porch table, pointing
and laughing.

Years later, Julie sends me a letter my dad wrote him in response to some old correspondence Julie had saved and sent
him from when they were kids:

Dear Julie—
Granted that the enclosed represent the memorabilia of a couple
of aging men and nothing more—you can't imagine the joy they
gave me or how I went into a raging gust of screaming laughter
that brought tears. "The Summer of 42"—and we were the
principal players. . . .

Passing sentiment: your letters reinforced a feeling I've had gut
deep for a whole lot of years. You were and are a dear and valued
friend, Julie. And if that doesn't elicit a small catch in the
esophagus, then there never was a tune called MacNamara's
Band and nary A Broome County farmer ever purchased a pair
of work gloves at Louie's.

Affectionately,
Rod

Shortly after Julie and Rhoda leave, my dad drives back to his hometown in Binghamton, New York—a small, once bucolic city in upstate New York where down a tree-lined street there stands a white, two-story house with dark shutters. It isn't difficult to find; head down Front Street, straight onto Riverside Drive, right on Beethoven Street, then two blocks and you're there.

This is a pilgrimage my father takes every summer until his death. It is 1965. He is forty years old. In ten years he will be gone.

He starts the car and waits as we call, "Good-bye." He is going back, he says, "just for a few hours," and leaning out of the car window, waves. His paratrooper bracelet glints in the sun. I listen as the car's tires crunch through the gravel road of our cottage. I watch him go.

I imagine him driving slowly down Bennett Avenue, his old street, and passing by his house, now slightly in need of painting, a little worse for wear. I wonder if, stopping briefly, he pictures his mother still there, opening the front door, seeing him suddenly, a vision she cannot quite be certain of, holding up her hand to block the afternoon sun. Or maybe it is his father he sees out in the driveway, washing the old Ford, suddenly dropping the hose, which snakes through the air, spraying memories my dad can almost touch as he imagines both his parents running toward him in a kind of dreamlike, slow-motion reverie that only this level of recall can recreate. Or perhaps, driving a little farther, he sees the ghosts of his boyhood friends running barefoot alongside the car or calling out to him from their porches, waving to him and calling, "Come on, Roddy, come on," until the sounds of the present bring him back and the passage of years and everything he has imagined are gone again.

I recognize that these visits re-center my dad. One day I will see the *Twilight Zone* episode inspired by these trips— "Walking Distance." "The idea," my dad will say, "came from walking through the streets of my hometown and then taking a long evening stroll to a place called Recreation Park three blocks from my old house and seeing the merry-go-round and remembering that wondrous, bittersweet time of growing up." In the closing narration of that episode he says:

> Martin Sloan, age thirty-six, vice-president in charge of media. Successful in most things but not in the one effort that all men try at some time in their lives—trying to go home again. And also like all men perhaps there'll be an occasion, maybe a summer night sometime, when he'll look up from what he's doing and listen to the distant music of a calliope, and hear the voices and the laughter of the people and the places of his past. And perhaps across his mind there'll flit a little errant wish, that a man might not have to become old, never outgrow the parks and the merry-go-rounds of his youth. And he'll smile then, too, because he'll know it is just an errant wish, some wisp of memory not too important really, some laughing ghosts that cross a man's mind, that are a part of The Twilight Zone.

I know early on that within my dad there is a kind of desperateness, an urge to go back, a need to touch home plate, to have things the way they were. And one day I will understand it on more than a farsighted level.

Occasionally my parents meet friends in Ithaca, a nearby college town twenty minutes from our cottage, and they always have the identical conversation when my mother takes too long getting ready. My dad will start pacing and growing annoyed. "Come on honey!" and she'll yell back, "For Christ's sake, Rod, I'm almost ready! Go start the car." To which he will always respond, "I don't have to crank the God damn thing!" When she arrives, he often does this prank (he does to all of us) when, just as she, or one of us, is about to reach the car handle to open the door, he'll drive a few feet forward. He does this to my mother all the time promising each time, "Okay. Okay. I won't do it anymore. Get in," at which point she'll reach for the door and he will drive off again. After about the third time, she is completely exasperated, yells, "Rod!" and may storm inside, but I always hear her laughing.

For years, on the last night of summer, in a tradition I have passed on to my own children, we carve little boats from the leftover wood in the scrap pile. In the center of the boats, a hole is dug for a candle. We spread newspaper on the picnic table, and with our friends, we paint the boats and scratch in our names.

At sundown, when they are dry, we walk down the steep path through the woods to the lake and light the candles. Our parents sit on the dock beside us, and we lie on our stomachs and push the boats out into the dark water. Sometimes a breeze immediately sweeps across the lake and extinguishes the light. Sometimes the boats float for a long time, small flames in the distance, growing dimmer and dimmer, away from us, our shadowed figures huddled on the dock.

Year after year, we watch these little boats decorated by our small hands as they carry away that last gasp of summer's glow.

When we are back in California, my dad and I have a ritual to speed the days until we can return to the lake. He takes me to a diner, where on late afternoons, we sit across from each other in a booth by the window, have a sundae, and play our private little game of "Only A Few More Months Until Summer," both of us despairing of the long wait; my father, because Los Angeles is already beginning to wear on him again and I, because I treasure the uninterrupted time with him. He will say, "And then there's Christmas, which is actually right around the corner. After all, this is practically November, which leads to December . . ." I am giggling, knowing what comes next, knowing this script so well, but saying excitedly anyway, "And then what?!"

He smiles. "You can eliminate the first fifteen days, which brings us to January, and February doesn't count."

"Why not?" I'll ask as if on cue.

"Too few days."

"And March?"

"Forget March! That whizzes by! So there's just," and he ticks them off on his fingers, "April, May, and then June and then Bunny..."

"Summer!" we'll both shout in unison and explode into laughter.

Chapter 4

I EASILY IMAGINE MY dad as a little boy, because even as an adult there is something magically childlike about him, so endearingly silly, that I feel in some ways I know the boy almost as well as I know the man.

Frequently, he talks about his parents. He called his mother "Dearest." He adored her, and she him, but it is his father, Sam, he will most often tell me about. It is the memories of my grandfather that make my dad stop midsentence, immobilized, and look away for a moment while he gathers back his voice. He doesn't just miss his father; these aren't merely transitory emotions. This loss, for my dad, is like an amputation. It is an almost constant, unvarying ache.

Sue Fisher Hersch, a close lifetime friend of his, told me once, "Sam worshipped your dad." Clearly it was mutual.

I did not know either of my father's parents. His mother, Esther, died when I was a baby; and Sam, long before. I've often envisioned their lives, their joys, regrets, their voices and personalities, more as an extension of my father than the other way around. In my grandfather's face, there is a certain amused expression, much like my father's, although physically, my dad looks more like his mother, her coloring, her tanned complexion, her black, wavy hair and dark brown eyes. I am struck by the similarities in a particular photograph of the three of them together, all turned toward the camera, grinning, the bull terrier—Tony—on my grandfather's lap. I imagine the moments that follow. My father waving to his parents, running off to play, this boy with the sparkling brown eyes who in just a little time will go off to war with his friends and be forever changed.

When we sit outside in the sun together, my father tells me fragments of my grandparents' past. He tells me what brought them to upstate New York, the deplorable conditions that drove his parents to leave Eastern Europe.

His mother Esther was born in Lithuania. Her father, Meyer Cooper, came to the States—leaving behind his wife and nine children—to escape famine and religious persecution and to earn enough to bring his family over. Since he did not have any trade or profession, his brother helped him buy a horse and wagon, and he started buying and selling scrap iron and discarded materials for a living. He continued his peddling for about three years, alone, covering the roads of Cayuga and Onondaga County between Auburn and Syracuse in upstate New York. Finally he accumulated enough money, and when Esther, my grandmother, was three, she and her mother and eight siblings came to America. By then Meyer had opened a meat market in Auburn, New York, which he was able to develop into a chain of successful grocery stores.

Meyer had a short, pointed beard and was very stern looking. Eventually he became successful and respected, but he always had trouble with English. He held picnics for his employees during the prosperous days of the business. Every year he made a speech that some didn't want to hear, and they would go around the corner and shoot craps. Meyer found out about this, and one year before beginning his speech warned, to the amusement of all, "No crappin' on the grass."

Not much is known of my grandfather's family except that he was born in Detroit. His father, Isaac, moved there from Russia and married a fifteen-year-old girl, Anna, who was deaf. They moved to Syracuse where Isaac owned a junk business.

Sam and Esther met in Auburn. When they decided to marry, they were given five hundred dollars as a wedding present and went to Panama for their honeymoon. Sam had been offered a job there as a stenographer for Colonel George Washington Goethals, who was overseeing the massive task of constructing the new Panama Canal.

The year was 1915. My grandparents were just beginning their new life together. They knew no one in Panama. One day Sam must have tapped a stranger's shoulder, asking, "Please, we're on our honeymoon, could you take our picture?" And waiting, he pulled Esther closer and draped his arm around her. There they are in black and white, palm trees in the distance. Esther is looking at Sam, not at the camera. Their clothing looks dated now. Their smiles are not.

A corner of the photograph has peeled away, a part of the image gone; some of the history lost. With Sam away working, it is not an easy time; Esther did not anticipate the extended stay. She is far away from her family and friends and, I imagine, lonely. I wonder, while my grandfather worked, did she send postcards home? Did she write, "The days are tedious; they are hot and long and hard"?

Esther, in fact, contracts yellow fever during their stay in Panama and almost dies.

They are gone for two years and finally move back to the United States, to Syracuse, New York, where Sam goes to work for his father-in-law. Esther is pregnant with Robert, my father's older brother. But because of the residual effects of yellow fever, it is a difficult birth.

After Bob is born, the doctor gives them the crushing news: this will be their only child. He says it is impossible for her to carry another, and true to his warning, a baby girl is stillborn a few years later. Seven years later, however, the doctor is proven wrong.

December 25, 1924, Esther and Sam are rushing to the Good Shepherd Hospital. Hurriedly, they call a neighbor to watch Bob. A few hours later, a healthy baby boy is born. They name him Rodman Edward Serling.

Although Jewish, the family also celebrates Christmas, and my dad will one day say, "I was a Christmas present that was delivered unwrapped."

Bob does not recall this arrival so idyllically. No one has time to put together his new toy, an electric train, that Christmas morning. His parents are still at the hospital, and only a neighbor is there to watch him. He sits on the floor, tears through the red wrapping, and attempts to put the train together himself. He connects the tracks, lines up the engine, baggage car, and two passenger cars, but because he doesn't know what he is doing he shoves the rheostat too far, causing the cars to circle too fast, out of control, and they crash. Bob remembers, "My first realization that I had a brother was that I hated the little son of a bitch 'cause he'd wrecked my train."

Eventually, though, Bob grows to adore his kid brother. In an interview he gives Marc Zicree for *The Twilight Zone Companion* almost sixty years later, Bob says: "Rod and I were fairly close as kids and we played a lot, despite the seven-year age difference. The two of us used to read *Amazing Stories, Astounding Stories, Weird Tales*—all of the pulps. If we saw a movie together, we'd come home and act it out. Our bikes became airplanes with machine guns on them. We were always playing cowboys...Rod was about the greatest extrovert you could imagine. He was a good-looking kid. Very popular, very articulate, very outspoken. He had no arrogance—it was confidence. There's a helluva difference."

Sam continues managing his father-in-law's store in Syracuse.

It is not the job he may have daydreamed about while staring out of a classroom window as a child, but he has a wife and two small boys to support, and although he is extraordinarily bright, he has never had the means to go to college. He is a voracious reader, though, often reading late into the night. One of his favorite books is *The Education of Hyman Kaplan* by the Jewish writer Leo Rosten, and some nights, sitting alone in his overstuffed chair, he laughs so loud he wakes up the whole family.

Shortly after my father is born, the family, along with the dog, "Tony," move to Binghamton, New York, where Sam manages one of his father-in-law's wholesale meat markets.

Every morning Sam leaves early to open up the market, kissing Esther at the door, sometimes in a dramatic pose or twirling her around, that makes my dad, standing there in his pajamas, laugh.

My father hugs his dad around the knees and runs to the window to watch Sam get into the car and wave before pulling away.

My dad told me that one day Meyer went to Sam's store and told the secretary not to work late because, "Someone will come in and stick it up in you a gun," which always made my dad laugh.

My dad goes to the Hamilton Elementary School. He carries his lunch in a brown paper bag—sometimes a cheese sandwich, or peanut butter, always with a pickle. He also loves chocolate egg creams and often shares them with his friends.

In his report cards he receives E for excellent in reading, spelling, and geography. In fourth grade he is not doing so well in drawing and receives only a "fair." In writing, too, he seems to struggle and gets only "S" (satisfactory). Under citizenship he receives E's in everything: manners, obedience, dependableness, respect for property, patriotism, and reverence.

He likes school. In all of the class pictures he is smiling somewhat impishly. Because he is short, he is near the front, tucked in close to his friends.

Esther frames most of these photos but keeps some in a baby book she calls "Roddy's book," where she saves all of the mementos: the notes, the cards, and a lock of his hair. Under "Milestones," where it reads, "When did your baby first crawl?" she writes, "I never let my baby down to crawl."

She dotes on her curly-haired son. She knits him socks from complicated patterns that last through decades. (I still wear them.)

Despite Sam's long work hours, he makes time for the family to drive back to Syracuse, seventy miles away, to visit Esther's brother Ben. The trip takes about two and a half hours, and once, when my father is about six years old, Sam asks Esther and Bob not to say anything during the ride. "Just let Roddy keep talking." My father never stops from the time they get into the car until they arrive in Syracuse. He sings and talks to his parents and to Bob about everything he sees out the window without waiting for anyone to respond. He just keeps talking.

When I hear this family story, I think of my dad in his office in back of our house, dictating his script into the tightly clutched microphone, acting out every part, creating an extraordinary world of his own. One of these scripts will be a *Twilight Zone* episode titled: "The Silence," in which a compulsive talker bets he can remain silent for a year.

These are joyful, almost idyllic days for my father, when industry, to some extent, shields the city from the desperation of the Great Depression. One of those industries is a shoe manufacturer, Endicott-Johnson. George Johnson, in addition to his other contributions to the Binghamton community, gives six carousels to local parks. His only stipulation is that at no time should money be charged for the "magic ride."

DEPARTMENT *of* EDUCATION

BINGHAMTON

QUARTERLY REPORT

of

Rodman Serling

School *Hamilton* Grade *4 B*

A. O. Spaulding Teacher

Promoted to *4 A*

TO PARENTS AND GUARDIANS:

This Report Card is to bring to you a message directly from the teacher to show what in her estimation your child is doing in school. If you find the marks satisfactory it is hoped that you will express your satisfaction. If they are below the proper standard you are requested to ascertain the cause and to aid in making the desired improvement. It is especially important that you become personally acquainted with the teacher of your boy or girl and also learn of the general conditions in your school.

After examining kindly sign the card and return it promptly.

F. T. Mann Principal

A. P. S.

SCHOOL YEAR 1933 1934

TERM *Spring*

Class Work and Attendance

	1st Q	2d Q	3d Q	4th Q	Avrg
Reading	....	E.	E.	E.	....
Writing	....	S.	S.	S.	....
Drawing	....	F.	F.	F.	....
Music	....	S.	S.	S.	....
Spelling	....	E.	E.	E.	....
Arithmetic	....	S.	S.	S.	....
English	....	S.	S.	S.	....
Geography	....	E.	E.	E.	....
History	....	....	....	....	....
Manual Training	....	....	....	....	....
....	....	....	....	....	....
....	....	....	....	....	....
....	....	....	....	....	....
Days Attendance	....	32	31	29	92
Half days Absent, legal	....	5	....	11	16
Half days Absent, illegal	....	....	....	....	....
Times Tardy, legal	..	....	....	....	....
Times Tardy, illegal	....	....	....	....	....

Prompt and regular attendance is essential to good work.

E indicates excellent work
S indicates satisfactory work
F indicates fair work
N indicates improvement necessary

Citizenship

Object: To develop an appreciation of what it means to be an American citizen, thereby creating a desire to meet intelligently the opportunities and to discharge faithfully the duties of such citizenship.

		1st Q	2d Q	3d Q	4th Q	Avrg
I	*Manners*		E	E	E	
	Courtesy to teachers					
	Kindness to associates					
	Consideration for rights of others					
	Cleanliness and civility of speech					
	Cheerfulness					
II	*Obedience*		E	E	E	
	Respect for law, order and authority					
	Willingness to respond to directions					
III	*Dependableness*		E	E	E	
	Truthfulness					
	Honesty					
	Self-control					
IV	*Workmanship*		S	E	E	
	Interested in work					
	Effort to do the best work		E	E	E	
V	*Respect for property*		E	E	E	
	Care of building, furniture and books					
	Consideration for property of others					
	Care of own property		E	E	E	
VI	*Patriotism*		E	E	E	
	Interest in community welfare					
	Willingness to render public service		E	E	E	
VII	*Reverence*		E	E	E	
	Attitude toward things sacred		E	E	E	
VIII	*Attendance*					
	Regularity					
	Punctuality				E	
	Average					

Health Education

Object: To make Health Habits automatic through education, thereby adding years to the lives of the coming generation and increasing the total of their efficiency and happiness by the training they receive today.

		1st Q	2d Q	3d Q	4th Q	Avrg
I	Personal Appearance.......	....	....	....	....	....
	1 Neatness of Dress					
	Clothing repaired					
	Clothing clean					
	Shoes clean					
	2 Neatness of Person					
	Face clean					
	Hands clean					
	Nails clean					
	Teeth clean					
	Hair brushed					
II	Housekeeping..............	....	....	....	....	....
	Neatness of desk					
	Neatness of floor					
	Order of cloak room					
	Care of books					
III	Posture...................	....	....	....	....	....
	Standing					
	Sitting					
	Walking					
	Setting-up drills					
IV	Playground Activities	....	....	....	....	....
V	Class Work in Hygiene	....	....	....	....	....
VI	Height	....	47	....	....	....
VII	Weight	....	51	51	51	....
VIII	~~Weight should be~~	....	....	....	51¼	....
	Average..........	....	E	E	E	....

Signature of Parent

1st Quarter	*Samuel F. Carling*
2nd Quarter	*Mrs S L Seitz*
3rd Quarter	

20 M G68 G64

"Carousels," he says, "contribute to a happy life and will help youngsters grow into strong and useful citizens."

In spite of the influence of Endicott Johnson, International Business Machines, and others, my grandfather begins to worry about money. Although he tries to shield this from the boys, my father will remember hearing him in the bedroom above, his footsteps pacing back and forth, and some mornings he is gone, already at work, before my dad wakes up.

When my father is about twelve, he gets his first job, working in a local toy store. His employer writes in his job performance record: "Roddy: Nice kid, but plays with the toys too much."

In school, my dad wants to play varsity football. He talks to the coach, who promptly discourages him. My father remembered: "The late and beloved Henry Merz tried to explain to me why I couldn't get onto the varsity football team because he found it difficult to reconcile playing a quarterback who weighed less than the team bulldog."

Inevitably I am always drawn back to his books and papers. I sit on the floor looking through his yearbooks, opening the pages to this growing, handsome child who will one day be my father. He is pictured in almost every extracurricular activity—the debate team, student council, the drama team, editor of the school paper and member of the honor society. He is always at least a head shorter than the other students and always looking back with that wide, captivating smile and those dark eyes I know so well.

Chapter 5

"WAS YOUR FATHER RELIGIOUS?" people often ask me. Did he follow his faith? Is it true, as someone has written, that your mother forced him to give up his religion and become a Unitarian?"

No one forced my father to do anything. He grew up in a Reform Jewish family and they were involved in the Binghamton Jewish Community Center, but the Center was said to have been held together more by shared ethnic values than religious beliefs. Sam was vice president of the Reform Temple, but his family did not attend synagogue regularly, the exception being the High Holy Days.

One day Sam sits Bob and my father down and says, "I am not a good Jew, but I think I'm a good person. If you want to be very religious, that's up to you. My own philosophy is, I take people for what they are, not where they go to pray."

These are powerful and compelling words to my father. Something clearly resonates that day and lasts a lifetime.

My parents always remain wary of organized religion. They

agree that my sister and I will go to the Unitarian Church Sunday mornings when we are younger. This is acceptable to my dad because the messages taught are intellectually open-minded. It is a liberal religion. Nothing is compulsory, and many of the ideals are similar to Judaism. My mother, who was raised Unitarian, likes the free thinking, the permission to believe what one wants.

My dad doesn't accompany us to church, but I do distinctly recall him dropping us off one Sunday and my friend Elizabeth Arlen and I sneaking off instead to the local grocery store. As we are racing carts down the aisles, suddenly, at the end of one, we see my dad. We abruptly go into reverse. I am sure he sees us, but knowing my dad, I am confident he won't say a word to my mother. And he doesn't.

Throughout his life, my father holds on to many Jewish values and traditions. For years I see him light Yahrzeit memorial candles at sundown on the anniversaries of his parents' deaths. The candlelight glows in the darkness of the room, flickering when we walk by, burning into the following day. Sometimes he stops and stares for just a moment. It is the same expression he has when he carries that box of old letters outside and sits in the yard at the cottage. I watch as he gently removes them from their envelopes and unfolds them. Many, I know, are from his parents. He reads them and then carefully folds them back up, replacing them in their envelopes. And then I see that same inaccessible look I will come to know and, even as a child, understand.

I remember his childhood bedtime prayer that he taught me. For some reason I memorize this, and both my children know it as well. "God bless Dearest and Daddy and big brother Bobby and all my relations and all my friends and God, help me to be a good boy and a good Jew. Amen."

For years, my father and Bob go to the Jewish Community Center. The director Isidore Friedland and his wife are philosophical humanists and spiritual mentors to many of Binghamton's Jewish youth.

My father can imitate Mr. Friedland's voice flawlessly and loves to do impersonations and play jokes on people. His brother Bob, always gullible, is the perfect target. One day, when Bob is home visiting from Antioch College and my dad is about ten, he calls Bob from the upstairs phone and pretends to be Mr. Friedland. "Hello Bobby? Why haven't you called me? I know you've been home for days." Bob stammers. "Hello, Mr. Friedland, yes, yes, I've been meaning to call you . . ." It isn't until he hears my father laughing on the other phone that Bob realizes who he is actually apologizing to. "God damn it, Rod!"

At the Community Center, my dad and his friend Julie Golden join a local Boy Scout troop. As Julie pointed out, in a now famous photo of Troop 36, my dad sits in the center, the shortest kid with the biggest smile. "Among those 'tenderfeet,' two grew up to be doctors, another a lawyer, yet another a college professor."

Julie and my father attend Sunday school and play a lot of Ping-Pong. "Your dad was a good player," says Julie, "but I was better." They go to each other's houses and hang out for hours. "Your grandfather, Sam," Julie remembers, "had a great sense of humor and loved to talk, just like your dad." He describes Esther, my grandmother, as "an elegant, soft-spoken woman who physically reminded me of Margaret Dumont, the tall, somewhat matronly actress who was often a foil for Groucho Marx. She was always charming."

Often they ride their bikes to the park with the carousel. My dad carves his name on a post of the bandstand, as in a scene he will later recreate in "Walking Distance."

Soon the boys enter Binghamton Central High School where, Julie says, "Your dad was very popular among most of his contemporaries. A lot of us were members of Upsilon Lambda Phi, a Jewish high school fraternity, and participated in social events in Binghamton, Scranton, and Wilkes-Barre. Your father, however, was blackballed by some ULPS members because he dated non-Jewish girls."

It is ironic that this first experience of discrimination comes from my dad's own Jewish contemporaries. The fight against discrimination and prejudice will remain central throughout his life.

Julie tells me my dad was adventurous long before he became famous and that the adventures often included him. "One winter afternoon, for example, your dad and I were visiting a high school friend, just chatting in the living room. Suddenly, he jumped up, ran outside, climbed up on the roof, and jumped off into the snow."

Julie remembers that they played a fair amount of tennis at Recreation Park, but that a typical Serling/Golden afternoon would be: "We would meet at my father's clothing store on Water Street, then walk next door to the Lyric Theater for a terrific double feature; the absolute best we ever saw was *Frankenstein* and *Dracula.*"

Thousands of miles away from this small town and these boys in the Lyric Theater, the world is on fire. Without warning, Russia has been attacked by Germany. The United States, no longer neutral, is actively aiding the allies. Japanese armed forces attack Pearl Harbor, and war, for the United States, begins the next day: December 8, 1941. A front-page headline proclaims: "THE UNITED STATES DECLARES WAR ON JAPAN." Twenty-four hours later: "GERMANY AND ITALY DECLARE WAR ON THE UNITED STATES." Congress reestablishes the draft.

My father's childhood ends.

Chapter 6

I HAVE BEEN TOLD that very little has changed in the auditorium of the Binghamton High School since my father was there. The curtains, the wood flooring on the stage, the old windows, now covered, and even the chairs where my dad and his friends sat are all still there.

And so it takes little imagination to visualize that day in January 1943 when my father and his classmates graduate midyear. Their joy, perhaps naive but not curtailed, despite a war that will soon alter the lives of so many of them.

I see them beneath that downpour of light, their diplomas hoisted high in the air as they walk across that stage. An orchestra plays "Pomp and Circumstance," just slightly off-key. There are smiles and laughter and shouting to family and friends waving programs madly from their seats below.

The next day, at seven a.m., my dad, along with some of his buddies, stands in a long line outside the recruiting center on Chenango Street in downtown Binghamton and enlists in the U.S. Army's 11th Airborne Division. He is barely eighteen

years old and the letters he will soon begin writing home
from training camp are achingly reflective of his age:

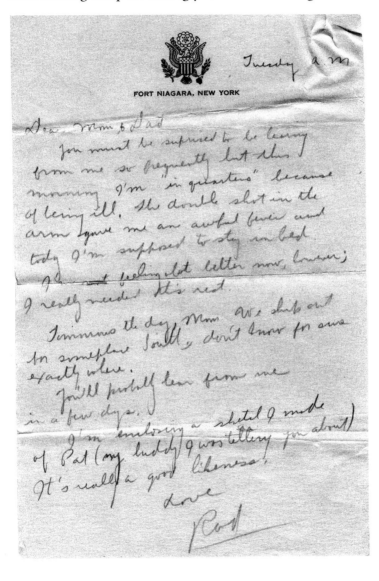

Friday February 12 1943
From HQ C) 511th Parachute Infantry
Dear Mom & Dad,
So much has happened and there is so much to tell you that I
hardly know where to begin. First I am at Camp Toccoa in
Northern Georgia. I travelled in a Pullman with 40 other guys.
The Pullman has a swell sleeper and excellent dining car. It
wasn't a regular troop train—merely a car added to a regular
train . . .

The story of how I passed my Paratrooper tests today is really
one for the books. You know it's tough as hell to get in and over
forty percent flunk out at the start. I went right through physical
passing everything until I reached the final officer who looked
over the physical report. He looked at my weight and said, "I'm
afraid you are just a little too light and small." Well, Mom, I
was so damned anxious to get in I went through a regular Bob
{brother} routine. I begged, I pleaded, I beseeched—and it
worked with the help of my Corporal who put in a good word
for me. He erased the original rejection and put down "O.K."
My Corporal said I was the littlest damn paratrooper he ever
saw. Later on he told me that the Major and the Captain who
forced the final review board here remarked about my "guts" and
said I should do O.K.

Here's my tentative training plans: thirteen weeks basic
training and four weeks jumping school. And here's a surprise,
folks—Mom I think you'll like it. I've been selected for radio
training. I'm to take charge of one of those walkie-talkie radio
sets after jumping. I was chosen for this particular job because I
had a very high mark on a sort of radio sound test . . .

Now after I finish my jumping school someplace I'll be sent to
radio school someplace so you won't have to worry about me
being sent out of the country too soon . . .

God this outfit is tough. I'm in for thirteen weeks of the
hardest training the army offers, but I'll be a far better soldier and
a better man, believe me.

Well. Mom, I'm writing this Fri night but I'm not sure when

I'll mail it. You see I'm only barracked in this particular company temporarily and there's a chance I might be sent away from here for my basic training in a short while . . .

Sunday February 21st 1943
Dear Folks,
Arrived here at Camp Hoffman in North Carolina this morning at eight o'clock. I'll probably be stationed here for at least six weeks, so you can write me here, preferably airmail. We've sort of been taking it easy these past few days—preparing for the trip which involved the transporting of our entire regiment—almost two thousand men, meant a complete termination of training. Tomorrow, however, we'll shoot back into training; I think I'm getting a little bit accustomed to it now, however.

The weather here today was beautiful—sunny and about 68 degrees. They tell us we'll probably see colder weather though, before spring sets in.

I wish you'd send me the following:

Shoeshine kit
Sewing kit
Pen & pencil set
Money belt
Pipe cleaners
Underwear (I don't like the GI kind)

I got a letter from Bevy the other day—also one from Muriel. It's really a thrill getting your name called off during mail call. It's also an awful let-down if you go away day after day with no letters. Please Mom, write and write and write and tell me all the news from home.

Gosh Mom and Dad, there's so darn much I'd like to tell you I can't get it down on paper—if only we could discuss it over one of Mom's home cooked meals—that would be paradise . . .

. . . I'm a member of the 511th Parachute Infantry regiment . . .

I've got quite a bit of money from Dad's ten and my partial pay often more. I get paid approximately 30 dollars the end of this month after my insurance, laundry and war bonds get deducted.

I'm going to send at least 8 or 10 dollars home every month—I have plenty for myself. Here's what you do Mom. Put the money away for me until I'm eligible for a furlough, then I'll send for it and have plenty of money to get home. Please use as much of it as you want in case you run short!

I've been sort of thinking Mom, I'm told that we had a chance for a furlough but there was just as much of a chance that we might not receive any. I couldn't take going overseas without seeing you once more so I was wondering if it were plausible to think that you and Dad might travel south to see me. I'll be getting 3 day passes after I finish my jump training at Fort Benning, Georgia (in June). That wouldn't be enough to get home but I could go to Atlanta, 94 miles away and meet you for three days. I realize it's war time but you could use the dough I'll be sending home and perhaps Dad could get away and you could travel by train. Oh hell, I guess I'm getting just pipe dreams. They are thoughts, however! (This sounds like Aunt Rose.)

How's business? Is meat getting harder to secure; down south we read in the papers all the time of big meat concerns going out of business because of the security of meat and prevalence of Black Markets. Please let me know what's going on.

Well, I still can't say I'm actually happy in the army. For my first six weeks I have almost complete lack of freedom—we march to meals, march to the PX, march all the time and are restricted to our company area (almost 300 yards).

Well, please write often and send me the stuff I asked for when you get the chance.

Love to the both of you,

                        Rod

In a letter a few weeks later, after not having heard from him, his mom writes:

We wondered and worried where our little soldier boy was... I'll be honest with you, we weren't so enthusiastic about you joining the paratroops. It is a very dangerous service to be in. However if that is what you wanted, I know you will do well in it. We have that confidence in your ability... We miss you too Rod. I miss having to scold my boy for throwing his things around. I have put your thousands of airplanes away in a box. On your first furlough you will have my permission to count them all on your bunk. I didn't disturb them, they are just as you left them... I will write you often and so will Dad...

March 11th, 1943, from his father:

Dear Rod:
An individualized son to father letter deserves a prompt father to
son answer—and that immediately—yours being received just
this morning.
    Your assurances of being happier naturally makes me much
more contented with your lot. I have experienced many qualms
knowing that you were pretty young to become too soon
acclimated to such a drastic change from your former sheltered
lifetime. These qualms were assuaged by the knowledge that the
C.O. in Niagara was right when he stated that you had the
"guts"—or more elegantly—"What it takes."
    I appreciate it must get pretty monotonous sticking to the
same routine but it will have its compensations, we pray. Your
response to Mother's question as to whether you would enlist if
you were to do it again—"No" does not surprise me in the
least. Far be it for me to say, "I told you so." But I do not agree
with you. The fact that you enlisted gives you some advantage,
even though it may be questionable, over the draftees. Your so-
called "guts" asserted itself when you enlisted . . .

My dad sends his parents a copy of *The Pictorial Review of*
the 511th Airborne. "To Dearest and Dad by their son Rod." The
combination of unwavering patriotism and questioning of
authority and bureaucracy that so characterized my dad's life
is evident. In a written dedication he refers to the paratroops
as: "The greatest fighting unit in the world," yet throughout
the printed copy he amends his own comments to offer the
"true" story. He underlines the printed sentence: "At no time
is any attempt made to push, cajole or talk a student out of a
plane." In the margin he writes: "A lot of bull—the gentle art
of pushing, shoving and 'Squeezing out' is commonly em-
ployed!"
    Among the yearbook-like autographs covering the final
pages of the *511th Pictorial* are such lines as: "Loads of luck to
the guy that brings laughter to our barracks." One sergeant

writes: "Good Luck and Happy Landings, Short Stuff." Several people refer to him as a swell guy or swell fellow and one writes: "Here's to a swell little guy—may we meet after this mess is over."

March 14, 1943
Dear Mom and Dad,
. . . Still doing ok with the paratroopers. When I'm marching quick time (with my exceedingly short legs) and feel so tired I don't feel I can move any further, I always do. And when my arms are tired and sore from holding my long M1 rifle and I figure I can't hold it up anymore—I always do. I don't know whether it's guts, determination, or plain stubbornness on my part but I'm always in there and always will be . . .

The only news is that I think I leave for Fort Benning in about three weeks. There I take my jump training, which is the most exciting part and really the climax of all paratroop training. I spend three weeks in rigid instruction and then take five parachute jumps from 8,000 to 800 feet respectively out of a plane. Upon completion of five jumps, I win my wings and boots—that will be the day.

After that I come back here or else go to some camp for six weeks radio training. I'm sure to receive some stripes after my technical training but OCS (Officer's Candidate School) seems pretty far away. It's tough to get into and my age and rather youthful appearance is against me. My lieutenant told me that though I'm really not worrying about it since it's too premature to be important as yet.

Spent the whole morning washing clothes. I'm really quite adept at it now. The laundry takes two weeks and I'm usually so short of clean clothes I need to take on the job myself.

Had a dance here a few nights ago—girls came from all around and I met a cute brunette who's a nurse. I got a date with her my first pass into town. We also start getting movies in camp next week.

I'm all tanned up—it's been very warm here.

The underwear you sent comes in handy.

Can't wait until I get to Benning. There I have evenings free and also weekends. I wrote Sue for her mother's address, maybe I'll be able to meet her in town.

Heard from Bob? I'm awfully anxious to hear what his assignment will be. Guys tell me here that when a big group leaves Woltes(?) it very often means an overseas assignment so maybe it's just as well that he didn't leave with his group.

Well folks, write me as often as you have been and give my best to everybody.

He closes the letter with:

PVT Rodman wants: towels, hangers, Fanny Farmer candy, another cloth for shoe shining, flashlight, Garrison belt.
Best Love,

Rod.

After a brief time in the infirmary, he writes home about his doctor, a Jewish lieutenant. "*He attends my ward. He's about 37, married and comes from Manhattan. We've had some nice talks and he tells me one of the Jewish captains is going to conduct Friday evening services for us because there is no Jewish chaplain.*"

SAMUEL L. SERLING
117 Washington St.
BINGHAMTON, N. Y.

16TH MARCH 1943.

DEAR ROD:

THIS IS IN ANSWER TO YOUR LETTER OF THE ELEVENTH; PLEASED
THAT YOU RECEIVED THE PACKAGE, AND THAT YOU ENJOYED SOME
OF THE EDIBLE CONTENTS.   WE SHOULD VERY MUCH LIKE TO
KEEP SENDING YOU SOME EDIBLES FROM HOME BUT AT A LOSS AS
TO WHAT IN PARTICULAR YOU MIGHT LIKE.   WOULD YOU LIKE
SOME MORE NUTS, COOKIES OR THE LIKE?   ARE YOU EATING
CANDY AGAIN - WE RECALL YOU WERE SORT OF LAYING OFF
CHOCOLATES FOR FEAR OF EFFECTING YOUR COMPLEXION. PLEASE
LET US KNOW WHAT YOU WOULD LIKE.

RECEIVED THE REMITTANCE OF $15.00 WHICH WITH THE CHECK FROM
AUNT BELLE WE STARTED AN ACCOUNT IN THE MORRIS PLAN WITH
$25.00.   IT WILL BE SPLENDID TO SEND AS MUCH AS YOU CAN
WITHOUT TOO MUCH STINTING OF YOUR SPENDING MONEY AND THIS
WILL COME IN MIGHTY HANDY WHEN THIS IS ALL OVER.   DOESN'T
THE DEDUCTIONS APPEAR ON YOUR PAY CHECK INDICATING VARIOUS
ITEMS?

"YANK" THE ARMY PAPER MENTIONED CHARLIE BDOOM'S DEATH AS HE
WAS ACTIVE IN LEGION AFFAIRS - PAST COMMANDER OF THE JEWISH
LEGION AND THE LIKE.   THEY STILL DON'T KNOW WHETHER IT
WAS MURDER OR SELF INFLICTION.

NOTE YOU WERE GOING TO A DANCE THE NIGHT YOU WROTE.   DO
THEY HAVE A U. S. O. AUXILLIARY AT YOUR CAMP?   HOPE YOU
HAD A GOOD TIME.

LOOKING FORWARD TO FURTHER ADVICES AS TO PROSPECTIVE
ACTIVITIES YOU WILL BE IN - AND ESPECIALLY ADVICES AS TO
WHETHER OR NOT YOU WILL BE IN LINE FOR OFFICER'S TRAINING.

BUSINESS IS VERY GOOD AND FRANKLY LOOKING FORWARD TO A
BREATHING SPELL WHEN POINT RATIONING OF MEATS TAKE EFFECT
THE LAST OF THIS MONTH.

ALL WE HEAR FROM IN THE FAMILY ARE WELL AND WHEN WE SEE THEM
OR ANY OF YOUR FRIENDS THEY ALL WANT TO BE REMEMBERED TO YOU.

THIS IS A DAMN SHORT LETTER AND LACKING IN NEWSSNESS BUT
THERE IS SO LITTLE OF INTEREST TO WRITE ABOUT OCCURRING, SO
THAT YOU WILL HAVE TO FORGIVE THE DRYNESS OF SOME OF OUR
LETTERS, BEARING ALWAYS IN MIND THAT YOU WILL BE APPRISED
OF ANYTHING MOMENTOUS HAPPENING.   WE WON'T FORGET.

FOR NOW, MUCH LOVE, AND FROM MOTHER TOO, OF COURSE. *Dad*
PS I THINK YOU KNEW ABOUT THE BUNGALOW; SOLD IT SATURDAY FOR
$2300. MAKING ME A VERY NICE PROFIT.

He also expresses his homesickness: "*Mom when you told me about seeing me if possible this summer, it boosted my spirits right up. I'm so damn homesick, the very thought that I'll see you—even if months from now is something I can look forward to and think about . . .*"

In one of his mother's letters, she writes:

Are you getting used to the service army training? Are you happy, Rod? I often stay awake nights wondering what my boy is doing. I think the happiest day of my life will be when this war is over and our boys are home again.

She signs it: "*Lots of love to the nicest boy I know.*"

She includes a note from Tony, the dog. "*I miss you so much, bow wow.*"

His father writes (in part):

4th April 1943
Dear Rod,
Seven-thirty Sunday night and here in the office writing you. Mother is leaving for Syracuse on the nine-ten bus as Uncle Si passed away this P.M. and will be buried tomorrow. Mother is naturally broken up about it but can do naught else but be philosophical about it. Will drive up myself to attend the funeral tomorrow. Writing tonight as I realize I will be too busy tomorrow. And I don't want you to be without mail for too long a period . . .

Will act on your requisition by forwarding a package tomorrow which will contain considerable reading matter; a shoe-shining outfit and if I can rustle up some brownies will do so; if this latter item is not obtainable you will have had at least the package of candy mother sent you last week from your friend Fannie's and the brownies will wait until mother can take care of it herself . . .

Had an extremely profitable month last month, but still playing with the idea of disposing of the business . . .

Nothing further to add, except to ask that you keep writing as often as you possibly can; send us your requisitions for whatever you want and keep well and happy.

Much Love,

Dad

A week later my grandfather writes my dad a letter that, in part, could be any note sent to a child who is simply away at summer camp.

12th April 1943
SERLING'S WHOLESALE MARKET
Food Distributors
117 Washington St.
Binghamton, New York
Dear Rod,
'Twas swell hearing from you Saturday by phone and to know that you are getting along so well. Any Sunday morning that you can we would be only too tickled to have you call. Don't let a little thing like the loss of your wrist watch bother you; there are so many big things to think and fret about now. Sent you a package to-day containing:

25 Funny Books
1 wallet—(Sue's) to use for dress
1 wallet—mine for rough wear
1 carton with packing, stamped and addressed to forward your glasses to Hills, Schenectady for replacement of lens you broke.

Your name is on the service board at the center and also at the court house.

You requisitioned candies and cookies in your last letter, but this crossed a shipment on its way to you. Will send you more right a long, and don't hesitate to keep your orders coming and will fill to the best of our ability.

Still working on the potential disposition of the meat business. Don't know how successful I will be but will keep you advised of anything momentous occurring—naturally.

Point rationing in our business is considerable of a headache.
Taking twice as long to wait on the trade at retail and much
more time taken up in billing out the wholesale what with
having to figure the points per pound which the instigators of the
system had to make it as hard as possible by stipulating
fractional points so that it is exercising my mathematical acumen
to figure out the fractional points and the fractional ounces. Can
you visualize how nervous I would be on a Saturday morning?
Taking it all in my stride, however, my nervousness being
assuaged somewhat with the hope that it won't be long before
someone else will have to take it and all the rest of the grief this
type of business is subject to.
Nothing further to add except much love as usual.

Dad

April 1943, from his mother:

I watch for the mailman every day, when he hands me a letter from
you or Bob he sure gets a smile from me. I am proud of you honey.
All my friends say, "Don't you worry about Rod. He will get any
where he wants to. He has what it takes. Personality Plus."

That same month—a letter from his friend Julie Golden:

Jack talks as if you'll be overseas this month. My God, you
weren't kidding in March, were you? Just how long before you'll
be going, Roddy, or don't you know? If it's soon, I can't think of
a helluva lot to say to you. Personally I wish you'd never have
to go, but that won't help things. And the two guys in your
regiment getting killed won't help things either. They got theirs
merely in training, not in conflict. It's sad and sickening, but I
don't think I'm going to worry about you. You can take care of
yourself as well as if not better than anyone I know, and I'm
satisfied that nothing is going to happen to you . . . Write soon,
Ro. If you're being shipped, write sooner. You know I wish you
the best luck in the world Private Serling. See you later . . . Julie

During basic training, my father wants to make a little extra money and earn some privileges. He decides to take up boxing and is trained by an ex-pro who had sixty-eight fights of his own.

My father has a lucky streak and wins seventeen fights in the flyweight division.

Monday april 26 - 43.

My dear boy-

We sure did get a laugh out of your last letter. So you are now a feather weight boxer. I wish you could see Dad's grin when he read that you won the fight. (quote Dad) That little devil, Can you imagine him fighting and winning." He told all the men in the store. Than about 1 hr after we received your letter. Dad got a telegram from Bob. "Money stollen, Please wire me ten dollars. Isn't there some way the army could put a stop to all this stealing?

We received a letter from Bob. He officially has been transferred to intelligence unit. He seems very happy. No doubt has written to you all about himself.

Sent you the dog chain, stamps & brush that you asked for in your last letter. (nuts too).

Julie has been transferred to Endicot store

A week later, May 1, his mother writes, "*So you are the offi-
cial champion boxer. What a tough lug you must be. Don't you dare
get your good looking face all slammed up.*"

In the eighteenth fight, a professional boxer breaks his nose
and knocks him out in the third round. My father gives up
boxing. He doesn't give it up in his imagination, though.
Boxing will be a recurring theme in several stories to come.

A newspaper, praising his boxing ability, says that he has
"the ring in his blood." Years later my father says, "In truth, I'd
left a helluva lot of my blood in several rings!" (I remember
him pointing to his nose one time, indicating to me where it
was broken in two places.)

There is a gap here where letters exist, I am certain, but I
don't have them and then on December 2, 1943, Sam writes
my father:

> *Dear Rod, Naturally we were disappointed to get the
> information that the leaves have been cancelled, but when we
> philosophized of the wrench the leave-taking always gives we
> were somewhat reconciled. Then too, while we were more
> concerned over the way you felt, we must remember this is war—
> and disappointments, heart-aches and other miseries must be
> almost constantly borne, hoping and praying always that the
> compensations when it's all over will heal the ravages caused by
> the miseries . . .*
>
> *If we could only be sure that you do not feel too keenly the
> disappointment of not getting home once more before you leave
> we could be more easily reconciled. Perhaps we were too devoted
> parents in our constant efforts to shield you from disappointments
> so your training in this direction is somewhat lacking. I hope I
> haven't failed as a father. I know I have been lacking in lots of
> ways. I have been harsh and allowed my unreasonable temper to
> control my better judgment—which I should have had. Another
> complex which I very much regret is my being undemonstrative. I*

never dreamed that you wanted to get closer to me; it would have been worth everything to me to let you indulge your impulses or inclinations, but your not appreciating my complex and my not knowing your desires, we both missed out. Pray God I will have the opportunity to change this . . .

My grandfather goes on to talk about cutting back his business and how he is *"beginning to see the possibility of a well-earned rest."* He writes, *"I need one badly—at least a mental relaxation. Physically I never worked too hard, but would have preferred this to the constant strain mentally."*

Sam closes the letter: *"I hope this letter doesn't strike you as maudlin. There I go again letting my complex rule my judgment. But, Rod, I want you to know that no father was more fond of a son than I am—always have been—and always will be of you. Forget, please, the infrequent lapses into actions, reprehensible and always regretted. All My love, Rod, in which mother of course joins me."*

The letters to and from my dad's parents then continue: *"Hello to our dear boy . . . we miss you . . ."* until one day, training is complete and my father is put on a troop ship and sent to the Pacific as part of an assault and demolitions team.

And here the letters stop.

Chapter 7

"New Guinea Nightmare"

Down here there are no Ten Commandments
And a man can raise a thirst,
Here live the outcasts of Civilization
Life's Victims at their worst.

Down the steaming Guinea coast
Live the men that God forgot,
Battling the ever present fever,
The itch and the tropical rot.

Living with the natives,
Down in the sweltering zone,
Rooting like hogs in a wallow,
Ten thousand miles from home.

Nobody knows we're living,
Nobody gives a damn;
Back home we're soon forgotten—
We soldiers of Uncle Sam.

Drenched with sweat in the evenings
We stew in foxholes and dream,
Killing ourselves with alkie
To dam up memory's stream.

At night we lie on our pillows
With ills no doctor can cure.
Hell no, we're not convicts,
Just soldiers on a tour.

We have but one consolation,
And that to you I shall tell,
When we die we'll all go to heaven,
Because we've done our hitch in hell.

—ROD SERLING, verses sent home
while on deployment

I SIT AGAIN ON the floor surrounded by my father's letters from training camp. They are now more than fifty years old. I am overwhelmed, barely able to get through this poignant collection. Letters from his mom and dad and his friends, and the ones he wrote to them before he is shipped overseas, are yellowed and musty and brittle. I handle them with care, as if they will dissolve in my touch and disappear forever.

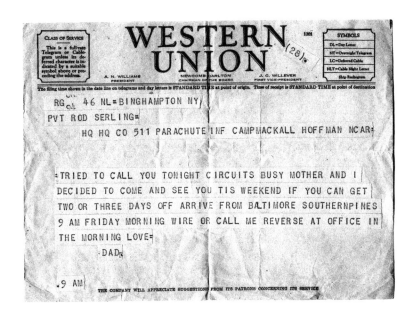

I open them slowly, tentatively. Some are typed, some of the words in ink have vanished. I get out a magnifying glass and try to recapture them. I think of my dad at eighteen, a boy sitting on a cot beside other boys on their cots, also just eighteen, reading letters from home for the first time, unknowingly about to step into their own Twilight Zones.

At the bottom of this box of letters is my dad's high school yearbook, *The Panorama 1943*. I leaf through it and look at the faces of his friends and acquaintances smiling back. They look so young, so expectant and happy. This is truly the last glimpse of their youth.

His belt buckle that says: "11th Airborne Div." is also in the box. Beneath it is where I find the *Airborne 511* booklet. After the pages my father has annotated are the rows of tiny photographs, no larger than postage stamps, below which are the names of the boys in his platoon. They wear their brand-new army Garrison caps and uniforms, and I know, with this dreadful gift of hindsight, who won't make it back.

I think of a *Twilight Zone* from the first season, a war episode called "The Purple Testament," about a lieutenant who, while looking into the faces of the soldiers in his combat platoon, sees a strange light that reveals who among them are about to die. In his opening narration, my father says:

> *Infantry Platoon, U.S. Army. Philippine Islands, 1945.*
> *These are the faces of the young men who fight. As if some omniscient painter has mixed a tube of oils that were at one time earth brown, dust gray, blood red, beard black, and fear-yellow white, and these men were the models. For this is the province of combat and these are the faces of war.*

When passing a small shaving mirror, the lieutenant sees the light glow off his own reflection. As I watch this episode years later, I understand what my father is saying; you can't experience the deaths of your fellow soldiers without a piece of you dying as well.

In October 1944, my father's division—the 511th Airborne—lands at Bito Beach on the east side of Leyte Island in the Philippines. The tough living conditions are de-scribed in a worn news clipping also tucked into the box:

> *When it rains they walk in a gumbo of mud. When the sun*
> *shines they sweat in temperatures approaching 100 degrees. At*
> *night they shiver in the chill mists that billow down from the*
> *mountains . . . High in the central part of this island they are*
> *surrounded by a sun-baked airstrip hewed out of a tangled jungle*
> *forest. The camp is entirely supplied by air and none but the*
> *hardy, jungle-trained fighters and natives can negotiate the trail*
> *that leads to the outside world.*

My father's first brush with death comes in one of the bat-tles for Leyte. Suddenly, out of the jungle a Japanese soldier is standing right before him, his gun pointed directly at my fa-ther. My dad freezes, staring back. He can't move; there is nothing he can do. The soldier has a perfect shot, and my fa-ther knows that. In that instant his war buddy, Richard, see-ing the enemy, shoots him over my father's shoulder. I first hear this story when this friend visits my dad at the cottage so many, many years later and I follow them down the path to the lake and listen to them talk. I hear my dad say, "I have never been so God damn scared in my life" and his friend re-sponding but I am only about seven, too young to compre-hend the significance of the words or the depth of this friendship. Now, though, I imagine that terrible day where, in an excruciating instant, my father's friend altered everything that would happen from that day forward. I think, too, of these young soldiers, kids, thrust into unimaginable condi-tions.

The battle of Leyte is considered by many historians to be among the fiercest fighting of the war. Recently, Amy Boyles Johnston, a writer researching my father's early work, found a folder of his early writings among a collection of his college papers archived at the University of Wisconsin. It contained a short story called, "First Squad, First Platoon." It opened with a dedication to his unborn children:

To My Children
I'm dedicating my little story to you; doubtless you will be among the very few who will ever read it. It seems war stories aren't very well received at this point. I'm told they're out-dated, untimely and as might be expected—make some unpleasant reading. And, as you have no doubt already perceived, human beings don't like to remember unpleasant things. They gird themselves with the armor of wishful thinking, protect themselves with a shield of impenetrable optimism, and, with a few exceptions, seem to accomplish their "forgetting" quite admirably.

But you, my children, I don't want you to be among those who choose to forget. I want you to read my stories and a lot of others like them. I want you to fill your heads with Remarque and Tolstoy and Ernie Pyle. I want you to know what shrapnel, and "88's" and mortar shells and mustard gas mean. I want you to feel, no matter how vicariously, a semblance of the feeling of a torn limb, a burnt patch of flesh, the crippling, numbing sensation of fear, the hopeless emptiness of fatigue. All these things are complimentary to the province of War and they should be taught and demonstrated in classrooms along with the more heroic aspects of uniforms, and flags, and honor and patriotism. I have no idea what your generation will be like. In mine we were to enjoy "Peace in our time." A very well meaning gentleman waved his umbrella and shouted those very words . . . less than a year before the whole world went to war. But this gentleman was suffering the worldly disease of insufferable optimism. He and his fellow humans kept polishing the rose colored glasses when actually they should have taken them off. They were sacrificing reason and reality for a brief and temporal peace of mind, the same peace of mind that many of my contemporaries derive by steadfastly refraining from remembering the War that came before.

All this was in my time, youngsters—I hope not in yours. Perhaps some day men's—

The rest of the letter is missing. But the story begins:

*The Pacific rain thundered down from the skies, smashing in
sheets against the heavy jungle foliage, driving into the muddy
ground like millions of bullets. Driving, incessant rain that
dissolved the earth in a fluid mass; uncomfortable hostile rain
that caked mud on weapons, uniforms and equipment . . .*

*They all listened . . . and heard . . . the dull, roaring throb of
the airplane motors. A hundred throats became dry and throbbing
with hope and excitement. Everything was riding with those
planes . . . relief was coming on wings . . . food was en route from
the sky . . . food food food to end their gnawing hunger pains . . .
food and ammunition to keep them going and best of all
discovery! The regiment had found out where they were.*

Corporal Levy suddenly found his sense of humor.

*"Scorecards," he screamed. "Scorecards. Can't tell a piper Cub
from a P-40 without a scorecard!"*

Men yelled their laughter.

*"Chow call." He screamed again, "Chow call boys . . . ham
and eggs by airmail . . . ham and eggs and fried potatoes
boys . . ."*

*He didn't even know what he was saying . . . only knew that
something inside him made him scream out of his happiness.*

*"Chow call!" It boomed and echoed down the ranks of
yelling, overjoyed men.*

*Then the planes were visable . . . three . . . four . . . five piper
cubs winging their way in at less than six hundred feet . . . the
blue Air Force Stars plainly visible on their wings.*

*First pass over the clearing—tiny men at the plane door could
be seen pushing out bundles. There goes a red chute popping open
like a flower bud . . . there goes a green chute another red.
Beautifully dropped, gentleman of the Air Corps . . . the
equipment chutes were landing directly inside the perimeter—
dead center aiming.*

*The planes circled the clearing and came in for another
pass . . . this time heavy crates, unchuted, were falling in clusters*

*from the sky . . . fifty pound boxes of K-rations . . . a hundred or
more of them hurtling earthward.*

*"Make it kosher, boys," Levy screamed, tears rolling down his
cheeks. "Make it Kosher . . . even if you have to drop a Rabbi."*

Men convulsed with laughter.

*But suddenly the new danger was recognized. The heavy
crates were smashing into the earth close to their holes. Men
started shouting in alarm.*

*Lieutenant Panders raced around the perimeter, slipping and
sliding in the mud, shouting for the men to take cover. Once he
threw himself headlong into a puddle to narrowly escape getting
crushed by one of the boxes.*

*The men leaped into their holes as box after box plowed into
the earth and fell closer and closer to them.*

*Levy just stood there where he was waving his arms and
shouting, Sergeant Etherson pulling at him from behind trying to
get him down in the hole. But Levy was oblivious to all around
him except the food which poured down.*

*"It's raining chow boys . . . it's raining chow." His shrill voice
pierced the air all around.*

*Then there was a sudden dull thud as a crate hit the ground
near the first squad's positions, throwing mud into the air and all
but covering up the holes with it.*

*Sergeant Etherson climbed slowly out of his hole, wiping the
mud from his eyes and grinning broadly. He noticed Levy lying
face down a few feet from him. "Ok Mel . . . you can come up for
air. Ok Mel start singin' they quit droppin" . . . Hey Mel . . .
Mel . . . Levy!"*

*He stopped short and noticed all at once that Levy's head
rested a few feet from the rest of his body.*

Mel Levy was one of my father's best friends.

On patrol in the jungle one afternoon my father is wounded
when an exploding mortar shell sends shrapnel into his wrist
and knee. He is awarded the Purple Heart for his wounds and

Bronze Star for bravery in combat on Leyte. Years later he keeps these medals in his dresser drawer in their cases and sometimes takes them out and shows them to me.

The knee injury, an omnipresent ghost, will haunt him throughout his life as a painful souvenir of the devastation of war; a constant reminder, too, of his friends who never made it home.

Frequently his knee gives out and spontaneously begins to bleed. Often he wears a knee brace, but occasionally he goes without it, and walking down the stairs, suddenly having no control, he will fall. It is frightening to watch. My sister and I witness this many times and cry. From where he has fallen, my dad always tells us he is fine, but it takes a while for him to get up, and the strain on his face is heartbreaking.

In 1945, while still in combat, my father meets Russell Schwen. "I first met your dad in April 1945 in the Philippines," he tells me. "The fighting in Luzon was winding down, and we were bivouac'd at the base of Mount Malpunyo just outside the village of Lipa. Your dad's company and mine were in the same area. I think the reason we first gave a 'Hi' was that we were both somewhat vertically challenged among a bunch of six-footers. We found out that we had many common interests in books, old movies, religion, and general philosophy of life. We were both affected greatly by the war, as I think everyone who was in combat situations was, especially in the Infantry, which was many times a face-to-face encounter. Killing is not easily forgotten. I still have combat nightmares after sixty-five years... We spent many hours talking. I was so impressed with your dad's knowledge of things. At the time he was nineteen and I was eighteen. We both grew up reading the dime novels in the drug store. Sci-Fi, *Amazing Stories, Adventures of the Lafayette Escadrille*— flying in World War One, et cetera. Your dad loved to perform. I remember the short stories he used to write and recite with great flourish for our small group. I can picture him so clearly; almost hear his voice..."

My father continues to serve in the Pacific until the end. Russ recalls the celebration when they heard the first A-bomb was dropped: "In the coming invasion of Japan, the Eleventh Airborne Division was scheduled to jump over the Tokyo area which would have been a slaughter for both us and the Japanese. Doubtful that we would have survived. A couple of days later we were loaded into planes and flown to Okinawa to a war that was still in progress. While there, the second bomb was dropped and we knew the war was over. We flew into Japan and landed at Atsugi airfield in Yokohama on August 29, 1945. On September second we were at Yokosuku naval base in Tokyo and we could see the battleship *Missouri* where the surrender was being signed. We were then loaded on a train to Morioka. Your dad was with us through all of this. When the point system started, everyone was looking forward to the trip going home. Your dad was in slightly before I was; he had more points, and so we would not be going home on the same shipment."

Shortly before my father's group is ready, he gets the terrible news from the American Red Cross that his father has died of a heart attack. Sam was fifty-two years old. My father immediately asks for an emergency leave. It is refused. Sam's death in the midst of the horror of war, coupled with the army's refusal to allow him to go home, destroys something within my dad. It is a loss of such magnitude that he will never truly recover.

Russ recalls: "I met your dad in the hall right after he received news of his father's death...I have never seen anyone so devastated."

I can only hope that my dad remembered a letter he wrote his father (that my mother just sent me):

January 7th
Philippines
Dear Dad,
*Your letters, though infrequent, are never read less than two or
three times over at a sitting and I never fail to read parts of them
to the guys; they're letters any son would be proud to receive. See
what you can do, Dad, about putting a few more through to
me—they'd be appreciated.*

   *Just as you and Mom thought mainly about some future
Christmas—my thoughts were along the same line on my
birthday. We were still in combat—but you'd be surprised—a
guy can do some thinking in a fox hole. You know Dad—if you
and I have had differences—and little run-ins occasionally it's
not for you to apologize. All my life you've given me everything
I've wanted—I never so much as gave it a thought that you
might find it tough to keep supplying me with every whim and
the idea of repaying you never entered my head. Accordingly my
gratefulness was a shallow, momentary thing that couldn't of made
you understand that your efforts were REALLY appreciated.*

   *So Dad—when that future Christmas when we're together
again rolls around—you can put aside all thoughts of making up
for the past—it'll be for me to start showing that twenty years of
your slaving away and worrying just for my benefit wasn't
thrown away on a selfish and thoughtless kid. Sure I've had it
pretty tough at times—I've had my share of being wet and cold
and hungry. I've dodged plenty of lead and faced the Japs but it's
made a man out of me Dad—it made me realize that I had to
put out for myself because I didn't have a self-sacrificing Dad
around to look out for me. It's done some good, I guess Dad.*

   *Hope I don't sound too maudlin—I guess that may be the
case when you think so much of a person as I do of you.
However, be assured that my every thought, and hope and prayer
is of our eventual reunion—that's something worth fighting
for—right there.*

   Tell Dearest I'll write tomorrow—I feel fine.

Rod.

Over the following weeks there is a great deal of trauma. Russ remembers they were living in what had been a Japanese agricultural school. "Our building caught fire in the middle of the night and we had to go out the windows. Lost all our guarded stuff we were going to take home. Just before that happened, our first sergeant committed suicide in the orderly room right next door. He was such a nice guy, much older than most of us . . . I think he was 28. I could not understand why after going through the whole war, he would shoot himself . . . I can remember several suicides. War and killing is a devastating experience for people."

Years after the war, my father will say, "I was bitter about everything and at loose ends when I got out of the service. I think I turned to writing to get it off my chest."

He will be plagued by nightmares of war throughout his life; yet will forever wear his silver paratrooper bracelet. Sometimes I hear him scream in the middle of the night, and in the morning he tells me, "I dreamed the Japanese were coming at me." He transforms one nightmare into a *Twilight Zone* titled "A Quality of Mercy."

It's August, 1945, the last grimy pages of a dirty, torn book of war. The place is the Philippine Islands. The men are what's left of a platoon of American Infantry, where dulled and tired eyes set deep in dulled and tired faces can now look toward a miracle. That moment when the nightmare appears to be coming to an end. But they've got one more battle to fight, and in a moment, we'll observe that battle. August 1945, Philippine Islands. But in reality, it's high noon in The Twilight Zone.

Although my father's physical wounds are a daily reminder of the war, they pale against the emotional scars he and many war veterans endure. He turns to writing as catharsis. Like so many writers of his generation, the war continues to provide material and motivation throughout his career. While teaching an adult writing class at Antioch College in the 1960s, he sums up the effects of war like this: "Shrapnel wounds and mangled, bullet ridden bodies are not the only casualties of war. There are casualties of the mind. Every war produces a backwash, a residue of pain and grief."

My dad returns home almost three years to the day after he enlisted. In this dark time in the South Pacific, he has narrowly escaped death, his father has died, and several of his war buddies have been killed. He is, in fact, one of the few who survived from the squad he started with.

On the final page of his story, "First Squad, First Platoon," he writes about the day he left, January 13, 1946:

> Snow was falling in bleak, gray Yokahama harbor and the troops boarding the ship huddled closer together in line by the gangplank awaiting orders to board it. The big ship sitting at the dock was covered with flags and gaily festooned paper and signs.
>
> "Stateside Express" the one huge sign read on the side of the ship.
>
> Serling looked at the decorations and wondered to himself why they seemed so hollow and incongruous.
>
> He was going home, he kept telling himself—going home. How many times during the past three years had he pictured this scene, how many hopes and dreams and plans he'd pictured in his mind . . .
>
> The boat whistle sent smoke and shrill noise into the sky and the troops started shuffling ahead up the gangplank.
>
> Home.
>
> Warm comfortable home.
>
> Peaceful, quiet, happy home.
>
> Serling put his jaws close together and forced the other images out of his mind's eye . . .

*Out of his mind he pushed them . . . or tried to push them,
but as he came to the top of the gangplank and stepped aboard,
the images still stuck, still persisted, still ran up and down his
consciousness.*

A sailor approaches and says:

*"This way soldier—down those steps . . . whatsa matter—you
don't look happy."*

"Happy? Hell, I'm the happiest goddamn guy aboard."

The sailor laughed.

"I doubt that . . ."

*And as Serling lugged his duffle bag down the narrow steps to
the hold, he said under his breath, "I doubt it too." And little
formless ghosts inside his mind echoed his words, "I doubt it . . . I
doubt it too . . ."*

I envision my dad on that day as he is leaving, twenty-one
years old and weighing one hundred and eighteen pounds,
wearing, still, his combat boots and uniform. I imagine his
hands, cut and calloused, holding that filthy bag on his shoulder as he descends into the Liberty ship, the USS *Herald Of
The Morning*, and begins the long trip home.

I look at a photograph of the ship, a steel gray monster, and
think of it plowing through rough waters, the troops quar-
tered below on their bunks five high and close together. I
imagine them convening on deck, shoulder to shoulder, leaning against the rails, sharing a smoke, and when they catch
sight of each other, I wonder, do they startle for a moment?
Just before they turn away, do they see the ghosts of the boys
they once were dissolving in the eyes of the men staring
back?

Two decades after the war, in 1965, my father decides to go
back to the Philippines, back to his past. My mother is meeting him there a few days later. He writes to two of his

friends—Alden Schwimmer (a vet who fought in Europe)
and Bill Lindau, who was in the Philippines with my dad.

Dear Ald,
Been an odd day . . . It's all quite incredible—not that twenty
years have gone by nor even that I survived . . . it is just to walk
over the same ground after so much has happened and to
remember it all with such infinite clarity.
    Last week, I went back to a little village outside of Manila
called Paranaque. My last visit there was February 4, 1945, and
I spent one day and one night getting shelled. So I took the
nostalgic walk one early morning and drank it all in and began
to feel sad because nobody came up to me as they did twenty
years ago and grin and say, "Victory, Joe!" So three hours later I
went through a tiny alley and wound up on a dirty beach
overlooking the ocean, and this little grimy 8-year-old kid comes
up to me and says, "What are you looking for, Joe?" And I cup
this dirty little brown face in my hand and I answer, "My youth,
Joe."
    Hey, Ald! You can't go back. At least you can't go back and
experience. You return as a tourist just to observe. Like visiting a
cemetery. Nobody's around to talk to you and reminisce, even
though deep in your gut you have this urge to tap some ghost on
a shoulder and say, "Hey, buddy, remember that afternoon . . ."

And to his friend Bill Lindau:

You walk in the place and suddenly somebody does something to
the years. And you're back. You're a long way back . . . from
where you landed a couple of eternities ago. And you break into
a sweat because the recollections are so damned bitter-sweet and
so incredibly clear . . .
    So what the hell do I tell you about this trip? . . . You don't
purge any of the stuff that's been eating there for so long. All it
really does is bring it up to the surface and makes you wonder
about your attitude of the day before yesterday and the sort of

person you were and how in the hell have you aged so much in the ensuing time. It's not cathartic for the imposed ills of the lifelong post-war regrets. But it does take them out of the pores and lets you examine them in daylight. And then I guess somewhere along the line you put them back inside you.

Chapter 8

*I never had a master plan that included a built-in
compulsion to write. I really didn't know what the hell I
wanted to do with my life. I went to Antioch because my
brother went there. I thought I'd major in physical
education because I was interested in working with kids.
This was a pretty amorphous thing, not really thought
out or planned—but it constituted some vague objective,
which, of course, the war put to an end.*

—ROD SERLING

THE YEAR IS 1946. The place is Yellow Springs, Ohio.

By all appearances, he looks like any other college student
with his stack of books and pens and papers, but he and the
other GIs who returned from World War II are not archetypal
college freshmen. They carry something unique yet indis-
cernible and, in those days, not fully defined. The condition
will one day be known colloquially as "Battle Fatigue," "Traumatic War Neurosis," or, ultimately, "Post Traumatic Stress
Disorder." But in 1946, my dad and these other young vets feel
desperately overwhelmed by something then labeled "Shell
Shock"—a condition still sometimes misinterpreted and for
which treatment is, at best, primitive. Many vets suffer the
aftermath—terrible insomnia, panic, and haunting flashbacks.

Monroe "Mike" Newman, a prominent economist and old
college friend of my dad's remembers those years at Antioch:

*I first met your father in 1946 when, as a freshman, I was housed
in a dorm room at Antioch that was a few doors away from his.*

The informal social structure in the dorm has to be understood.
There was a group of veterans, older and better financed (thanks
to the GI Bill) and the non-veterans (younger and generally
poorer), of which I was one. Within the veterans group, there was
a sub-group of combat veterans, to which your dad adhered. In
present day terms, the combat veterans showed signs of PTSD.
(One friend was by far the worst, depressed and frequently
drunk.) Despite these allegiances, there was a high degree of
personal interaction among the dorm residents and your dad soon
became a dominant force. I recall him being very close to his
mother. He was obviously very smart, never reticent, had strong
convictions, was quick to angrily express them and seemed to
have no patience with levity. Some examples:

A group was sitting on the floor in the dorm hallway,
discussing the wisdom and ethics of the death penalty. Your dad
came out of his room (looking tall since we were all on the floor)
and told us we'd overlooked a key. (I think that was his word.)
The key was that some part of the executioner died with each
execution. Immediately, he returned to his room and slammed the
door.

Your father's convictions and anger were focused on anyone
who did either of the following: Got a haircut from anyone but
Mr. Pemberton, the only barber in town who would cut the hair
of African-Americans. Did not go to the Old Trail Tavern but
rather to the establishment across Xenia Avenue which did not
serve African-Americans.

In the early fall of that first year at Antioch, my dad often
goes to an infrequently used golf course and sits there alone.
Sometimes he goes and drinks Southern Comfort. Sometimes he goes just to think, to turn down the noises in his
head. But he soon realizes the isolation is only serving to augment his wounded thoughts. He begins to feel what he eventually describes as "a kind of compulsion to get some
thoughts down and the desperate sense of a terrible need for
some sort of therapy...I needed to get it out of my gut,
write it down. This is the way it began for me."

He changes his major from physical education to language and literature, and slowly, gradually, as time affords some distance from the war, some of the old, gregarious Rod reemerges. He is writing, directing, and acting in weekly productions on a local radio station. He begins to enjoy Antioch, of which he will one day say: "The freedom to speak, the freedom to reason, and above all, the right to question—this I think is tradition at Antioch."

My dad is moved by the words of Horace Mann, the first president of the college. "Be ashamed to die until you have won some victory for humanity." Twenty years later, he uses these very words in a poignant *Twilight Zone* episode, "The Changing of the Guard." British actor Donald Pleasence portrays Professor Ellis Fowler—"a gentle, bookish guide to the young," who is being forced to retire after a long teaching career at a boys' school. Convinced that his life has no meaning left and that, in fact, he has accomplished nothing in his lifetime and will quickly be forgotten, he resolves to commit suicide with an old pistol in front of a campus statue of Horace Mann, on whose base the quotation is inscribed. But then, mysteriously, he hears school bells and returns to his classroom to find the ghosts of some of his dead former students who convince him that the lessons from his teaching are what inspired each of them to their individual acts of heroism, courage, and self-sacrifice. When the ghosts depart, he realizes Mann's words do apply to him, and he can retire, and live, in peace with himself. He tells his housekeeper:

> *I do believe . . . I do believe that I have left my mark. "Be ashamed to die until you have won some victory for humanity." I didn't win them but I helped others to win them. I believe that now. So in that way—even in small measure—they are victories I can share.*

I realize how much this episode reveals of my dad's thoughts and feelings: the great appreciation he had of mentors and teachers, the struggle for self-worth, the fear of being forgotten, and the reverence for valor and sacrifice.

Throughout his life he kept in touch with his high school teacher and mentor, Helen Foley. In a 1968 Binghamton Central High School commencement speech, he refers to her as his "dear friend." He even names a *Twilight Zone* character after her—a teacher in the episode, "Nightmare as a Child."

At Antioch, there are not many coeds on campus my father does not know or has not dated by the time he first sees Carolyn Kramer from Columbus, Ohio. She is at Antioch despite the initial misgivings of her grandparents, who raised her after the death of her mother, when she was only two. Her grandmother Louise had wanted her to go to Wellesley, where both she and her daughter had gone. This, despite the fact that Louise's father Edward had been president of Antioch in the 1870s.

My mother somehow convinces her grandparents, and soon their reservations completely dissipate as they see she is immersing herself in college life. Warren, her father, is not a part of this decision, having left her upbringing to her maternal grandparents.

One day my father is with some friends, out on the student quad, when my mother walks by. She has her books tucked beneath her arm. She sees him but pretends not to, mindful of his reputation as a "lady's man." Still, she is drawn to his rugged, dark good looks and perhaps, unwittingly, smiles as she rushes by.

I picture them, those early years, he twenty-two, she just eighteen. Her hair, dark, falls to her shoulders and shines in the early morning sun. She has her hand up to shield her eyes.

Her smile is shy, reserved, so unlike his. One day she'll tell me that when she first sees him, he is pretending to be a monkey, an impersonation that becomes part of his permanent repertoire to the later delight of my sister and me. My mother thinks he is a bit of an idiot, but funny, and she hears from friends he is bright.

And him? What is he thinking? He is looking at her. She is stunning. Her skin slightly tanned, her hair in a headband. The way, he will tell me one day, he loves it. He doesn't know who she is, only that her name is Carol.

My father makes it a point to seek out this striking girl, maneuvering himself into a situation where they can formally meet. They have coffee and make plans to get together for lunch, for dinner, another date, and then another. Soon they are inseparable.

They marry on July 31, 1948. My mother wears a simple ivory knee-length dress she has saved up for. My dad wears a suit that must have been secondhand because I cannot imagine he could afford a new one. The camera catches them on their way out of the church in Columbus. There, waving on the steps, my great-grandparents, my grandmother Esther, my uncle Bob, some friends, and my young parents waving back. Today, the framed picture hangs on the cottage wall.

The next photo captures my parents running through a shower of colored confetti, my father just ahead, holding my mother's hand, pulling her along with him as they get into a waiting car parked on the street below.

I imagine my father is driving, my mother beside him. They are turned around, looking at the people left behind. Their hands, again midair, waving. A string of cans tied to the bumper, clanging as the car pulls away.

They spend their honeymoon and late summer months at the cottage. They drag stones from a pasture and some from the ravine below to build a terrace. When it is done, they put out a table that even then is slightly rickety, but will last for decades.

My mother writes captions for the pictures. In one, my dad is at the table: "first breakfast": Another is of my mother knee-deep in the water of Cayuga Lake, hair piled high on her head: "Madam Butterfly." In another, my dad at a type-writer: "Rod hard at work." A few of the photographs are black and white, others in fading colors, and all are labeled, capturing these first moments of their marriage; a marriage that will last until my father's death, twenty-seven years later.

When my mother informed her grandparents that she wanted to marry my father, they had some initial concerns; she was so young. My great-grandmother writes in her diary:

> About a year ago Carol made it known that she had met a young man, also an Antioch student, and they wished to be married and continue their respective courses together. She seemed so "perilously" young that we had grave doubts about the wisdom of that step. But as time went on, and we saw how strong the attachment was on both sides, we felt that we had no right to obstruct this union. They were married last July. They are very busy and very happy. Carol is now Mrs. Rodman E. Serling and the more we see of Rod, the better we like him. He has an interesting mind and a warm, affectionate nature. They both definitely expect to graduate in 1950. Rod is specializing in radio and Carol in child psychology.

It has been written that my mother's family disowned her because of her marriage to my dad, but this isn't true. It was only her father who objected and as far as my mother was concerned he did not have a voice in her decision. Suddenly, though, deciding that he has a say, her father told her, "You are not to marry that black-eyed Jew." Brought up in Mississippi, her father from a young age had been surrounded with prejudice. Clearly, he never changed and there was concern he might attempt to stop the wedding, but he did not show up.

My dad had an absolute antipathy toward any form of prejudice. He wrote about it throughout his career, and everyone who knew him acknowledges it. In 1967, he told a *Los Angeles Times* reporter, "I happen to think the singular evil of our time is prejudice. It is from this evil that all other evils grow and multiply. In almost everything I've written, there is a thread of this: man's seemingly palpable need to dislike someone other than himself."

Decades later, in an interview with Linda Brevelle for *Writer's Digest Magazine*, even more impassioned, he talked about how deeply, personally, it affected him:

> *Bias and prejudice make me angry . . . more than anything. Somebody sent me a copy of the American Nazi newspaper the other day—published in, I guess, Arlington, Virginia—there were words in it like "coon" and "kike" and things like that, and I was very distraught. That made me terribly angry. Viciously angry. Even to creating daydreams about how I could go there and bump off some of these pricks. But it's short-lived. I'm much too logical for that. That ticks me off. I can't think of anything else that really makes me angry.*

At some point, both my parents must have forgiven my mother's father. I recall Christmas gifts exchanged with Warren and him visiting us at the cottage. There is a photo of him standing behind me when I am about six. On the back of the photo, my mother writes, "Thought you might want this picture—perhaps the only one of your 'grandfather.'"

Despite this documented presence, he leaves no lasting impression. In fact, if not for the photo, I do not even remember him being there. Ever. My only memory of this man who, I shamefully admit, was my grandfather is when he dies.

I am eight years old when I attend his funeral with my mother and don't remember why my sister isn't there as well. Standing outside in the cold Missouri air, I look at the people gathered by his gravesite. My mother's half sister, Deedie, is weeping.

My mother is not.

When my parents first married, they lived on the Antioch campus in student housing set up to accommodate returning GIs with families, war surplus trailers without running water. In the photo album, my mother labels their home, "Trailer #10." It is small, with a kitchen and a tiny living room with a couch that pulls out into a bed. In the corner sits a table that is moved to the center of the room when my parents and their friends play cards under the pale yellow light.

The ceiling has two hatches that open to allow in light and fresh air. One night, while my mother is out, my dad has one of his crazy ideas. He crawls on top of the trailer and, upside down, he hangs his head through the open hatch. He waits a long time for my mother's return, and when she finally arrives he blurts from the ceiling, "*Good Evening*!" and scares the hell out of her. As my mother remembers, "In the darkness of the trailer he looked horrible and I screamed. He got stuck in the hatch . . . I thought he deserved it. Friends had to come and help him out."

On weekends and evenings, my dad is writing whenever he can, typing frantically with two fingers. That spring, when he is twenty-four years old, he receives his first big break. *Dr. Christian's* radio show wires him that his script, "To Live a Dream," about a prizefighter dying of leukemia who wants to help a young fighter succeed, has won second prize. The show bills itself as "The only show on radio where the audience writes the scripts."

The prize for the *Dr. Christian* contest is five hundred dollars and an all-expense-paid trip to New York City. My future parents leave after class on a Friday afternoon and arrive in midtown Manhattan at the Savoy Plaza. Earl Hamner, who will write eight *Twilight Zone* episodes and then the autobiographical series *The Waltons,* has also won. He and my dad first cross paths that day when both are presented their prizes on the show.

Years after my father died, Earl told me, "Your dad changed my life in so many ways and made it possible for me to have accomplished a rich and rewarding career in Hollywood." In a tribute on his website he writes:

> Rod, more than any other man in my professional life, had the greatest influence on me through his kindness, his encouragement, his example, and his unique talent. I have only one regret. I thanked him from time to time, but that afternoon when I heard he was hospitalized I said to myself, "I will call him tomorrow." He died the next day, and I did not get a chance to say good-bye or let him know how very much he had meant to me.

Winning this contest for the radio show is a tremendous and defining moment for my dad, one he will never forget: "For the very first time in your life, somebody has given you money for words that you've written, and that's terribly important. It's a tremendous boon to the ego, to your sense of self-reliance, to your feeling about your own talent."

Prizefighters will appear again several times in my dad's works. In his book *Patterns*—four of his television plays and a personal commentary—my dad talks about the average fighter . . . "He is one of the vast army who never become champions and who are lost to memory as one by one they fall by the ringside." He says, "What seems to give this idea the stature of tragedy is that the business of prizefighting never allows an alternate preparation for another field of endeavor. To be a fighter you have to live as a fighter. Everything you do, every action you take, every moment you live is part of and preparation for the next fight on schedule. And when your career is finished, the profession discards you."

I recall a *Twilight Zone* episode he wrote for the first season titled "The Big Tall Wish." It was broadcast on April 8, 1960, though I saw it much later.

The majority of the actors in "Big Tall Wish" were African American. As Marc Zicree wrote in *The Twilight Zone Companion*:"In 1960, casting blacks in a dramatic show not dealing with racial issues was something practically unheard of, but this was a deliberate move on Serling's part."

"Television," my dad explained, "like its big sister, the motion picture, has been guilty of a sin of omission. Hungry for talent, desperate for the so-called 'new face,' constantly searching for a transfusion of new blood, it has overlooked a source of wondrous talent that resides under its nose. This is the Negro actor."

The episode was about the relationship between Bolie Jackson, a has-been, broken-down boxer and Henry, a little boy living in his ghetto apartment building who adores him. Henry, believing in magic, wishes Bolie a win with "the big tall wish."

In the opening narration my father says:

In this corner of the universe, a prizefighter named Bolie Jackson, one hundred and eighty-three pounds and an hour and a half away from a comeback at St. Nick's arena. Mr. Bolie Jackson, who by the standards of his profession is an aging, over-the-hill relic of what was, and who now sees a reflection of a man who has left too many pieces of his youth in too many stadiums for too many years before too many screaming people. Mr. Bolie Jackson, who might do well to look for some gentle magic in the hard-surfaced glass that stares back at him.

In the locker room before the fight that could save his career, Bolie overreacts to a crooked manager, punches the wall, and breaks his right hand. The match is all downhill and he finds himself going down for the count. Watching on television, Henry wishes so hard that the reality is reversed and it is Bolie who wins the fight. However, when the triumphant Bolie returns home, he cannot accept the magic of Henry's wish.

"If you don't believe it, it won't be true!" Henry pleads.
But Bolie professes he is too old to believe in magic and the
results are reversed. Bolie suddenly finds himself on his back
in the ring as the referee completes the ten-count. This time,
Bolie returns—injured, defeated, and dejected. But Henry
still believes in him and still idolizes him: "You looked like a
tiger even so. You looked like a real tiger. I was proud of you,
real proud."

In my dad's closing narration:

*Mr. Bolie Jackson, who left a second chance lying on a heap on a
rosin-spattered canvas at St. Nick's arena. Mr. Bolie Jackson,
who shares the most common ailment of all men, the strange and
perverse disinclination to believe in a miracle, the kind of miracle
to come from a little boy, perhaps only to be found in The
Twilight Zone.*

When I see this episode years after it first airs, long after
my father died, I am struck by the tenderness of the relationship between Bolie and this little boy. The program, although
sentimental, has an edge of steel and never glosses over the
harsh reality and struggle of day-to-day survival for the poor
and marginalized. In the end, it is the magic between this little boy and a down-and-out fighter that triumphs:

*Bolie Jackson went into his room and thought about what he
would have to do next. There would be no more fighting, no
more comeback . . . But tomorrow he and a little boy were going
to the baseball game. "Tomorrow," Bolie had told him, "we'll get
some hot dogs in the park, you and me."*

Chapter 9

ON JUNE 24, 1950, Antioch College is completing last-minute details for its ninety-fifth graduation. It is to begin any moment. There, waiting, sitting in chairs on the lawn, are my father's mother, brother, and my mother's grandparents, all watching as my young parents and their classmates walk across an outdoor stage and graduate to thunderous applause.

My parents move to Cincinnati, about an hour's drive southwest, where my dad works as a staff writer with radio station WLW. It was the job Earl Hamner had just resigned from. He told me, "I took time off to write a novel. Rod stepped into the job I vacated. Years later, when we would run into each other at Hollywood events, your dad would introduce me as 'the man who gave him his first job.'"

Part of his job, as my dad describes it, is to write "folksy" dialogue for two "hayseed" entertainers: "One was a girl yodeler whose falsetto could break a beer bottle at 20 paces." He also writes phony testimonials for a patent-medicine remedy. "It had about twelve percent alcohol by volume and, if the testimonials were to be believed, could cure everything from arthritis to a fractured pelvis."

This experience with patent miracle cures will one day find its way into a *Twilight Zone* script, a western titled "Mr. Denton on Doomsday."

Another part of his job is to write scripts honoring small towns. "In most cases," he said, "the towns I was assigned to honor had little to distinguish them save antiquity. Any dramatization beyond the fact that they existed physically, usually had one major industry, a population, and a founding date, was more fabrication than documentation."

All of this begins to wear on my dad. He tosses and turns at night, gets out of bed, lights a cigarette, goes to the window, pulls away the curtain, and looks at the blackened world outside. Night after night he walks the same path across the cold floor. He grows increasingly frustrated, knowing unequivocally what he wants to do. The drudgery at the radio station is not his destiny. He wants to write something serious, something of substance. And so he begins to work two jobs. His days are spent creating copy at the station, and his nights are devoted to script writing.

In retrospect, he will say:

I used to come home at seven o'clock in the evening, gulp down a dinner and set up my antique portable typewriter on the kitchen table. The first hour would then be spent closing all the mental gates and blacking out all the impressions of a previous eight hours of writing. You have to have a pretty selective brain for this sort of operation. There has to be the innate ability to single track the creative processes. And after a year or so of this kind of problem, you have rent receipts, fuel for the furnace and a record of regular eating; but you have also denied yourself, as I did, a basic "must" for every writer. And this is simple solitude— physical and mental. It was during this double-shift period that I collected forty rejection slips in a row. Nobody but a beginning writer can realize just how crushing this is to the ego.

In his final interview, decades later, he sums it up like this:
"In the old days, you were rejected, and not only was a piece
of your flesh cut to pieces, your pocketbook was destroyed.
You know—you don't have bread for rent."

Things begin to change when he sells two radio scripts to
the series "Grand Central Station" and, in 1950, a script to
Stars Over Hollywood, an NBC film series. The script is called
"Grady Everett for the People." He doesn't remember too
much about the story but does distinctly recall that he sells it,
along with all television rights, for one hundred dollars. Years
later, with his typical self-deprecating manner, he says, "As of
this writing the show has aired at least twenty-four times at
odd hours and on odd channels. I will claim immodestly that
it surpassed wrestling; beyond that I'll make no value judgment whatsoever."

My dad is now even more certain he wants to quit WLW
and take the leap to freelancing. One night, he and my
mother go to dinner and discuss his career. This is a pivotal
moment, one that he will summarize in his book *Patterns* and
that my mother will tell me was exactly as he wrote it.

*I sat that night with my wife, Carol, at a Howard Johnson's
restaurant and after a few false starts— "You know, honey, a man
could make a lot of money freelancing"—I talked out my hope.
Freelance writing would no longer be a kind of errant hope to
augment our economy, to be done around the midnight hour on a
kitchen table. Freelance writing would now be our bread, our
butter, and the now-or-never of our whole existence. My wife was
twenty-one, three months pregnant, and a most adept reader of
the score. She knew all about freelance writing. She'd lived with
it with me through college and the two years afterward. She knew
that in my best year I had netted exactly $790. She was well
aware that it was a hit-or-miss profession where the lush days are
followed by the lean. She knew it was seasonal, and there was no
definition of the seasons. She knew that it was a frustrating,
insecure, bleeding business at best, and the guy she was married*

*to could get his pride, his composure and his confidence eaten
away with the acid of disappointment. All this she knew sitting
at a table in Howard Johnson's in 1951. And as it turned out,
this was a scene with no dialogue at all. All she did was to take
my hand. Then she winked at me and picked up a menu and
studied it. And at that given moment, the vision of medicine
bottles, girl yodelers, and guitar-strumming M.C.s faded away
into happy obscurity. For lush or lean, good or bad, Sardi's or
malnutrition, I'd launched a career.*

*I'll grant you the perhaps inordinate amount of sentiment
attached to all the above, but if this were a novel, patent
medicines, Howard Johnson's, and my wife, Carol, would all be
part of an obligatory first chapter.*

In the early fifties, television was evolving into a major medium. To say my dad "was at the right place at the right time" could not be truer. He sells scripts to three of the major dramatic anthology series: *Kraft Television Theater, Studio One,* and *Lux Video Theater.*

"The medium had progressed somewhat past the primitive stage," he recalled in the commentary in *Patterns.*

*There was still a sense of bewilderment on the part of everyone
connected with the shows. And it was still more the rule than the
exception to find the opening camera shot of almost every
television play trained on the behind of one of the cameramen.*

*The television writer's claim to the title "playwright" had been
made, but as yet was not universally accepted. The TV play, once
called by Paddy Chayefsky "the most perishable item known to
man," enjoyed no longevity through the good offices of the
legitimate stage and the motion pictures. The motion-picture
industry looked down at its newborn cousin somewhat as the
president of a gourmet club might examine an aborigine gnawing
a slab of meat.*

Between 1951 and 1954 my dad flies from Ohio to New York City to participate in story conferences and rehearsals of his shows. Despite his gregarious and outgoing personality, he is a young writer trying to establish himself, the proverbial kid from a small town, and still new at the game. He says, "Every time I walked into the network or agency office I had the strange and persistent feeling that I was wearing overalls and Li'l Abner shoes."

One incident he recalls involves a rewrite on a script for *Lux Video Theater* titled "You Be the Bad Guy." My dad says:

> *The script editor asked if I'd like to meet the star of the show. I was ushered into a small office and was introduced to MacDonald Carey, an extremely pleasant, affable guy who stood up and shook my hand and complimented me on the script. I remember standing in the center of the room wondering what the hell I could do next, and deciding that I had outworn my welcome and my purpose and should at this time beat a retreat. I looked busily and professionally at my watch, nodded tersely to all assembled, mumbled something about it being a pleasure to see them all but I had to catch a plane going west, and then turned and crashed into the wall, missing the door by two feet. Then I ran into an oncoming secretary and dropped my briefcase, exposing not only scripts and writing material, but a couple of pairs of socks, some handkerchiefs and some underwear. I traveled light in those days.*

It is the end of the year 1952. November. An endless stretch of gray, rain-soaked days. My dad sits before his typewriter, the wastebasket on the floor beside him overflowing with balled-up papers, each one indistinguishable from the next. He is experiencing every writer's nightmare—a dry period. He writes, "My diet consisted chiefly of black coffee and fingernails. I'd written six half-hour television plays and each one had been rejected at least five times . . . what this kind of thing does to the family budget is obvious; and what it does to the personality of the writer is even worse."

He says he used to stare at his typewriter "like it was a black monster that came up with the mortgage. I had to throttle that panicky fear that rises up in your throat when you get a frantic feeling that you've lost what grip you had—and should have gone into insurance or chicken farming."

He is eager for any opportunity and writes to Raymond Crossett, a story editor at Universal Pictures in Los Angeles, "I'd appreciate the opportunity of meeting you and perhaps querying you on film writing. If the industry is actually looking for new blood—I'd be most appreciative of giving some of mine."

He continues to persevere, and his luck changes. *Lux Theater* buys eleven of his twelve scripts. If there was a glimmer of hope before, this, he says, is the turning point. "You announce your name at the reception desk and the girl nods knowingly and doesn't ask you to repeat it or query you as to its spelling."

As he noted in *Patterns*, the form itself had begun to change:

> *The major advance in the television play was a thematic one. The medium began to show a cognizance of its own particular fortes. It had the immediacy of the living theater, some of the flexibility of the motion picture, and the coverage of radio. It utilized all three in developing and improving what was actually a new art form . . . One could see that the television play was beginning to show depth and a preoccupation with character. Its plots and its people were becoming meaningful. Its stories had something to say.*

My father and mother and two-year-old Jodi move from Cincinnati to Westport, Connecticut. It is the fall of 1954. Outside the window, just past my dad's desk, there is an explosion of fall colors, and in a nearby room my sister plays on the floor, talking to her stuffed animals. My dad begins his seventy-second television script, typing *Patterns* on the title page.

Four months later, he has completed and sold his script. He describes it as:

> *A story of ambition and the price tag that hangs on success. If it professes actually to have a message, it is simply that every human being has a minimum set of ethics from which he operates. This minimum set of ethics often injects itself into a man's own journey upward against competition. When he refuses to compromise those ethics, his career must suffer; when he does compromise them, his conscience does the suffering. There are tragic overtones to this because our society is a competitive one. For every man who goes up, someone has to leave. And when the departure of the aged is neither philosophical nor graceful, there is a kind of aching poignancy in this changing of the guard.*

In an interview in *The Toledo Blade* my dad says he is not a writer who can imagine characters. "They have to be people I've known. I've never known any businessmen very well, but I had a captain during the war who had the same kind of viciousness as the executive in *Patterns* played by Everett Sloane. In the script, I simply put him into a business suit."

He and my mother, now four months pregnant with me, are taking an overnight trip to Ithaca. My dad holds their suitcase and opens the door. A fresh coat of snow blankets the drive but not enough that he'll have to shovel. They hug Jodi good-bye and tell the babysitter, "We just moved here, don't worry, no one will call us."

Kraft Television Theater airs the show (which also stars Richard Kiley, Ed Begley, and Elizabeth Montgomery) while they are in Ithaca. It is Wednesday, January 12, 1955.

The next morning Jack Gould writes in the *New York Times:*

> Nothing in months has excited the television industry as much as the Kraft Television Theater's production of *Patterns*—an original play by Rod Serling. The enthusiasm

is justified. In writing, acting and direction, *Patterns* will stand as one of the high points in the TV medium's evolution. For sheer power of narrative, forcefulness of characterization and brilliant climax, Mr. Serling's work is a creative triumph that can stand on its own.

As my dad said, "One minute after the show went off the air, my phone started to ring and it's been ringing ever since."

In a commentary about writing for television, my dad writes:

There are two ways for a writer to achieve success. One is the long haul, the establishing of a record of consistent quality in his work. The other way is the so-called overnight success, charged and generated by a single piece of writing that captures the imagination and the fancy of the public and the critics. Patterns was that kind of piece. It came on the air unheralded, but pushed me into the limelight with a fabled kind of entry.

Two weeks after its initial production, in an unprecedented move, *Patterns* was again performed live by popular demand. My dad writes about the anatomy of success:

In two weeks after Patterns' initial production, the following happened to me:
 I received 23 firm offers for television writing assignments.
 I received three motion picture offers for screenplay assignments.
 I had fourteen requests for interviews from leading magazines and newspapers.
 I had offers of lunch from Broadway producers.
 I had two offers to discuss novels with publishers.

He has also learned much about his craft. In an article in *The San Diego Union* in October, he comments,

The movies can stress the physical, the horizontal. But TV
learned from the start that in this medium you have to
emphasize the vertical aspects, the story itself and faces in closeup.
Something else that TV writers learned right off is that the little
screen needs human beings—it won't take stark villainy or lily-
white heroism. You had to deal in all the greys that make up
character and try to get at the truth.

The following year, *Patterns* wins my dad his first Emmy. The category is Best Teleplay Writing. He accepts the fact that writers are always considered among the least important participants of the show, and in that moment, when he hears his name called and walks up to accept his award, in a tux he can now afford, there is no one on the stage to present the Emmy. Ed Sullivan, who is supposed to be the presenter, has been called away by photographers. A nervous laughter begins to erupt in the audience. My dad stands there, "lonelier than I shall ever again be, wondering what the hell I should do next." Recognizing the screw-up, someone from Price Waterhouse—in what my dad calls "a perfect spasm of compassion"—grabs an Emmy, meets my dad on stage, and hands it to him.

Despite this inauspicious moment on stage, my dad says, "No matter how you slice it, the little bronze statuette is recognition. It's identity. It's a reward and a compliment and a culmination that comes after a lot of years after banging a typewriter."

My dad is now known as "the guy who wrote *Patterns*." He writes of his overnight fame:

All of a sudden, with no preparation and no expectations, I had
a velvet mantel draped over my shoulders. I treaded my way
through a brand new world of dollar sign mobiles hanging from
the sky, shaking hands with my right hand, depositing checks
with my left, watching my bank account grow, reading my name
in the papers and magazines, listening to myself being
complimented undeservedly and extravagantly.

He finds that he can sell everything, and he does. Years later he will say he shouldn't have been so impetuous; he should have kept many of the old teleplays in the trunk.

Yet with humility that I later know to be typical of him, he does not consider himself at the top of the television-writing heap. "In a given year I might have two successes with other plays in between that weren't so good," he tells J.P. Shanley of *The New York Times*. "Of all the television playwrights I know, Paddy Chayefsky seems to be the only one who has escaped that. He has a fine record of consistency."

Several years later he confirms his admiration for the creator of the New York–bred "Marty" and "The Tenth Man." "Paddy Chayefsky is my idol. He has the gift of melting significance and meaning and humor into one play, often into a single situation. He gave stature to television."

My dad sells six new scripts in a row and some others that are never released. One of them, "The Rack," is produced on *The United States Steel Hour*. It is about the after-effects of mental torture on American prisoners of war in Korea. With compassion and realism, he shows that there are no easy answers to the profound moral questions posed by war. He made that point in a different context the year before on *Studio One* with "The Strike," in which an army major is forced to call a bombing strike on his own platoon.

Paul Newman stars in the film version of "The Rack." My dad thinks it is better than *Patterns*. He feels it was one of the most honest things he has ever written. But *Patterns*, he says, seems to obscure everything he's done, and he is desperate to change that. A year later, turning back to prizefighting, his script "Requiem for a Heavyweight" does just that. He is quoted in *The Pittsburgh Press:* "All writers grab on to what represents them qualitatively, and 'Requiem' represents me."

"Requiem" is the story of a once successful boxer, played by Jack Palance, who is on his way down. My dad says:

*I had one basic idea . . . I wanted to analyze a human being who
fought for a living but who was nonetheless a human being. I
wanted a guy who would act, react, feel and think without
sounding like the stereotyped, cauliflower-eared, punchy human
wreck who has now become so familiar that he's funny. I wanted
the dull, slow, painfully halting speech to elicit sympathy and
understanding, but not a laugh . . . Requiem's basic premise is
that every man can and must search for his own dignity.*

The producer, Martin Manulis, says, "After the live broadcast, CBS chairman William Paley called the control room
and told the crew, 'That show has advanced TV by ten
years.'"

My dad is truly on his way.

Chapter 10

We had tilted at the same dragons for seven or eight
years and, when the smoke cleared, the dragons had
won. Live television was history. So the summons came,
and the writers moved west.

——ROD SERLING

THE TELEVISION INDUSTRY IS booming, and prerecorded
broadcasts are becoming the norm. In 1958 we move to Pacific Palisades, California. I am three years old, standing, for
the first time, in the Tudor-style house on Monaco Drive, our
new home. My mother, holding my hand, shows me the
room that will be mine—the one closest to theirs, and Jodi's
just a little farther than mine.

Men in white are painting, their ladders leaning against the
banister, and they smile when we walk past.

This is my first memory, this house whose doors, even
today, decades later, I reenter in dreams. The sounds and colors are just as vivid—the abundance of sunlight throughout,
the blue of my parents' room, the darker blue of Jodi's, the
flowered wallpaper of mine, and the tree that brushed against
the window when the wind blew. It is always the same in this
recurring dream. I am calling my father, looking for him in
vacant rooms where beds have been stripped bare, furniture
moved, closets emptied. No one is home; no one lives there
anymore. Beyond the emptiness and the silence, there is unfamiliarity. As if walls have been rearranged, structures changed,
leaving behind a maze of altered routes, a kind of house of

mirrors. I always wake with a start and with an attendant, lingering sadness. It takes a while to shake away this imaginary house and recall the one of my childhood. In those first moments of wakening, I make a conscious effort. In my mind I go back, I turn the handle, push open the front door, and I begin again.

The revisiting is not unlike a *Wizard of Oz* moment. I open the door to a profusion of color and light and see us standing there, the people we were, my family that passed in and out, in and out, countless times through that heavy wooden front door. Invariably, inevitably, time distorts memories, lightening some, diffusing others, and although the telephoto lens that roams through my recollections tends to obscure things, this is what is there; this is what remains when I go back: We have a red guest room, and sometimes I hear my father there, in the middle of the night, and when I am older I know he is there because he is again having trouble sleeping. He is probably suffering through more war nightmares.

In the living room, the couch and the carpet are white. This room is used only for company, but for some reason this is also the favored spot for the setters—Michael and Maggie—to relieve themselves; they always pee on that carpet. My dad will say, "God damn it," and he or my mother or my sister or I will clean it up, time after time.

I don't recall celebrities frequently in our house, but one night Betty White visits my parents. Although I have seen her on television, I am most impressed by the fact that she loves our dogs and bends down to pet them. My parents lead her into the living room. I follow and sit on the couch, staring up at her, while she tells me all about her animals. She holds our setters' faces in her hands and talks to them inches away. "Hello big beautiful fella." I fall instantly in love with this kind, gracious lady.

Our kitchen is green and long like a hall. I see my sister

and me sitting there, our younger selves, ages six and three, playing the "Milk Game," which is my father's way to get Jodi and me to drink our milk. He pretends to be the monster that doesn't want the milk touched. "Don't drink that!" he growls, and then looks away, and we take large swallows before he turns around again to find our half-empty glasses. "*Who* drank my milk!" he says in a ferocious, growling voice. This goes on until the milk is gone, my sister and I giggling convulsively until we can barely breathe.

On weekends my parents often go out. My mother sometimes wears a green silk dress—my favorite. She promises to save it for me. I love peering at her from around the doorway—watching her get ready to go, putting her makeup on, combing her dark brown hair. I study her closely, thinking how beautiful she is.

Eventually she shoos me away, and I go downstairs to my father. When I am older, he and I sit in the family room waiting for the babysitter Mrs. West to arrive. Mrs. West is an enormous woman, likely about forty, but to Jodi and me she seems ancient.

At the round table beneath the white light, my dad and I play "Crazy Eights" or "Go Fish," calling for twos, fours, announcing our matching cards, waiting for my mother to descend the stairs and announce that she is ready. We leave our cards exactly as they are, to return to later, and my father stands, pushes back his chair, and helps my mother with her coat. They say good-bye to Jodi and me and tell Mrs. West, now there, that they won't be too late.

As they open the front door, a few faded, fall leaves blow in, and I rush to the window to watch them go.

Mrs. West always watches television downstairs, programs Jodi and I don't like, like *Jackie Gleason,* so we are pretty much on our own and sometimes, I run to my parents' room and slip into one of my mother's dresses and pointed shoes dyed to match and, twirling before the mirror, pretend for an instant to be her. I must have been a ridiculous sight—this small, chubby girl staring back.

My bedroom overlooks the driveway. At night, if I am still awake when they come home, I see the headlights shine through the curtain and hear the car doors close. I hear my parents' voices wafting up to my window and their footsteps as they walk to the front door. I can count the seconds, almost exactly, until they check on me. If I am in their room sneaking television and hear the car, I race back to my bed where I hear Mrs. West saying good night and driving away, and I know how long it takes for my parents to hang up their coats, climb the stairs, and walk down the hall. (Sixty-five seconds.) I lie waiting, finally seeing my parents there, silhouetted at my door by the yellow hall light. My mother leans over me, her perfume filling my room like flowers. She kisses my cheek, and then I feel my father's cool hand on my forehead and hear him start our whispered routine, "Who's your best friend, Pops?" And eyes still closed, I'll whisper back, "You are," and he'll pull my blanket up and walk quietly to the door.

On nights when I feel scared, and only my dad can help, I call out to him, "Dad? Daddy? *Dad?*" And down the hall he will come, his voice soft in my ear, telling me all the reasons I should not fear the dark.

When we all go out together, my father dutifully checks under my bed upon our return and assures me there is nothing there. This inspection takes a while. I am convinced these creatures are not just hiding on the floor behind the bed skirts. My monsters are clever. They hang from the box spring where they cannot be seen with a cursory glance. "Daddy! Look again! You're not looking carefully!" I tell him, and he does but too hurriedly. "Dad, that's too quick. You have to look again." He mutters under his breath, "God damn it, Pops, there's nothing there!" but he double checks. There is never a doubt in my mind that my father can contend with anything that might be lurking there.

A decade later, I will watch him sleep at Strong Memorial in a hospital gown, frailer than we could have known, and I'll remember him, all those years before, invincible on his knees, on the orange and yellow carpet of my bedroom, peering beneath my bed, checking, assuring me there is nothing there, nothing hiding in the dark. And these contrasting images will forever do battle in my mind, and in my heart.

In my father's original study at the lake, a small, red wooden outbuilding that later becomes the dog house, there is a high shelf filled with model airplanes. My dad sits at a wooden table and, although not very mechanically minded, assembles these tiny warplanes, gluing and painting them. This is a favorite hobby of his and clearly relaxes him. I remember countless times watching him there, shirtless and tan, his strong arms flying the completed model planes through the air and then retiring them to the high shelf.

Putting together other things—toys, shelves, bicycles, tables—is not his strong suit, but rather my mother's. She will patiently stand back with a slight smile as my dad, directions spread before him, attempts to assemble something. Often I will hear, under his breath, "Shit," right before he gives up and throws over the booklet. "Rod, let me do it," my mother says, picking it up and reading the directions. She is the one who can follow the directions, put things together, read the maps, light the fires. She is the organizer, the coordinator, the pragmatic, practical one. She is the one who tries to persuade him that the sign that reads, DEER CROSSING NEXT TEN MILES means beware of deer *for* the next ten miles, not *after* the next ten miles. I remember sitting in the backseat, hearing this same argument over and over. I am fairly certain she never convinces him.

Once, when my sister is about sixteen, some older boys, looking dirty and unshaven, come to visit her. They tear down the cottage road on loud motorcycles, our dogs jump-

ing out of the way, and my dad, furious, shakes his finger, unable to utter a single word. It is my mother who calmly and
articulately states, "What my husband is trying to say is that
you're not welcome here." My dad, laughing, tells this story
for years.

My mother is cast in the role of disciplinarian and keeper
of order and, as such, she is the one who makes certain our
beds are made and our rooms cleaned. She is the one who
drills us on our multiplication and checks to make sure no
homework is left undone. She does, though, have a silly side.
She'll make up words like "heak" and say it in a squeaky voice
that makes my sister and me laugh.

My dad's anger can be formidable if he's had a particularly
long day or if he is stressed, but we know it is transitory;
whereas my mother can maintain hers and her disappointment for days. And so, for the most part, it is her anger we
fear. If my dad is out of town, and she threatens us with the
proverbial "Wait until your father gets home," her statement is
met with little trepidation by my sister or me. We know that
if he is irritated, the reaction will dissipate almost immediately.

The two exceptions to this are when we are teenagers and
make long distance phone calls or leave lights on in an empty
room. My dad has no patience for excessively long conversations with our friends back east or for the waste of electricity.
These ignite his impatience and his quick, explosive temper,
but I know it will be short-lived. He will stand in my bedroom, furious, yell, and then disappear, only to return within
moments, peek his head in, with that black, wavy hair, and
quietly ask, "Have you seen my twin brother anywhere?"
Sometimes he will reappear in a costume or with my lampshade on his head or some goofy expression on his face.

My mother, left with the harder job of keeping the house-
hold running, makes my dad seem the fun parent, the warm
parent, the one whose love is, without exception, uncondi-
tional.

It is my mother, though, who is the more hands-on parent, the one who knows our day-to-day lives and balances her own work in between. For years she volunteers at the Santa Monica Hospital gift shop, where she is in charge of purchasing all of the toys and children's books. She also volunteers as a clinical worker at a suicide prevention center. At the time this means little to me, but now, in retrospect, I think these choices indicate how both my parents were never swallowed up by the Hollywood scene and never lost touch with reality. Why our trips to the cottage grounded us, all of us, and why, perhaps my sister and I would settle on the East Coast, preferring that peace over the insanity of Los Angeles.

My dad "teaches" me to drive when I am four. I sit on his lap, holding the steering wheel, and he pushes the gas. For years we drive that white Lincoln down Monaco Drive, D'Este Drive, and Capri Drive. Just as the streetlights begin to come on, there we are, swerving through our neighborhood, singing at the top of our lungs.

In a 1959 interview on the ABC television program, *Mike Wallace Interview*, Wallace mentions that my father works twelve hours a day, seven days a week. I never feel, though, that his attention is in short supply or that he is unavailable. Perhaps because when you are in his presence, you are very much center stage, and he is continually entertaining you. Whether it is pulling quarters out of my ear, or appearing, suddenly, in the doorway wearing a poncho, playing endless games of "Go Fish," or walking with my sister and me through the ravine searching for salamanders—to be with my father is, almost always, exhilarating. And because he has an uncanny talent for impersonation and a seemingly endless number of different voices and dialects, funny expressions, and jokes, it is like having a different playmate every day. He also has an incredible ability to separate work from family. While he is playing with me in the little dog house/play-house, sitting in the tiny chairs and drinking the imaginary coffee I have set before him, he is under tremendous pressure with his writing and battling against the network censorship of many of his works. But I don't have the remotest idea that this is happening, and, in fact, I won't know this for years.

In one of the scripts he writes, the sponsors object because an office window scene shows the Chrysler Building in the New York skyline. It has to be blacked out because the show's sponsor is Ford. In another, his quote from Hamlet, "Neither a borrower nor a lender be," has to be cut because the sponsor is a savings and loan association.

His exasperation continues with a story he writes for *The United States Steel Hour* called "Noon on Doomsday." It is in-spired by the aftermath of the kidnapping and murder of Em-mett Till, the fourteen-year-old African American child from Chicago who was killed by two white men while visiting his cousins in the Mississippi delta in 1955. His killers, who later proudly boasted of their actions, were exonerated by an all-white jury. The case, and Till's mother's amazingly brave and resolute insistence on having an open casket at his public fu-neral to display his beaten and tortured body to all, galvanized the civil rights struggle and made a lasting impression on tens of millions of people. My dad was haunted by the case and the Till family's suffering, and knew he had to write about it.

But even though the case became a historic example of the despicable consequences of racism, American television could not handle it in anything other than masked parable form. So my dad engaged in what he later called "ritual track cover-ing," changing the locale to the North and the victim to an elderly Jew, hoping the point of the ugliness of all prejudice would still come through. He said:

The righteous and continuing wrath of the Northern press
opened no eyes and touched no consciences in the little town in
Mississippi where the two men were tried. It was like a cold
wind that made them huddle together for protection against an
outside force which they could equate with an adversary. It struck
me at the time that the trial and its aftermath was simply,
"They're bastards, but they're our bastards." So I wrote a play in
which my antagonist was not just a killer but a regional idea. It
was the story of a little town banding together to protect its own
against outside condemnation. At no point in the conception of
my story was there a black-white issue. The victim was an old
Jew who ran a pawn shop and the killer was a neurotic
malcontent . . . I felt that I was on sound ground. I felt that I was
dealing with a sociological phenomenon—the need of human
beings to have a scapegoat to rationalize their own
shortcomings . . .

Sometime before the airing, a reporter asked him point blank if he based his script on the Till case.

"If the shoe fits . . ." my dad replied.

As soon as *Variety* reported the remarks and other news outlets picked them up, thousands of outraged letters and phone calls poured in, the vast majority from the South, many of them threatening a boycott. That was all the network and the sponsor needed to hear. U.S. Steel and CBS demanded changes so as not to "offend" viewers.

My dad was incredulous at their reaction and lack of courage:

I asked the agency men at the time how the problem of a boycott
applied to the United States Steel company. Did that mean that
from then on all that construction from Tennessee on down would
be done with aluminum? Their answer was that the concern of
the sponsor was not so much an economic boycott as the resultant
strain in public relations.

Frankly, he doesn't see that what he writes is truly controversial at all and gripes about television's lack of courage. "I
wish they'd let us write about the Little Rock [Arkansas
school integration] situation. Funny, there were about seven
or eight dramatic treatments of the Hungarian uprising but
the spectacle of adult whites taunting a couple of defenseless
little Negro girls is considered controversial. Wrong? That's
not controversy. If anybody takes the pro side in that particular battle, they'd better change flags."

These were more instances of how my dad earned the title
of "TV's Angry Young Man." But the dye for "Noon on
Doomsday" was cast.

"That was all it took," he recalled.

> The murdered Jew was changed to suggest an unnamed foreigner,
> the locale moved from the south to New England . . . and
> ultimately it became a lukewarm, vitiated, emasculed kind of
> show. By the time they finished taking Coca-Cola bottles off of
> the set because the sponsor claimed that this had Southern
> connotation—suggesting to what depth they went to make this a
> clean, antiseptically rigidly acceptable show, why it bore no
> relationship to what we purported to say initially.

Despite the fact that my dad feels the script has been totally stripped of serious meaning, when the show airs it is
met with another flood of protest: about 15,000 letters and
wires from the White Citizens Council and other, similar
groups.

Emmett Till's fate continues to haunt my dad. Two years
later, he writes a script for *Playhouse 90* titled "A Town Has
Turned to Dust." When the outline is submitted to CBS it is
immediately rejected. An article appears in *Time Magazine* on
June 30, 1995, summing it up like this: "A précis of Serling's
first effort was rejected by all but one of the sponsors; they
would not lend their brand names or money to a treatment of

racism that might prejudice Southern customers against their products."

My dad tries again. He sets the story in 1890 and turns it into a Western. Although this time the script is accepted, changes are demanded and my dad says:

> By the time *A Town Has Turned to Dust* went before the cameras my script had turned to dust . . . Emmett Till became a romantic Mexican who loved the storekeeper's wife, but "only with his eyes." My sheriff couldn't commit suicide because one of our sponsors was an insurance firm, and they claimed that suicide often leads to complications in settling policy claims. The lynch victim was called Clemson, but we couldn't use this 'cause South Carolina had an all-white college by that name. The setting was moved to the Southwest in the 1870's . . . the phrase "twenty men in hoods" became "twenty men in homemade masks." They chopped it up like a roomful of butchers at work on a steer.

There were many more ludicrous demands from the sponsors, and my dad is quoted as saying, "I think it is criminal that we are not permitted to make dramatic note of social evils that exist, of controversial themes as they are inherent in our society."

It is not only the bigots and right-wingers whose ire my father arouses. On May 20, 1960, *Playhouse 90* presented its final offering, a teleplay of my dad's titled, "In the Presence of Mine Enemies." Starring Charles Laughton, Arthur Kennedy, Susan Kohner, and a young Robert Redford (who, two years later, will star in the *Twilight Zone* episode "Nothing in the Dark"), the drama takes place during World War II and focuses on a Jewish family in the Warsaw Ghetto, just as the Nazis are about to destroy it. Rabbi Heller (Laughton) a Talmudic man of peace, is at odds with his freedom fighter son (Kennedy), who seeks only violence and revenge. In the midst of this apocalypse, their daughter/sister, who has been raped by a Nazi captain, falls in love with a young German lieutenant (Redford) who, plagued by the conflict between his orders and his conscience, saves the girl.

Jack Gould, reviewing for *The New York Times*, leads off with

> Rod Serling and *Playhouse 90*, perhaps the most consistently fruitful partnership in television theatre, scored again last night with a drama of searing tragedy and nobility.
>
> In ninety minutes Mr. Serling searched beneath the anguish of the Jews who faced the indescribable torture of living death. But more specifically, in a series of brilliant characterizations, he examined the different courses chosen by victims to preserve their integrity. Whether it took the form of recourse to religion or the gun, the pursuit of honor was an individual decision... "In the Presence of Mine Enemies" attests to the continuing growth of Mr. Serling as a playwright.

Despite the fact that the other main German characters are thoroughly despicable, the program sets off an avalanche of protests from Jews and Jewish organizations, taking my dad to task for his sympathetic portrayal of the Redford character. *Exodus* author Leon Uris writes an open letter to CBS calling the show, "the most disgusting presentation in the history of American TV," and saying that "Joseph Goebbels himself could not have produced such a piece of Nazi apologetics. I demand that CBS burn the negative and publicly apologize for the scandal."

My dad responds to Uris, lamenting the fact that the prominent novelist cannot disagree without name-calling and accusations. Charles Beaumont, one of his fellow *Twilight Zone* writers, calls Uris's accusations "hysterical, vicious, and wholly irresponsible. As for his demand that CBS burn the film, the author of *Exodus* would do well to remember that that sort of thing was one of Herr Goebbels' specialties."

To a prominent Jewish leader my dad writes:

Neither my Pole nor the German soldier were designed to be representative or symbolic. As a dramatist, I was dealing with individuals—not symbols. As a matter of fact I thought I'd gone to great lengths to make the implication clear that these were exceptions to the rule.

The essence of playwriting is conflict and for me to have shown a Jewish point of view in this case would have been simply a restatement of a horror we are already too familiar with. All I was trying to dramatize was that even in a sea of madness, there can be a moment [involving] just a fragment of faith, hope, decency and humanity. Hence, an orthodox rabbi can put his hand on the quaking shoulder of a young German and offer him forgiveness that he cries out for.

To his friend Julie Golden my dad writes:

Good hearing from you and to know that you liked IN THE PRESENCE OF MINE ENEMIES . . . The show has engendered considerable comment both pro and con. I now stand in the middle between two poles of accusation. Either I'm a great and vicious anti-Semite (according to Leon Uris) or I'm a dirty, Jew-loving bastard (from the Steuben Societies of the United States). But I suppose that is what makes ballgames and church attendance.

It is no secret that my dad will not compromise his goals or his principles. In some ways, the "Presence of Mine Enemies" experience supports the statement he makes in a speech in Washington several years later: "The writer's role is to menace the public's conscience. He must have a position, a point of view. He must see the arts as a vehicle of social criticism and he must focus on the issues of his time."

And the struggle continues.

Though he has little professional experience in the field, science fiction and fantasy have, for a long time, been very appealing to my dad. Late at night, he reads ghost stories or H.P. Lovecraft. Sometimes Edgar Allan Poe. Eventually it dawns on him that fantasy can provide a natural forum for him to express himself and that networks and advertisers will accept scripts including controversial situations if they exist in another, fictional world or, as he notes, "A Martian can say things that a Republican or a Democrat can't."

In fact, he has considered the idea before, though he may not realize it. In the commentary in *Patterns: Four Television Plays* he writes:

> *Last year I was faced with such a problem when I wrote a script called "The Arena" which was done on Studio One. In this case, I was dealing with a political story where much of the physical action took place on the floor of the United States Senate.*
>
> *I was not permitted to have my Senators discuss any current or pressing problem. To talk of tariff was to align oneself with the Republicans; to talk of labor was to suggest control by the Democrats. To say a single thing germane to the current political scene was absolutely prohibited.*
>
> *In retrospect, I probably would have had a much more adult play had I made it science fiction, put it in the year 2057, and peopled the Senate with robots. This would probably have been more reasonable and no less dramatically incisive.*

My dad wants to beat the excessive censorship and still write meaningful and effective scripts. One weekend, while deliberating his next career move, he goes to visit his old friends, Julie Golden, now a copy director for an ad agency,

and his wife Rhoda, a clerk for United Merchants and Man-
ufacturers.

"Your dad often stayed in our apartment in Forest Hills
when he had business in New York," Julie explains. "We
blocked off part of the L-shaped living room with a screen so
that he could have his privacy, but he usually kept us awake
with jokes and stories. One night, he told us over the screen
that he had an idea for a TV series, and what did we think of
the name *The Twilight Zone*? Well, Rhoda and I liked it."

Chapter 11

The Twilight Zone is about people, about human beings involved in extraordinary circumstances, in strange problems of their own or of fate's making.

—ROD SERLING

IT TAKES A LOT of perseverance to get *The Twilight Zone* off the ground. The first pilot my dad submits, "The Time Element," is an expansion of a half-hour script he had written and sold shortly after graduating from Antioch. Although CBS buys the script, it is shelved for two years until it is picked up by Bill Granet, producer of *Westinghouse Desilu Playhouse*. Desilu, the production company owned by Lucille Ball and Desi Arnaz, wielded significant power in the world of 1950s television owing to the phenomenal success of *I Love Lucy*.

Despite strong opposition from the ad agency representing Westinghouse and network executives, Desi Arnaz backs Granet and they convince CBS to air the show as part of their 1958–1959 season.

In his book *The Twilight Zone Companion*, Marc Zicree will later write, " 'The Time Element' received more mail than any other episode of *Desilu Playhouse* that year, and the newspaper reviews were universally good."

New York Times reviewer Jack Gould wrote:

Serling once again came up with an absorbing and unusual drama . . . "The Time Element" is a story about a man visiting a psychiatrist. The patient complains of recurrent dreams in which he imagines he is living in Hawaii just before the attack on Pearl Harbor. In a series of flashbacks the man is shown living with his knowledge of what has happened in the seventeen years since. He bets on sure winners in sports events, for example. But more particularly he seeks to warn a newly-married couple, newspaper editors and anyone else who will listen that they will be attacked by the Japanese. But everyone is either too interested in a good time or too determinedly patriotic to give heed; the man only gets punched on the jaw. In a highly tricky ending the psychiatrist is left looking at a blank couch and to steady his own nerves he goes to a bar to get a drink. There he learns his patient was killed at Pearl Harbor.

Marc Zicree states, "The reviews were enough to convince CBS that it had made a mistake in shelving Serling's script. It was decided that a pilot of *The Twilight Zone* would be made."

Buoyed by a second chance (but with some trepidation) my father begins writing "Where Is Everybody?" the story of a man who finds himself inexplicably alone in a strange, completely vacant town. It turns out he is an astronaut preparing for the loneliness of deep space flight and the entire experience has been a hallucination. The story is bought, and after the episode has been produced, he travels to New York City and with CBS presents it to potential sponsors. William Self, a CBS executive, recalls, "It was the fastest sale that I have ever been involved with. In fact, the pilot sold just six hours after the screening."

It was *The Twilight Zone* that made my dad famous, transforming him from a well-respected television writer into a celebrity and a public personality. But that was almost accidental. As Self explained to Marc Zicree in *The Twilight Zone Companion*, "It was from the outset decided that there would be a narrator, someone who would set the stage or wrap it up. The first person we used was Westbrook Van Voorhis, who had done *The March of Time* and had that kind of big voice. But when we listened to it we decided it was a little too pompous-sounding."

Everyone at the network, the sponsors, their ad agency, and the talent agency representing my dad, want Orson Welles, who, they think, would add just the right note of drama, flair, and prestige to the show. But Welles's quoted fee is higher than the sponsors want to pay. They all scramble to come up with other names.

"Finally," Self continues, "Rod himself made the suggestion that maybe he should do it. It was received with skepticism. None of us knew Rod except as a writer. But he did a terrific job."

For the first season, viewers hear "the Voice" near the beginning and at the end of each episode. It is not until the second season that he appears on camera. Within months, he is the most recognizable writer in the short history of television.

My dad started and owned the production company (Cayuga Productions) that produced all of the *TZ*s and was completely committed to this show. He would get up very early and dictate scripts for hours. And then, around noon, he would drive over to the MGM studios, where the shows were recorded. Marc Zicree quotes Edward Denault, the assistant director: "Rod was instrumental in the development of the scripts and in the rewrites, was in on the post-production, always looked at the dailies. If we got in a jam and something had to be rewritten in an effort to get the show finished on time, or if we were short of minutes, he was always ready and could knock off a scene very quickly. He was very, very much involved."

Marc Zicree writes, "For all his involvement Serling also knew his own limitations and although he was credited as executive producer, he had no pretensions of being a producer." Buck Houghton, the producer, said my dad, despite his involvement "knew his limitations." He went on to say:

*You see Rod had a very short span of attention. He was a very
intense guy and he worked very hard and drove himself very
hard and he was very short of patience. He was not impatient;
patience was not something he had. A ten minute story
conference with him was the limit, then he'd go out and get an
ice cream soda or shoe shine. So, as far as sitting through a
dubbing session or going through the casting lists or sitting and
cueing the music . . . that sort of thing: no thanks. And that's
not to derogate the title of executive producer; he did have the
final say.*

When *The Twilight Zone* premieres on October 2, 1959, I
am four years old and still oblivious to what my father is
doing when he is not playing with us, showing us how to
blow on a blade of grass and make it whistle, or chasing us
around the yard.

For a while, his office is in the downstairs of our California
house in a room off the living room. He has a secretary
named Pat, who has beautiful red hair. Sometimes when Pat
leaves at the end of the day, Jodi leans out of the living room
window, singing, "Pat loves Daddy." But beyond that, I don't
remember her nearly as well as his subsequent secretary,
Margie, who I initially thought was still Pat, because she, too,
had red hair. Margie has a son, Rich, who is older than my
sister and I. Years later, Rich makes my dad countless tapes of
comedians doing Jewish jokes. My dad listens to them at the
cottage while he lies out in the sun in the hammock, chuckling away. He loves them.

In the spring of 1959, he has an office built in the backyard
of our home in California. You have to walk about one hundred feet in order to get there, either across the backyard or
along a stone sidewalk. The sidewalk is bordered by two gardens where my mother has planted snapdragons, roses, pan-
sies, chrysanthemums, and her grandfather's favorite, bleeding
hearts. I see her out there in her green and white garden

gloves, kneeling; digging in the dirt, wiping her brow, surrounded by a profusion of color. My father clearly appreciates
these gardens. Sometimes he stops for several moments on his
way to the office and looks at them. Later, he often comments
about them to my mother or to my sister and me.

Often my mother takes me with her when she goes to the
nursery. I cherish these trips; I love skipping through the gardens and returning home with armfuls of flowers. She gives
me my own little space, and we work out there together digging and talking and then standing back to examine our
work.

We have birthday parties in the yard near our gardens that
are all captured on home movies. Scavenger hunts and circle
games, relay races, and frenetic games of musical chairs—
always a flurry of children in pastel-colored dresses rushing
for a vacant seat and quick shots of my mother or my father
dragging one more chair away.

My mother is the one who organizes these parties, while
my father comes in and out of his office to see what we are
doing. He bends down, his hands on his knees, and talks to us.
Sometimes he'll even play, pretending to look for us when
we're hiding in plain sight. My friends adore him. He is always there when they are leaving, holding on to their colored
balloons trailing in the sky behind them. He is always there to
wave good-bye.

There is a general understanding that when my dad is in his
office, he is off-limits to us. When he is not working, the office is usually locked, but I happen to know that a key is hidden in a large planter just outside his door. So whenever we
can, we sneak in and grab a brownie or cookie or a piece of
candy. All the "good" food is in my dad's office; all of the treats
my mother wants to limit. My father loves sweets, so there
is always an abundance. He loves chocolate pies and often
brings them home from a shop called The House of Pies. For
some reason my sister calls him "Y from the House of Pies."

Entering the office through Margie's door leads to her long desk, a wall of cupboards, and file drawers. In one, my father keeps copies of all of the searing or supportive letters he has written. He writes strong political statements but also other, more mundane letters, one to the See's candy manufacturer because he loves their product. Another to a Mercury car dealership, explaining why he no longer uses their service department after having brought the car in several times for the same problem: "The engine would still race upon being started to a point where my wife would have won the Grand Prix without ever putting her foot on the accelerator."

On Margie's wall are some framed caricatures of my dad. Past her desk are a bathroom and then another door leading into my dad's area.

His is a large room with sliding glass doors. One entire wall is made up of bookshelves with an attached ladder. At the top is a small loft. Pictures of his parents and of us are on one of the shelves. There is a stone fireplace with a curved stone seating area and fitted, off-white cushions. My dad's Emmys are on the mantel.

Behind an accordion door is a tiny kitchen with a small sink and refrigerator. A coffeepot sits on the counter beside containers of the coveted junk food.

My father's built-in desk, large enough to crawl beneath, is in front of a picture window. On it is a Dictaphone. Although he is a whiz on the typewriter, his two fingers tapping away in rapid flight, he primarily uses the Dictaphone to write. I've heard him practicing different voices on it. Sometimes I think it's funny the way he can alter his voice. He says it allows him to hear his characters. His friend Mark Olshaker recalls my dad playing one of his recordings for him. Mark was impressed that he even dramatized the punctuation. In an interview, my dad repeats an expression, "Every writer is a frustrated actor who recites his lines in the hidden auditorium of his skull."

Mark also remembers that my dad had his own Xerox machine, which, at the time, impressed him tremendously.

I later realize that the Dictaphone is not confined to the office or producing my dad's scripts. Practical joker that he is, he sometimes hides it near the dinner table and records whatever happens during the meal. He then takes great delight in playing it back for us—laughter, arguments, all of us planning the next day's activities, Jodi and I bickering or my mother struggling to get us to talk about something important.

Years later, the first time I bring my fiancé Doug out to California, not long before my mother sells the house, I play him one of the recordings that somehow has been saved. We both laugh at the silliness of the whole thing, but hearing my dad's non-television voice without the dramatic intonation and his laughter again produces a wistfulness in me that is almost overpowering.

Next to my dad's desk is a student's old-fashioned wooden desk where Margie takes shorthand before retiring to her office to transcribe the Dictaphone tapes—the script ones, not the dinner ones.

When I am older, I remember my father occasionally struggling with dialogue for his female characters. Margie, who my father nicknamed "Parge," tells him one day that a certain scene isn't working. "Rod, Jane's conversation is stilted; it needs something more."

Frustrated but knowing she's right, my dad leaves her a note later that morning, folded on her desk. "Parge: Jane says to go fuck yourself."

Until I am six or seven I have no idea what my father does for a living. I know that he *writes*. I know he is a *writer* but what that means exactly, I haven't a clue. I know Margie is his secretary, but I am only vaguely aware of what she does.

This lack of knowledge comes into focus one evening at the lake when I overhear my parents talking on the cottage porch. It is the summer I turn seven. My father is leaning back in the green wicker chair; his feet are up on the railing, and he is blowing smoke rings in the humid night air. Between puffs he tells my mother he misses having a secretary. Standing, unseen, peering through the screen door, I listen. Before he can consider his options, I fly out the door and jumping up and down before him I tell him, "I can help! I will be your secretary for as long as you need me!" My dad looks over and smiles at my mother. I have no idea what the job entails or what the scope of it will be, or what I will need to do, but I have seen his secretary Margie sitting across from him at his desk in California. I have seen her taking notes in a small tanned-covered notebook. Certainly I can do the same and write down what he says, and besides, I am already deciding which skirt of my mother's and which high heels I will need to borrow for the job. My mother doesn't dress up much at the lake and so I know my choices will be slim.

I am the first one up the next morning, and I remember teetering in my mother's shoes, trying to walk on the toes so they won't clomp-clomp down the cottage hall and wake everyone.

Back then the kitchen is in a separate building off the back porch. I quietly push open the door and tiptoe across the porch and sit down at the small wooden table.

My father's cough is the first thing I hear and then his feet padding down the hall moments later.

When he sees me at the table, I have the notebook open and ready on my lap. My mother's dress is folded beneath me touching the floor. My legs are crossed so my dad can see the pretty matching blue shoes and see how grown up and ready for the job I am.

It is in that moment that I recall my father begins to laugh—one of his hysterical laughs where his eyes get all crinkly and for an instant he can't breathe.

When he finally gets control, he comes over and hugs me,

managing, "Thanks, Bunny." At the time, I am not certain just what, exactly, is so funny, but I am laughing, too.

I am too young to realize how ridiculous I look, but my father's laugh is so infectious and engaging.

We stay there in that kitchen a long time on that sunny summer morning years and years ago. Me in the long blue dress, and my father beside me, tears rolling down his face.

My dad is an early riser. I am as familiar with his morning sounds as I am with my own. Lying in my bed in California, I listen for him. His footsteps down the stairs, the front door opening as he walks out, shuffling his blue slipper heels to get the paper at the driveway's end. His footsteps coming back, the door opening again and closing, his chair scraping across the floor as he sits down, his spoon tapping the side of his coffee cup. I know he is reading the paper and talking to our Irish setters, Mike and Maggie.

If I hurry, I know I can see him there before he slides the glass door open, coffee and cigarette in hand, often humming or whistling the songs of Sinatra or Bennett or Dean Martin, as he walks the path to his office.

One day when I am in first or second grade, an older boy on the school playground runs up to me, taps me on the shoulder, close enough that I can see that the freckles on his right cheek form a perfect constellation, and asks, "Where does your dad get all of his ideas? Hanging from the ceiling?" He runs off hooting and laughing, and I stand there perplexed.

Later, while my dad and I are watching *The Flintstones* and my mother has taken my sister to ride her horse, I mention this boy's comment. I love that my father likes this show as much as I do. This is a coveted, secret time for us. My mother strictly prohibits watching television during the week. She feels it is a waste of time, that we should be reading or doing something productive. During the commercial I ask, "So why did that boy say that about you?"

My dad stubs out his cigarette in a large green ashtray he has balanced on his chest and explains, "It's a show I do that's on every week. There are other writers too. It's a series called *The Twilight Zone*. Some of the episodes are too old for you; some are maybe a little scary." He says more that I don't hear because the commercial is over and Wilma is saying something important to Fred.

He does take us, though, to the set at MGM where *The Twilight Zone* is filmed. In one of the family albums there are two black-and-white photographs of my dad, my sister, and me. He is holding our hands and leaning down, pointing at something just outside the camera's range. In the other we are standing on a stairway. I have a vague recollection of steps that lead nowhere.

A few years later, when we are at the cottage, I see *The Twilight Zone* for the first time. Sitting in twin wicker chairs pulled up close to the small television, my dad and I watch an episode starring William Shatner called "Nightmare at 20,000 Feet." Moving the chair closer to my father and looking from the television screen to him, I am stunned that *this* is what he does, writes these terrifying stories. I later learn that this particular episode "Nightmare" was written by Richard Matheson, but at the time that fact is of little consolation. It is still my father who appears at the beginning and the end of the show.

Although it is initially disturbing to think that my father is connected to this scary stuff, the thought almost immediately vanishes because this is not the dad I know. There is nothing scary about him. And I am excited to see him on television!

Chapter 12

IT IS ALMOST CHRISTMAS. My hands are cupped around my eyes as I look through the sliding glass doors into my father's study. Michael is beside me. His tail smacks the bricked ground with each wag. Together our breaths fog the window, creating our own distinctive, separate, murky pools.

My father doesn't see our obscured reflections right away. He is preoccupied, staring straight ahead, leaning back in his office chair; his legs are propped up on his desk and crossed at the ankle. In his right hand he holds a microphone, and I can see his mouth moving but I cannot hear a single word.

I still have only a vague grasp of what he is doing in there even though I am now eight. I know that he has won awards for his writing. (I carefully take the Emmys down and play with them sometimes.) But any real, tangible comprehension of his work is still lost on me, and I have still not seen many more *Twilight Zone* episodes.

I am not supposed to be there, standing by his door when

he is working. I know this. Is this rule spoken or presumed? I don't remember. Nevertheless, I stare unabashedly through the glass waiting for him to notice us. Michael's big red head is focused on him, too.

My yellow raincoat flaps conspicuously in the wind behind me. Perhaps it is this flash of color that catches my father's eye. With his free hand he waves us in and pushes some buttons on the Dictaphone. I watch as the reel stops, as he sets the microphone down and turns toward us and smiles.

He seems unfazed by my interruption, perhaps finished with what he was doing and intrinsically aware of why I am there. "Grumple? How many more days until Christmas?" he asks, petting Michael who is pawing him in the air. My dad and I both know the answer. The Advent calendar my mother has hung in the kitchen, with its sparkling pictures of snow-filled, starlit skies, shows only fifteen more windows to open, fifteen more days.

Although my father is Jewish and fiercely proud of his heritage, we celebrate Christmas, not as an acknowledgment of any religious significance, but rather for the spirit of it or, as he said, "The wondrous magic."

And that is why on that uncharacteristically cold, soggy LA day in December I am standing in his office, dripping rain on the slate floor. We are making plans for that evening when he will thread the sixteen-millimeter reel onto the projector, pull down the screen in front of the bookshelves, and together my family and our friends will watch "Night of the Meek"—one of the few *Twilight Zones* I *am* intimately familiar with. The lights will be shut off; my father will hit the switch on the machine and join us. The filmstrip, crackling in those first few moments in the darkness, will finally begin, and after the opening scenes, we will hear my father's voice and then see him on the enlarged screen, "snow" falling on his winter coat, on his head, and circling all around him. With his arms crossed in front of him, he will continue:

This is Mr. Henry Corwin, normally unemployed, who once a
year takes the lead role in the uniquely American Institution,
that of department-store Santa Claus in a road-company version
of "The Night Before Christmas." But in just a moment Mr.
Henry Corwin, ersatz Santa Claus, will enter a strange kind of
North Pole which is one part the wondrous spirit of Christmas
and one part the magic that can only be found in . . . The
Twilight Zone.

Beyond being enormously proud that it's my dad, *my dad,*
up there, the relevance of this particular episode is not lost on
me even then.

"Night of the Meek" is the story of a down-and-out department store Santa Claus, played by Art Carney, who, after
arriving at work drunk, is fired by the manager, Mr. Dundee.
In a wonderful scene, he tells the manager he would have reminded an irate customer: "Christmas is more than barging
up and down department store aisles and pushing people out
of the way! Someone has to tell her that Christmas is another
thing finer than that. Richer, truer, and should come with patience and love, charity, compassion. That's what I would have
told her if you'd given me a chance. You know another reason
why I drink, Mr. Dundee? So that when I walk down the
tenements, I can really think it's the North Pole and the children are elves and that I'm really Santa Claus bringing them a
bag of wondrous gifts for all of them. I just wish, Mr. Dundee,
on one Christmas, only one, that I could see some of the
hopeless ones and the dreamless ones, just on one Christmas,
I'd like to see the meek inherit the Earth."

He then discovers a garbage bag that magically contains
any gift wished for. He proceeds to give all the gifts away. At
the end, despondent that he no longer has any gifts to give, he
stumbles on the "real" Santa's sleigh in a back alley. And an elf
sitting in it urges him to join her and go back to the North
Pole. My dad's closing narration to this episode truly captures
his feelings about Christmas:

A word to the wise, to all the children of the twentieth century, whether their concern be pediatrics or geriatrics, whether they crawl on hands and knees and wear diapers or walk with a cane and comb their beards. There's a wondrous magic to Christmas, and there's a special power reserved for little people. In short, there's nothing mightier than the meek.

Both my parents love this season. My dad's sentimental streak is almost as intense as his crusading moralistic streak. Undoubtedly the sounds, the smells, the decorations, and the music all evoke something deep within him of another time and another place.

He tells me how, when he was little, his parents once had to hide a small Christmas tree under a bed when some of the more religious relatives came to visit.

He also loves Christmas carols and says they "melt" him. "Oh Holy Night" is a favorite of his, but we never can remember any words except "Fall on your knees," so together, we sing those and ad-lib the rest.

Every year he puts up the Christmas lights outside. One year he gets up on the ladder, tacks them all up, climbs back down, and moves the ladder to admire his work. He forgets the hammer he's left on the top rung, which falls and hits him on the head. It is a wonder, and a miracle, that he is not badly hurt.

At night, after he reads to me, he always says, "Blow out the light," and I blow while he turns the switch. He stays for a moment, and together we watch his multicolored Christmas lights blinking on and off, shadowing my bedroom wall.

The Super 8 camera, an enormous thing with a blinding bright light, is always brought out to document Christmas, other holidays, and family trips. Most of these home movies are "directed" and filmed by my mother, each beginning with a title sheet she tucks into fall leaves, or Christmas decorations, or Easter eggs, announcing the season or the occasion. On one Christmas morning the film begins with all of our feet getting out of bed.

Every year, when I am old enough to appreciate it, we watch Jimmy Stewart in *It's a Wonderful Life*, tears streaming down our faces at the end when George Bailey's little girl, Zuzu, says, "Look, Daddy! Teacher says, every time a bell rings, an angel gets his wings!" and George says, "Attaboy, Clarence."

My dad is nostalgic and childlike. This is never more apparent than at Christmastime. He never tires of tradition. He takes me to a place with shops and restaurants called the Brentwood Mart. When we get out of the car he holds my hand. "Holding paddles," he calls it. We have a hot chocolate by the fire pit. Every year he tells me, "So, here's what I got Mom, but first you have to promise not to tell, okay?" I always nod excitedly, feeling important that he is entrusting me with his secret. On Christmas Eve, my parents go to the home of Barbara and Dick Berg—friends from the days of live television, when the four of them lived in Westport. Dick was running an art supply store and gallery and writing in his spare time, before eventually moving to LA to become a film and television producer. He told me recently, "Your dad and I loved each other from the first night we met."

Dick and my dad exchange gag gifts at Christmas. An ugly pair of cuff links becomes a favorite, passing back and forth between them for decades.

Every year for New Year's Eve we fly to Columbus, Ohio, where my great-grandmother "Nana," my mother's grandmother, lives and where my mother grew up when she wasn't away at various schools. My great-grandfather Frank Caldwell, who my mother adored, died before I was born. I have seen photographs of this handsome, white-haired man. He designed their house following a trip they took to Switzerland. They fell in love with the architecture and built their Ohio home to look like a Swiss chalet. It has three stories. The upper two have small porches. One is a small indoor porch. Frank and his father also designed and built the red summer cottage on Cayuga Lake.

When we arrive, Jodi and I run through the house, through all of the mahogany-paneled rooms with the heavy, dark, antique furniture, and then, two steps at a time, we zoom up three flights of stairs to the attic. There we roller-skate, attaching our skates to our shoes with skate keys. For hours we skate back and forth, back and forth, across the worn, wooden floor, calling each other by the nicknames we have given each other, which we hate, but occasionally use playfully. Jodi yells, "Go! Caldie!" after my middle name Caldwell, and I answer, "Go! Joyce!"—her real name, but I am the only one who uses it.

An enormous wardrobe sits in a far corner on this attic floor. It holds some of my great-grandmother's coats and hats, and on the shelf, some of my great-grandfather's papers. I do not pay much attention to the contents of this wardrobe beyond pretending I can enter it and disappear to Narnia. I am a huge fan of the C.S. Lewis books. Like my dad, I love fantasy.

Downstairs in the living room is a brick fireplace, and beside it, a glass vase filled with hundreds of colored marbles. My sister and I play with them by the hearth. We divvy up the marbles and give them names—Bev for the blue ones, Wendy for white, et cetera. Sometimes my dad lies on the floor with us and we shoot them back and forth.

Nana's closet leads into the bathroom. This always feels magical to me, like a secret room.

Although she always seems very old to me, I adore my great-grandmother. Perhaps because I was named after her late daughter, my mother's mother, I sense a closeness, an unspoken attachment.

During these early years, she and I sit at the piano, and she plays, her head with its clouds of blue gray hair bent over the keys. I know that she cannot carry a tune. This is evident even with my untrained child's ear, and I know some of the chords she strikes cannot possibly be in the songbook, but that does not deter either one of us. We sing out our own version of "Silent Night," her scratchy voice and my little one wafting through the house.

We all treasure these trips back east, the change of climate, our breath in the wintry air, and being tucked into this wonderful old house surrounded by snow. For my father, these vacations are a respite from work, although when I am older I recognize that distant look he has when I know he is writing in his head.

Even in Columbus he gets up early, earlier even than we do. After breakfast he takes us outside and we trudge through the snow-filled, silent sidewalk and into the backyard. Although I loathe having to wear a snowsuit, I love being in the snow with him. He tirelessly pulls my sister and me up the hill in our sleds, over and over, up and down. He takes his brown mittens off and blows on his hands.

I didn't know it then, but my father had Raynaud's disease, a circulatory problem that is an additional complication from years of heavy smoking. He only stops for a few moments, though, to warm up his fingers, and then slides down with us again and pulls our sleds back up. Years later, I remember his fingers turning absolutely white. I remember him warning us of the dangers of smoking. "See?" he'd say, in his serious voice, blowing smoke through a white paper towel. "See it turning yellow? That's what nicotine does to your lungs."

When I am eight, my great-grandmother has a series of strokes. My parents have an electric lift installed that attaches to the banister, so she is still able to go up and down stairs, but I think Jodi and I ride in it more than she ever does.

My great-grandmother's nurse, Sylvia Dill—I always thought her name was Sylvia Miss Dill—and I play long games of checkers in the afternoon on the indoor porch while my grandmother rests. On sunny days, the light floods through the partially closed curtains and falls across the checkerboard, warming the pieces. She takes a long time planning her moves.

Gradually my great-grandmother grows more and more disabled until eventually she becomes bedridden. When we visit, I read to her from a chair pulled up close to the bed. She lies there, so still in her blue cotton nightgown, the sheets pulled up beneath her chin, her hair white against the pillow and her face expressionless.

In the end she is not always lucid and she becomes agitated. Her hands flap against the flowered bedspread and then in the air above her chest like trapped, colorless birds. She looks at me with unfamiliarity, telling me in a strange, whispery voice, "Don't let the little girl jump out the window."

I never know what to do in these moments. Afraid to leave her, I sit up straight in the chair beside her, my feet barely touching the floor, and watch as the person I know vanishes a little more each day, while I sit impotent, frozen, unable to summon the words to free her.

We are in California when the call comes that she has died. It is decided that I will go with my mother to Columbus.

It is late when we arrive. My mother carries the gray suitcase we share, and I follow her up the wooden stairs, watching as she sets it in a corner bedroom and then collapses, exhausted, on the covers.

I walk past her, straight ahead. The moon, huge, lights my great-grandmother's room, illuminating everything in an unfamiliar light.

I stand in the doorway, afraid to go farther, afraid of this empty, cold room still full of her things. I battle this growing comprehension of her absence. I choke down tears and swipe at my eyes.

Finally, I force myself to walk to her desk and turn on the little Tiffany light. Her desk still holds her glass figurines, her stamps, cards from friends, poems she likes, letters from my parents, and her notes from my dad. She wrote him frequently about *Twilight Zone*s she watched and he wrote her back. Toward the end, though, her writing became shaky, difficult to read, impaired by the strokes.

I pick up the small bottle of perfume on her dresser. I want to spray it in the air and close my eyes. I hold it up but then quickly set it back down, somehow knowing, even then, that the familiar scent of her in this vacant, still room will be devastating.

In the corner, her bed is made, the bedspread neatly tucked in, perfectly smooth, as if no one has lain there, ever.

I consider curling up there. Just for a while, a moment. But I am afraid. Afraid of the enormity of this loss pushing through me.

The next morning my mother and I go to her service. The church is full, mostly of older people with sad smiles and heavy coats. I notice a few who still have snow on their boots.

My mother sits beside me, and I stare at the white-haired heads in the pews beyond us. I remember how the sun from the tiny windows, way above, spills down as if through prisms, illuminating the minister as he talks far away in a quiet voice, saying my great-grandmother's name, "Louise," over and over.

I bite my lip and I try not to cry.

We leave for the airport later that day. My mother has called a cab. The driver helps us with our suitcase, and my mother locks the empty house behind us. We crawl into the backseat, and the cabbie starts the meter. My mother tells me, "Turn around and take one last look. You will probably never be back." We both turn in unison, and I see that my mother is crying. One day I will wonder what other memories she may have been doing battle with that day. Was she thinking about more than my great-grandmother as the house grew smaller in the distance? Who did she imagine at the door? Was she

Dad at about age three. He was born on Christmas Day, and although Jewish, he said, "I was a Christmas present that was delivered unwrapped."

My dad frequently talked about his parents. He called his mother "Dearest." He adored her and she him, but it was his father, Sam, he most often told me about.

Like my dad, his father loved cars.

My dad *(center)* with his Boy Scout troop.

Dad's Sunday school class at the Jewish Community Center. Julie Golden is next to him, and next to Julie is Alan Levy, who was killed in the war.

Season's Greetings

1937

Curiously, both my parents had Boston terriers as children—and their pets appeared with them on their family Christmas cards. (Top photo by Esther Serling; bottom photo by Frank Caldwell)

A Merry Christmas and a Happy New Year.

Greetings from Mr. and Mrs. Caldwell and Paul. '36

My dad with his father shortly before he was shipped overseas. This was likely the last photo taken of them together. (Photo by Esther Serling)

My dad in boot camp before going to the Philippines.

My dad's 511th Paratroopers regimental booklet, describing, among other things, the reality of what they did.

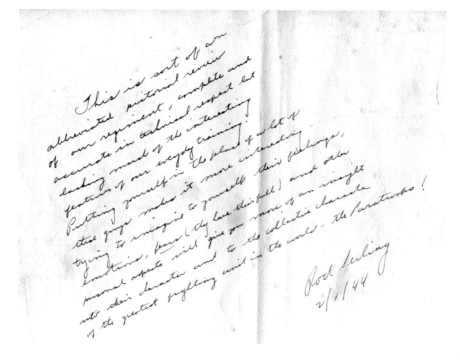

THIS COPY
OF THE
PICTORIAL REVIEW
OF THE
Five Eleven
IS PRESENTED
To Eleanor and Dad
By their son – Rod
February 1st, 1944

AIRBORNE
11

AUTOGRAPHS

My dad in his army uniform—a picture taken by his oldest friend.
(Photo by Julie Golden)

My parents leaving for their honeymoon.

My parents at Antioch College. My dad had dated just about every other coed before finding my mother.

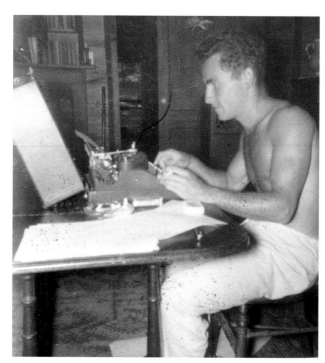

My dad wrote whenever he could, on weekends and evenings, typing frantically with two fingers. (Photo by Carol Serling)

In 1958 we moved to this house in Pacific Palisades, California. (Photo by Nick Springett)

On the way to bed for one of my dad's great bedtime stories.

My dad had an office built in the backyard. There was a wall of books, accessible by a ladder. (Photo by *Palisadian Post*)

Dad in front of the TV, relaxing with our setter, Michael. (Photo by Carol Serling)

My older sister, Jodi, and me at our family cottage near Ithaca, New York. (Photo by Carol Serling)

Dad often read us bedtime stories. He used different voices and intonations to make the characters come alive.

Although for years I had no idea what my dad did for a living, I have a vague recollection of him taking us to the MGM set where *The Twilight Zone* was filmed.

One of my favorite pictures with my dad. (Photo by Carol Serling)

My dad taught us how to blow through a blade of grass to make it whistle. (Photo by Carol Serling)

My dad loved spending time at the cottage, relaxing, swimming, and boating. (Photo by Carol Serling)

Sometimes my dad picked me up at school in his Excalibur. One Saturday morning he drove my friends and me, all piled in the back, around the neighborhood. (Photo by Carol Serling)

Jodi was married in the
summer of 1972 in
Ithaca, New York.
(Photo by Ron Prouty)

One of the last pictures of my mother and father. They were married for 27 years.
(Photo by Anne Serling)

Dancing with my dad at my sister's wedding. (Photo by Joan Barnes Flynn)

My dad would often appear in goofy costumes, and more than once he put my lampshade on his head. (Photo by Joan Barnes Flynn)

FOR GRUMPLE WITH GRITTED TEETH LOVE—

Dad

Dad on the set of *Night Gallery*. He inscribed the photo using the pet name he gave me, "Grumple." (Photo by NBC Universal Photo Bank)

My father loved our animals—particularly our dogs. He would often play on the ground with them like a littermate. (Photos by Anne Serling)

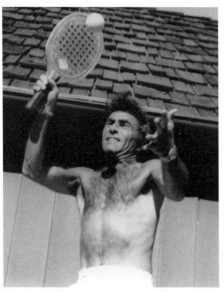

My dad loved paddle tennis and baseball.
He and his friend Dick Berg were forever
arguing about lines on the court,
and they would bet against each other
on professional baseball games.
(Photos by Anne Serling)

Not the first time the hammock broke under him. (Photo by Susan Woog Wagner)

(Photo by Broome Community College)

Summer 1974 or 1975—one of the last pictures taken of my dad and me.
(Photo by Joan Barnes Flynn)

thinking about all the years, in all those Februarys she waited as a child on that cold top step for a birthday card from her father? Or was she thinking about her grandfather standing in the garden waving up at her?

It begins to snow and we lose the house sooner than we might have, but, for a moment, just before it disappears through the heavy falling flakes, it looks like a perfect Christmas card, and I remember Nana, pressed at the glass, as she had all those winter mornings at the end of our trips, slowly waving good-bye as our yellow cab pulled away.

My parents establish scholarships at Ohio State in the names of my great-grandmother and my great-grandfather, Frank Caldwell, who had been the first professor of electrical engineering at Ohio State and chair of that department following graduation from Cornell University in Ithaca.

Some of my great-grandmother's belongings are eventually shipped to our house in California, and a few to the cottage: the desk from her room, the green Tiffany lamp that hung over her dining room table, a clock that chimed in the hall, a few trunks, some tables and chairs, and many miscellaneous items that throughout the years will evoke some memory of her.

Among these things, carefully wrapped in layers of newspaper deep in a box, are the photographs that hung on the wall by her bed. By the time she had her final stroke, her movement and mind were greatly impaired. I like to think, though, that alone there, when the afternoon sun illuminated the wall by her bed and passed over the faces of these people she loved and who loved her, she was still able to turn and know them.

Most are black-and-white, placed in the box in sequential order: her parents, both of her children, and her husband, all of whom she lost long before she died. Besides these are photos of my mother as a child, a picture of my mother and father on their wedding day, and a picture of her great-grand-children—Jodi and me.

And there, too, a photograph of my father at a typewriter, on which he wrote:

"To my amazing and remarkable Grandmother.

With Love, Rod."

Years later, the house will be given to the Ohio State University and sadly, eventually, torn down.

I will think of that a decade later when my mother sells our house in California and the new owners invite us back to show us how they will change it. But I have not been warned that construction has begun, and when the woman opens the front door, I realize the exterior is simply a façade and I freeze. I can go no farther. There are no interior walls, just blown-out space, and behind this stranger's smiling face, it is as if a bomb has gone off. The inside so shattered that even memory will struggle to restore what was.

Chapter 13

JODI AND I ARE aware of my father's growing celebrity, but fame back then is not the madness of today. There are no paparazzi, no blinding cameras flashing inches from your face. It is not the mayhem, the pandemonium, or the complete and disrespectful lack of privacy that exists now.

When we are out with my dad, someone passing on the street or someone in a store often recognizes him and stops and stares. They are usually polite; even in groups they are not a frenzied mob. Still, at times we hate this and will tug on his hand. We don't want anyone taking him away, even for a few moments. Frequently he is asked for his autograph. He is always cordial and gracious and obliging.

I remember a nervous fan who gets the wording wrong and exuberantly declares to my father, "Hey! You're *my* best fan!" My dad gets a kick out of this, and I remember him chuckling as we walk away.

Every year, from the time I am six until I am about twelve, my dad takes me to Disneyland for my birthday.

I look forward to these trips to Disneyland and having my dad all to myself. Much advance planning goes into these excursions. My dad and I decide where we will stay overnight, the precise time he will pick me up at school, where I should wait for him, what we should take, and so on. That he is as excited as I am is clearly evident. There is no pretense, no forced pleasure; these trips unquestionably appeal to the child within him.

Driving on the freeway, we play our usual pre-Disney game. He'll say, "Okay, Pops, the first one who sees the sign for Disneyland gets to pick the first ride." My dad never sees it. He must be blind, I think in my young mind.

We always spend the night in a motel close by and get up very early the next morning. We love the Swiss Family Robinson tree house, and the G.E. Carousel of Progress. I clutch his arm when we ride The Matterhorn and we rarely miss the Skyway to Tomorrowland. My father loves the Pirates of the Caribbean and always comments on the attention to detail, such as the hair on the pirates' legs.

Every year, he stands patiently beside me in the mile-long line to ride in the electric cars. For years I hope I'll reach the height requirement to drive, but I never do.

We generally leave the park in the late afternoon, exiting the gates tired but content, and back in the car, we manically talk about next year's trip as my Mickey Mouse balloon bounces from side to side in the backseat.

As we drive up the freeway on our way back home, it is not lost on me that I am fortunate to be able to go to places like Disneyland. To punctuate this fact, every year at Christmastime my mother has my sister and me read "The Hundred Neediest Cases" in *The New York Times*, and we decide which family we want to help.

For many years, my parents have foster children in Korea and the Philippines, and they visit them on several occasions.

Often Jodi and I write the monthly letters to them and send drawings.

In 1962, my father writes to Pan-Ki, a child in Korea.

Dear Pan-Ki,

We understand that we are to be your Foster Parents, for a time, and we wanted you to know that we have received your picture and were just delighted that we have taken on responsibility for such a fine looking man.

Here in the United States, I am a television writer and I've been wondering if you have television there, or have ever seen it.

I have two little girls and have always wanted a son. I'm hoping that you will write us whenever you can and tell us of your needs and what you're doing. We are tremendously interested in your welfare, and to that end we'll do all we can on your behalf. I'd also like to think that though I haven't any real son, perhaps you will fill the bill for me, and that perhaps someday we could meet.

Be sure to write us when you can.

With Affectionate regards,
Rod Serling

Many years after my dad and I last visited Disneyland together, and years after he died, Disney, in an effort to compete with the free-fall ride at Six Flags Theme Park, has built one of their own in Disney World. After several years of negotiations, the deal is sealed and the ride is completed. It is called "The Twilight Zone Tower of Terror."

I accompany my husband Doug and our children Erica and Sam, along with friends, my mother, Jodi, and her son Ryan to the opening ceremonies in Orlando. As we walk through the park, Erica (seven at the time), Sam (four), and Ryan (three), are all skipping around us and pointing at different rides and attractions, having a blast, completely immersed in the magic.

I think my dad would have been stunned that Disney would build a ride based on *The Twilight Zone*. He could never have imagined so many people waiting in a line for a ride involving *him*.

It begins with a visit to the lobby of an "abandoned" old Hollywood hotel and then snakes through to the eerie, cobweb-covered library where there is a film with my dad projected on a television screen, made up of hundreds of individual cuts that have been reassembled to have him introduce an attraction designed long after his death. From there visitors make their way into the boiler room in the hotel's basement, where they board one of the building's "service elevators."

According to Disney "lore," "In 1939, during a gloomy Halloween night, five unlucky souls were riding down the hotel's maintenance service elevator when a violent storm struck the building . . . and they were never seen again. Black scorch marks still scar The Twilight Zone Tower of Terror façade where lightning left its autograph."

Once you board the elevator, it rises several floors and opens its doors on surrealistic *Twilight Zone*–type illusions, then shuts the doors again and hauls you the rest of the way to the top before plunging down again in a seeming free fall.

There is actually little of the true spirit of *The Twilight Zone* about this attraction, lacking the commentary on the nature of man or imaginative explorations of "other dimensions." The entire experience, in fact, feels a little strange to me; dropping nearly two hundred feet in a haunted elevator is not exactly my cup of tea, and I am glad my kids are too young to ride it. But I think my dad, a former paratrooper, would have loved the ride.

Someone who apparently had been considered to do the fill-in portions of the voice-over is at the opening ceremony and follows us around the park, pretending to be my father. It is creepy, not to mention offensive, and I finally have to ask him to stop.

The next day, our last day, we go back to the other "Lands" with the tamer, more manageable rides—and where no one is following us: "The Carousel of Progress," "It's a Small World," "The Swiss Family Robinson Tree House," and other rides that have been updated from what I remembered.

When we pack up and head back to the airport for home, we hear our kids in the backseat: "That was fun!" "What was your favorite ride?" Erica asks Sam, and together, excitedly they say, "Mom, can we go again next year? Please! Please!" I turn to my husband, Doug, and smile, and for just a moment I'm back in time and I hear my own voice and my father answering.

Chapter 14

MOST OF MY PARENTS' friends are either not in the business or are the writers, producers, and the directors behind the scenes. I beg my dad, though, to introduce me to Shari Lewis (host and puppeteer/ventriloquist of her own TV show). I don't know how he knows her, but one night she does come for dinner. On the appointed evening, I wait and wait, my forehead pressed against my bedroom window. Finally, she pulls in and I run downstairs, holding my father's hand at the front door. I am speechless and in awe. Later, she brings out her famous puppet "Lamb Chop." In our very own house!

Barbara Billingsley, the mother in *Leave It to Beaver*, also comes for dinner once. At the time I am only vaguely familiar with the show and actually find her to be, from my very young perspective, rude. She asks me to get her something every time I sit down and then never thanks me.

When I am about seven, I go on a television program with my dad titled *First Impressions*. There are four or five other little girls, and the panel is to guess which one of us is his daughter. My father sits me down in the hall of the studio and whispers, "Don't forget, don't look at me when you answer a question. Act like you don't know me."

I nod dutifully in my brand-new, puffy, itchy blue dress, tapping together the toes of my new patent leather shoes, and notice someone who looks familiar. Within moments of my dad's directions, I yell out, "Daddy? Who's that?" I don't know if I am overheard by the panelists nearby or if they see a resemblance (people sometimes say I look like him), but everyone on the panel guesses that I am his daughter.

Anne Francis is one of the celebrity panelists. At the time I don't know who she is, but a few weeks later, I am at a shoe store with my mother and I see her. I don't remember if she speaks, but I remember her smiling at me. Even at a young age, completely naïve to any celebrity status, I am taken with this act of kindness.

My father is a great fan of actress and comedienne Carol Burnett. She is in *The Twilight Zone* episode "Cavender Is Coming," about an angel who has twenty-four hours to help a woman who is unemployed and behind on her rent. After she is given a luxurious apartment, money, and friends, the woman realizes she wants her old life back.

For my thirteenth birthday my father takes me to the taping of Carol Burnett's variety show. Someone must have told her he was there because when they turn the house lights up and she does her question-and-answer segment at the beginning of the show, she finds us in the audience and says hello. I feel a little embarrassed when I suddenly find myself smiling manically and am tremendously relieved when my dad answers all her questions so that I only have to sit there.

Around this time, after graduating from sixth grade, I am attending a small private day school. I don't like the school and never feel comfortable; never really feel a part of it. I think I was sent to this school because the public schools were so enormous, the class size unmanageable. Not an extrovert like my dad, I find it hard to navigate my way.

One day, a few months after my dad took me to Carol Burnett's show, I look up from my desk in French class and see her walk by, past an open door. The red hair and the warm smile are unmistakable. It is Carol Burnett! She stops and waves. I am astonished and moved that she remembers me. I hear she is looking at the school for one of her daughters.

My instinct is to get up from my seat and tell her, "Don't send her here; she'll hate it." But I say nothing. I don't move. I just sit there, star-struck and silent, waving back.

Chapter 15

OUR HOUSE ALWAYS SEEMS full of people and noise, with the front door continuously opening and closing, the phone ringing, dogs barking, friends running in and out, and my dad and his friend Dick Berg playing gin rummy downstairs on rainy Sundays.

I hear the slapping of their cards against the table, their voices rising, and a sudden eruption of laughter. No one can laugh like my dad. Listening to him tell a joke, any joke, is a story in itself. He acts out voices and mannerisms with an impeccable sense of dialect and timing, usually slapping his knee and losing himself in his own hysteria before ever arriving at the punch line.

The comedian David Brenner remembers that laugh. He told me how one day he boarded the first-class section of a jumbo 747 and saw my dad sitting in the middle, front seat. He said they talked for the entire five-hour flight. "I knew your dad was short and I asked him if I could bounce a joke off of him that had just popped into my head to see if it was too offensive. Your dad said, 'Sure.' So I said, 'I feel sorry for short people. It must be frightening to wake up in the morning and see your feet right here.' I held my open palms under my chin and continued talking to them. 'It's us! It's us!' Your dad literally slipped off his seat and was curled up on the floor hysterical with laughter."

I know my father's laugh anywhere. I can pick it out of a crowded room and, in fact, have. Years later, as a senior in high school I am in a stage version of *The Wizard of Oz*. For my great acting debut I am cast as the lead poppy and, as such, am the first out, wearing a green leotard and orange petals around my neck. This role must have been created because the teacher wanted to give everyone a part, no matter how dismal. When I dance out, I immediately hear my father's laugh in the crowded auditorium. I might have been hurt if I, too, hadn't thought the whole thing was pretty funny.

In the late sixties, my dad discovers paddle tennis, which doesn't put as much strain on his war-injured knee as regular tennis. He has a court built in our backyard. This becomes a favorite weekend activity for him and some of his buddies. Among the regulars are Dick Berg and Jerry Paris (a regular on *The Dick Van Dyke Show* and director of many TV shows, including *Happy Days)*, friend Tom Ryan, actor John Forsythe, and writer Bill Idelson.

Every weekend, they are out there unless it is pouring rain. From my bedroom, early in the morning, I hear the ball being hit back and forth, and I hear them talking, yelling, and swearing. Inevitably, there is some break in the game as an argument ensues about the boundaries and some heated "discussion" about the score takes place.

Years later, after his first heart attack, one of the funniest cards my dad receives in the hospital is from Jerry Paris: "Berg said you were dead... but he always calls 'em wrong."

During the week our days have a routine, a flow, even when my dad is in the middle of a project. He makes time for a quick game of basketball when I get home. In the earlier days if he was a little late, I played school with the dogs, leading them (with biscuits) into a little room off the kitchen I called their classroom. I have it all set up with pencils and papers and a tiny chalkboard I balance on my lap. I "teach" them addition and subtraction and then read to them. When they get restless, I call, "Okay, recess!" and we file back outside. My dad, who sometimes hears me, finds this very amusing.

He and I play basketball on the paddle tennis court, never keeping score; we just shoot the ball, and when I miss, he says, "You were robbed."

Sometimes, when his knee isn't hurting, he will do a Russian dance out there on the court, crossing his arms, squatting down, and kicking out his legs. I try it and fall down.

My dad and I continue to sneak in more than the occasional episode of *The Flintstones,* and he pays me a quarter if I tickle his feet.

One program, though, that we are never allowed to watch is *Hogan's Heroes,* about a Nazi prisoner-of-war camp. My father has a particular abhorrence of this show and no tolerance for how it perversely twists what happened in Nazi prison camps into something even remotely comical. Years later, in a speech at the Library of Congress in Washington, it is clearly still on his mind:

> *You take a show like Hogan's Heroes. Now, here you have a weekly, mirth-filled half hour that shows what a swinging ball it must have been in a Nazi POW camp. Now there's a slight deviation from the norm in that there are good guys on this show, certainly, but there are no bad guys, at least not in the sense that we're used to recognizing our enemies as they appeared in old Warner Brothers films. Now the Japanese in a Jack Warner production was very recognizable: big buckteeth, myopic eyes, he*

*lusted after Occidental women and he tortured nuns. And the
Nazis, of course, were all walking hymns of hate, totally
unregenerative and all looking like Erich von Stroheim.*

   *Now through the good offices of Hogan's Heroes, we meet the
new post-war version of the wartime Nazi: a thick, bumbling
fathead whose crime, singularly, is stupidity—nothing more. He's
kind of a lovable, affable, benign Herman Goering. Now this
may appeal to some students of comedy who refuse to let history
get in the way of their laughter. But what it does to history is to
distort, and what it does to a recollection of horror that is an ugly
matter of record is absolutely inexcusable. Satire is one thing,
because it bleeds, and it comments as it evokes laughter. But a
rank diminishment of what was once an era of appalling human
suffering, I don't believe is proper material for comedy.*

He goes on to suggest that the success of *Hogan's Heroes*
could lead to "*The Merry Men of Auschwitz*, or Milton Berle in
a new musical version of the Death March on Bataan, or a
single shot spectacular, *The Wit and Wisdom of Adolf Hitler*."
I don't recall any other television show about which he
feels such a singular repugnance or any other program being
banned in our house. On the topics of Nazis or the persecution of Jews, or prejudice of any kind, he is fierce and un-
equivocal. Never is this clearer or the message conveyed more
powerfully than in *The Twilight Zone* episode "Deaths-Head
Revisited," in which a former S.S. officer makes a nostalgic
post-war visit back to the Dachau concentration camp. Perhaps if it hadn't been broadcast four years earlier, "Deaths-
Head" would have been my father's response to *Hogan's
Heroes*.
The opening narration captures my father's disdain:

*Mr. Schmidt recently arrived in a small Bavarian village which
lies eight miles northeast of Munich, a picturesque, delightful
little spot onetime known for its scenery but more recently related
to other events having to do with the less positive pursuits of*

*man: human slaughter, torture, misery and anguish. Mr.
Schmidt, as we will soon perceive, has a vested interest in the
ruins of a concentration camp—for once, some seventeen years
ago, his name was Gunther Lutze. He held the rank of a captain
in the S.S. He was a black-uniformed strutting animal whose
function in life was to give pain, and like his colleagues of the
time he shared the one affliction most common amongst that
breed known as Nazis: he walked the Earth without a heart.
And now former S.S. Captain Lutze will revisit his old haunts,
satisfied perhaps that all that is awaiting him in the ruins on the
hill is an element of nostalgia. What he does not know, of course,
is that a place like Dachau cannot exist only in Bavaria. By its
nature, by its very nature, it must be one of the populated areas
of The Twilight Zone.*

In this episode, as in many *Twilight Zone* episodes, my dad
renders the justice that failed to occur in real life. He tells it
the way it should have been, where the evil get their comeuppance, their due. When former Captain Lutze returns to
the camp where he once held the power of life and death, he
has only a little time to reminisce before he is confronted by
one of his victims, Alfred Becker (played by Joseph Schild-
kraut, the Viennese-born actor who two years before had
portrayed Anne Frank's father on film). Becker says that he is
now the camp's "caretaker." Lutze soon realizes that Becker is
dead at the captain's own hand and intends to put him on
trial with the help of other ghosts from the camp. After the
guilty verdict has been delivered, Lutze stumbles around the
camp, experiencing the agonies he once inflicted on others.

When the taxi driver comes to fetch him, he calls the police and a doctor, reporting, "I heard him screaming. Such
screams. Like a . . . like a . . . wounded animal." He then asks
the doctor, "What happened to him? I drove him up here
myself not two hours ago. He was all right then. But his
screams . . . oh . . . his screams . . ."

To which the doctor replies, "I have no idea. All I know is

that he screams from pain. More than pain—agony. But there's not a mark on him. He's insane. A raving maniac. What could happen to a man in two hours to make him a raving maniac? Someone must tell me."

Almost all of my father's closing narrations end with the phrase, "The Twilight Zone." The message of this episode, however, was clearly so important to him, so central to his passion, that he felt the need to go beyond the fantasy.

The Dachaus, the Belsens, the Buchenwalds, the Auschwitzes— all of them. They must remain standing because they are a monument to a moment in time when some men decided to turn the Earth into a graveyard. Into it they shoveled all of their reason, their logic, their knowledge, but worst of all, their conscience. And the moment we forget this, the moment we cease to be haunted by its remembrance, then we become the gravediggers. Something to dwell on and remember, not only in The Twilight Zone but wherever men walk God's earth.

There are shows my father likes or shows we watch regularly when I am young—*Disney*, and all of the popular family shows. We also watch many cartoons besides *The Flintstones*. We love *Huckleberry Hound*. My dad can do Augie Doggie's voice to a tee, repeating Augie's catchphrase "Dear old Dad." Sometimes I grab his arm on his way out to his office or on his way down the stairs and beg him, "Come on. Do it. Be Augie one more time."

Our house is also never without a myriad of pets. We have dogs, cats, birds, fish, and turtles, and Jodi has a horse stabled in a canyon nearby. She names him "Highbeam" and writes his name on her wall by her bed. Years later, we find her writing again, laughing when we read: "Highbeam, Highbeam,

Highbeam" all over her wall in tiny letters and then an occasional "Highbeam rules."

Our cats were a Christmas present from my parents, a well-
kept secret until Christmas morning. But early one foggy
morning, two years after we get them, my cat, Harry, is hit by
a car.

My sister runs home to tell me. She stands on the threshold
of my bedroom, wiping away tears, yelling, motioning, waving her arms. It takes a while for me to comprehend what she
is saying. "Harry's dead," she finally manages. "A truck hit him
in the driveway where they're building that new house."

She stands there for a moment—the older sister passing on
the terrible news, the ill-equipped courier— waiting, as if she
is thinking of something more to say. But, at only eleven, she
is no more prepared to deliver the news than I am to receive
it and silent for a moment more, she then backs out of my
room and runs down the stairs.

My father helps me gently place Harry in a box with a
blanket and flowers and a note. We carry him to the end of
the driveway and say a few words about what a fine cat he
was and what a good, albeit short, life he had. My father tells
me a special truck will pick him up and he will go to cat
heaven.

I stay on the front stoop throughout much of the morning,
waiting for the truck, assured that my cat is going to a safe
place. My dad finally coaxes me inside, and by late afternoon,
the cat is gone.

Perhaps today that kind of parental dissembling would be
discouraged, but it certainly made this loss more bearable at
the time.

Eventually our menagerie grows to include another cat
and even black and white pet rats. Throughout the years, I
will name all of mine, "Mary" or "Junior." I think we got the
rats because my mother had heard they were very social and
great pets. We dress the rats in Barbie doll clothes. They crawl

over the cats in little skirts left open so they'll fit and the cats just lie there, oblivious, purring, unfazed.

Flying with all the animals between California and upstate New York, is, at best, a complicated endeavor, although we are able to take the rats to our seats in their cages with the little fabric covers my mother sewed for them.

One summer my sister's rat Berta gets loose and runs under the cottage. Jodi gets a flashlight and, lying on the ground, shines it under the porch in a futile attempt to point Berta home. She finally gives up and stands, her face tear-streaked and dirty. My dad has to return to L.A. for some un-expected business and promises to bring her a new rat. (In those days, pet stores in upstate New York did not sell rats.) On the flight back, he leaves the little cage on his seat when he gets up to go to the bathroom. Upon returning, he discov-ers the cage is open and the rat has gotten loose. Not wanting to alarm his fellow passengers, he quietly makes his way down the aisle, looking for her. Unsuccessful and beginning to panic, he gets on his hands and knees, literally crawling down the aisle until coming to the feet of the flight attendant.

"May I help you?" she asks him.

My dad stammers some response and goes back to his seat where, sitting on the armrest, is the rat. He grabs her and gets her safely back into her cage. Or so his story goes.

Twice my dad uses my nickname, "Nan," in his *Twilight Zone* show. In the first season episode "The Hitch-Hiker," the main character, Nan Adams, played by Inger Stevens, is driving across country and repeatedly sees a man hitchhiking. She be-comes terrified as she keeps passing him on the side of the road; no matter how fast she drives the man is always ahead of her. He turns out to be Mr. Death. When I eventually see this episode, I am not thrilled that my dad used my name in one of the creepier stories. In another episode later that season, "A Passage for Trumpet," one of my dad's personal favorites, he again uses my nickname, Nan, but in a much gentler, nostalgic story. It stars Jack Klugman as a depressed, alcoholic jazz musician who commits suicide but is then given a second chance at life:

> *Joey Crown, who makes music and who discovered something*
> *about life; that it can be rich and rewarding and full of beauty,*
> *just like the music he played, if a person would only pause to*
> *look and to listen.*

Two years later, my dad brings home one of the props, "Willy," the ventriloquist's dummy from the episode called "The Dummy," starring Cliff Robertson as an alcoholic, paranoid ventriloquist. Throughout the weekend Willy sits on my father's knee, and my dad, acting the part of the ventriloquist, animates him, making him move and talk and gesture, bringing him to life for Jodi and me. I remember Willy propped up, sitting at the dinner table with us, and later covering him up for bed. We are only able to keep him for a couple of days and are sad when he has to return to the studio.

When I finally see this episode, my view of Willy completely changes. He is controlling and malevolent, keeping the increasingly crazed Jerry in his thrall. The show ends with the two of them once again on stage, but this time it is Jerry sitting on a human-sized Willy's knee. I think about this weird and chilling story and the darker, sinister side of the human beings my dad often explores.

Chapter 16

IN 1962, MY FATHER is thirty-seven years old. That spring, CBS drops *The Twilight Zone* at the end of its third season, after 102 episodes have aired. They had not yet found a sponsor for the fourth season, and CBS had scheduled a new show in *Twilight Zone*'s regular time slot. My father is offered a teaching position at Antioch College, his alma mater, in Yellow Springs, Ohio. Although CBS later renews the contract for the series, my dad accepts the position at Antioch before he learns of *Twilight Zone*'s resuscitation:

> *Antioch is liable to drop my option, too. I've never taught before. If that happens, and if CBS doesn't go ahead with the hour show, I may go fishing the rest of my life. I have three reasons for accepting the position. First is extreme fatigue. Secondly, I'm desperate for a change of scene, and third is a chance to exhale, with the opportunity for picking up a little knowledge instead of trying to spew it out . . . I need to regain my perspective, do a*

little work and spend the rest of my time getting acquainted with
my wife and children.

I am in the second grade, and Jodi in fifth, when we move
to Ohio. CBS does renew *The Twilight Zone* but changes it
from a half hour to an hour-long format, perhaps because "a
bigger *Twilight Zone* might attract a bigger audience." The
show will air on a Thursday (rather than a Friday) night. Although my dad will still be writing a great number of the
scripts, he decides to take a step back from his day-to-day involvement.

We pack up the dogs, cats, and our two pet rats and head

east. Although my sister and I are sad about leaving our friends, we are all excited about this move and recognize it's only temporary; we'll be home again in six months.

On the flight to Ohio, as on many of the airplane trips we take, my father and I play cards. We play "Go Fish," for money, and I am up to $40 before I lose it all. We also write notes back and forth and play Tic-Tac-Toe and Hangman. After a while, having reached his saturation point, he writes me, "No more notes. Daddy-boy is busy reading." I look over across the aisle and both my mother and sister have fallen asleep.

In Yellow Springs we rent a white, two-story house. When we are first settling in, my father leaves to go to the college, and my mother tells my sister and me to walk around the block. Jodi runs ahead and I become hopelessly lost. All of the streets look the same, all of the houses unfamiliar, and all of the dogs look ferocious. By the time I find my way back, it is late. I am terrified and in tears.

I have only a few memories of specific rooms in this house, the threadbare stairs we run up and down each day, and the bedroom that, for those few months, is mine. It has dormers and red wallpaper that I love. It is an old house, and I pretend we are living in another time.

The elementary school is close enough that we can bike to it and return home for lunch. For the first time we are allowed to call our teachers by their first name. My teacher, Mary Chase, sometimes brings her dog to school—a basset hound who obediently sits in the corner of the classroom looking adorable.

Jodi and I make friends fairly quickly, but before we do, we sometimes settle for each other. One of our favorite things to do is to build houses for our little two-inch Steiff bears. We build the houses out of boxes. The liquor store boxes are the best because they have dividers that make for ready rooms. We use contact paper for wall paper, or sometimes paint the walls and floors and fill them with tiny doll furniture. We lie on her bedroom floor or mine, in our flowered pajamas, rearranging rooms, talking in "bear voices" as they travel from one house to the other.

Eventually we plan our weekends and overnights with friends. My best friend is Roz and she understands when, on Saturday mornings, I have to leave early. I don't tell her the exact reason but it is because I have discovered that I love vacuuming and I can't wait to get home so I can vacuum all of the rugs.

When I come in, my dad is sometimes on the couch in his light blue robe, reading the newspaper. He looks up at me over the paper, smiles, and picks up his feet so that I can vacuum the area before him. Often, though, he is upstairs working while I, still wearing my yellow winter coat, lug that huge Hoover vacuum throughout the house, backing away as I go so as not to leave a single footprint.

One of the classes my dad is teaching is a night class, "Drama in the Mass Media." I feel his absence profoundly in the evening and stand by the window, watching, waiting for him to come home.

Often he has to fly back to California, balancing work on both coasts. I hate it when he is gone. My mother must, too. She seems happier when he's around. My sister, as is usual for her, is busy, off with friends much of the time, probably missing her horse. We haven't played with our bear houses for a while; the bears sit in the same position we last left them, posed and motionless in our absence.

We are all aware of the quiet, still house when my father is away. Even the dogs Michael and Maggie stare at the door, waiting, joining us when Jodi and I jump around him when he returns.

Some weekend mornings we spend time with old family friends who live in Yellow Springs—Dorothy and Jim Mitchell. "Aunt Dottie" and "Uncle Peabody." We name Jim after a cartoon character who, like him, also bird-watches. We play with Dottie's makeup, loving her bright red lipstick and blue eye shadow. We make snickerdoodle cookies, eating them hot out of the oven, and later we roll around with their dalmatian Binky.

Dottie remembers my dad's students loving him. Recently she reminded me about the time my dad asked her and Jim to come over to play bridge. "The snow was about a foot deep. We told him we wouldn't be able to get there. Well, he said he would come get us and he did—in that sorta pink station wagon he had."

That Christmas we go with Dottie and Jim to choose a Christmas tree. A Boy Scout goes with us and helps us cut down the tree. My mother is filming with a heavy 8mm camera. Later we will watch this silent home movie.

There we are, in colored coats and hats and bright orange mittens. Suddenly my sister and I begin to run farther into the glen. The camera follows us for a while and then shifts to my dad, skipping behind, holding my mother's purse, hamming it up for the camera. My mother must be laughing because the camera begins to shake wildly as it pans over the shadowed paths. It follows my father, who now pretends to be a monkey, jumping around the pine needles, stooped to the ground, picking at his hair, a perfect primate.

The camera shifts again to all of us waving, always waving, and silently the film ends, our hands suspended in midair.

While teaching, my dad is still writing *Twilight Zone* scripts and receiving potential scripts from other writers. He is also writing a screenplay adaptation of the best-selling novel *Seven Days in May*, by Fletcher Knebel and Charles W. Bailey II, about U.S. military leaders plotting to overthrow the president because he supports a nuclear disarmament treaty and they fear a Soviet sneak attack. The film, a political thriller directed by John Frankenheimer, just off another taut political thriller, *The Manchurian Candidate*, turns out to be a critical and popular success that very much captures the tensions of the times. Frankenheimer had asked my dad to write the screenplay, figuring their attitudes, interests, and styles would complement each other.

Since the beginning of his administration, President Kennedy had been criticized by the right wing for being soft on Communism and weak on defense. My father picks up on these issues in his portrayal of President Jordan Lyman. On a deeper level, the film displays several themes that are important to my father throughout his career. Prime among these is not succumbing to fear born of ignorance. In the nuclear age, he seems to be telling us, we can't throw up our hands in helplessness over the enormity of the problem. With the stakes as dire as they are, we must all work positively to change things for the better. I think that is why he believes so firmly in the idea of the United Nations. As in *Twilight Zone*'s "The Monsters Are Due on Maple Street," my dad is warning us that the greatest threat we face is if a potential enemy uses our fears to get us to start destroying ourselves.

When my father flies back to LA to attend to other business, he also goes directly to the MGM studio to shoot several opening narrations for *The Twilight Zone.* Contrary to his plans to relax, he is under tremendous pressure during our time in Yellow Springs. Clearly, the six months there are not the respite he intends. And his attempts to revitalize, to reenergize, himself prove to be increasingly compromised.

But back then I know none of this. I only know when he walks down the stairs, his suitcase bumping against his leg, my father is leaving.

Had I looked closer, had I not been so young, would I have seen this? Could I have asked him to stay? Could I have slowed my father down?

When his teaching position ends and we are days away from going back to California, our rats have babies, tons of babies, hairless, pink, tiny things. In a mad rush my sister and I try to sell them and then try to give them away, but we are not successful. No one wants them. We have to leave a cage full of these baby rats with a friend whose parents agree to try to find them homes. By then, the rats have hair and are cute. (Well, cute for a rat.)

We leave in the spring of 1963. Leaning out of the car windows, on the way to the airport, we wave to our friends. We wave and wave, shouting "Good-bye, good-bye!" until we can barely see them. We drive farther away, picking up a little speed, and watch as they disappear entirely. Our hands fall to our laps, we stare straight ahead, and are quiet then.

Jeanne Marshall, a student who took my father's writing class, remembers: "At our last seminar meeting in 1963, Rod cried while saying good-bye to all of us. He told us we would all be together again sometime, somewhere."

Chapter 17

IT IS DIFFICULT TO imagine my father without a cigarette. It is his trademark. He smokes incessantly. In the car, the smoke wafts out of the sliver of space where the window is cracked open. At the dinner table there is always an ashtray pushed back and forth between my mother and him, although his habit far exceeds hers. When we watch television, the ashtray sits on his chest; sometimes I wave the smoke away and he apologizes, stubbing out the cigarette. During intermissions in plays or long movies, he works his way down the aisles, into lobbies, out the heavy doors, and there, on the street, beneath the neon lights, holding his cigarette between his thumb and forefinger, my father blows the smoke into the sky.

My sister and I know smoking isn't good for him and we both throw his cigarettes away. One day, I throw an entire carton into the fireplace. He arrives too late to pull the burning packs out. I think I am helping, but he is furious. "God damn it! What were you thinking?! Do you have any idea what a carton of cigarettes costs?"

I tell him, "I was just trying to save your life!" and hurt, I fly upstairs to my room. A few minutes later he quietly knocks on my door and apologizes to me. "Look, Nanny, I'm sorry. I know you're just trying to help. Don't get like this. Don't smoke. Don't fall prey to this God damn addiction."

I often wonder if he would have succumbed to the alienation a smoker experiences today and quit, but back then smoking was much more acceptable. Certainly he knew, though, that he was gambling; his own father, also a smoker, had died of a heart attack at fifty-two. Although I continue to nag him, I never again throw his cigarettes out.

Many times he tries to quit; his Raynaud's disease is causing increasing pain in his fingers. In a letter he writes to his close friend Dick Berg, he says: "No doubt you've heard rumors of my sudden onslaught of ill health. I won't belabor it now because it takes a great deal of explaining. Suffice it to say I'm under medication now and I'm out of cigarettes and they tell me I'm much improved . . . It all has to do with some sort of vascular ailment in the extremities (not the extremities you're thinking of, you schmuck!").

And in a letter to me while I'm at camp.

July 14
Dear "Momma,"
You know what a God-awful typist I am. I'm way out of practice and I'm just beginning to use my hand again. No cigarettes for eight weeks—you better be proud of me, Pops!

But he is never able to stop entirely, and almost immediately is back to his three packs or more a day.

Despite the heavy smoking and complications from Raynaud's, it does not occur to me, ever, that my father could be an invalid or that he will be gone while he is still young. Even following an incident a decade earlier, when after delivering a speech in Washington, D.C., he suffers chest pains and has to be hospitalized. The diagnosis is stress and fatigue; the doctor says he will be fine.

If there is something more serious or if health problems are imminent, I don't know, and won't know until many years later when my mother will say, "Your dad had to sit down after carrying his suitcase through the airport. He was out of breath."

But even she is unaware of the time bomb within him, the fragility of his health, and is oblivious to what looms. He is traveling alone and doesn't tell her until after the fact. By then he is on a perilous course, ignoring symptoms and well on his way to having what ultimately will be a very serious heart attack.

But that darkness is still light-years away.

For now, it is still the early sixties, and in a memory so palpable, so brilliantly clear, I don't need even to close my eyes or search for a confirming home movie or photograph. I simply reach back.

It is summer. I am six or seven. My father and I are walking down to the beach below our cottage. It has rained the night before and the path is slippery. We need to hold hands— "paddles," as he calls them. We are taking our time. My pink flip-flops are on the wrong feet, but neither of us notices until we get to the beach.

At the shoreline, he drags two lawn chairs over and places them side-by-side. He hands me my red pail he has carried down for me. I am going to collect stones with holes through them, lucky stones.

The sun is still warm for late afternoon, and the sky a cloudless, perfect blue, is broken only by the flight of seagulls passing above. They land on the dock in continuous swarms. My mother has tried to deter them. Earlier in the summer, she draped rope around the posts and tied on pieces of tinfoil.

It worked for a while, but the birds are onto her now. They simply sit on the rope, turned away from the foil, shrieking to one another.

My father is reading a paperback novel. He is stretched out on the lawn chair. His knees are bent, and one arm hangs down, petting Michael. Every once in a while, he feels for his sunglasses on his head, puts them on, and looks out at the lake or up at the sky. "Daddy, I am going to put on my bathing suit," I say, and go off into a tiny little room off the beach house we call the dressing room. I am pulling the suit on with some difficulty because it is still damp from yesterday's swim. I almost have it on when I feel a piercing pain and I scream. My father comes running, "Nanny! What happened?!" nearly tripping on the stoop. I whip off the suit and there, on the floor, is a large black wasp. It has fallen from my suit but not before stinging me twice.

My dad grabs a fly swatter and hits it, over and over. I wrap myself in a towel, watching him and wiping away my tears. He picks up the wasp by one wing, says, "Little bugger," and takes it outside. Then he hits it with a rock. By now I am no longer crying; my dad is taking care of things.

For the final retribution, he picks up what is left of this wasp and drowns it in the water. "Just let that little SOB try that again," he tells me, holding my hand, as we stand there together looking out at the lake where the wasp has disappeared.

A week later all pain, humiliation, and subsequent itching I once felt are completely gone and I go away to a sleepover camp for a two-week session. The camp is not more than ten miles away but I hate it. I don't know why I don't ask a counselor to call home. I don't know why I don't leave. Those just don't seem, for some reason, to be options. Perhaps I am afraid of disappointing my parents, who must have thought it was something I'd like, or be "good for me." My father promises to go by on the boat every day. I look for him during swim time. I hold my hand up to shield my eyes from the blinding sun bouncing off of the glistening water, and I sit on my towel on the stones and wait. The timing, though, is never right, and we never see each other. Later, he assures me he drove by.

In Arts & Crafts I paint my mother a picture with stars and hearts and make a box out of Popsicle sticks for my dad. It sits on his dresser at the lake to this day. Unable to decide which color to paint it, I paint it every color available. On the lid, in a child's big scrawl, I write "Daddy."

Summer ends. We walk down the drive one final time. A few leaves have already begun to fall, splashes of color along the gravel, the irrefutable sign of a new season giving notice that we need to go.

The ritual begins, we close the cottage. Beds are stripped, sheets are thrown over lamps like ghosts, floors are washed, porch furniture dragged back in, and the windows and doors are boarded. Suddenly, once again, another year has passed and we are gone.

The flight back west is long. My mom brings little presents for us to occupy the time. Puzzles, coloring books, new crayons.

As is often the case, I have grabbed the seat beside my father. Jodi and my mother are across the aisle. I look at my dad; he winks and then returns to his book.

I remember the way the light from the small oval airplane window illuminates him that day. The way I can clearly see the tiny dark spot in his eye where he had been hit by shrapnel in the war. The plane shakes a little and I grab his hand. The pilot announces we have reached our cruising altitude, and the engines roar as we speed through the sky.

I look out the window at clouds close enough to jump into and think about all of us at the lake and the summer we are leaving behind. Leaning forward, I check in the seat pocket ahead of us for the new deck of cards my dad put there and then look over at my mother reading and my sister writing a letter, sketching horses in the corner. Sitting back, I rest my head on my father's shoulder, loving these moments I have him to myself. I close my eyes and think about the game we will later play.

Chapter 18

THE TWILIGHT ZONE AIRS its final show, after five seasons, in 1964. The CBS president James Aubrey says, "It has gone over budget far too many times, the ratings aren't good enough," and he is "sick of it."

Although not in the top ten, *Twilight Zone* is still getting good ratings, and because of this, my dad's agent, Ted Ashley, feels he might be able to sell it to another network. NBC is not interested, but ABC is. They won't be able to use the name *The Twilight Zone,* which CBS, at the time, contractually controls, and so the title *Witches, Warlocks and Werewolves* is suggested. This was the title of a paperback anthology of classic chiller short stories edited by my dad in 1963. My dad, though, loathes this idea and suggests something with which he is more comfortable. It will be called *Rod Serling's Wax Museum.* He proposes a series using the image of the castle built by George C. Boldt, a millionaire and proprietor of the Waldorf Astoria Hotel.

When my parents took boat trips to the Thousand Islands,

they would pass this massive fortress situated in the St. Lawrence River along the northern border of New York State. Boldt shaped the island into a heart. As the story goes:

> *Boldt, the millionaire proprietor of the world-famous Waldorf Astoria Hotel in New York City, set out to build a full-size Rhineland castle in Alexandria Bay on picturesque Heart Island. The grandiose structure was to be a display of his love for his wife, Louise. Beginning in 1900, Boldt's family shared four glorious summers on the island in the Alster Tower while 300 workers, including stonemasons, carpenters, and artists, fashioned the six story, 120-room castle, complete with tunnels, a powerhouse, Italian gardens, a drawbridge, and a dovecote. Not a single detail or expense was spared. But tragedy struck in 1904; Louise died suddenly. Boldt telegraphed the island and commanded the workers to immediately stop all construction. A broken-hearted Boldt could not imagine his dream castle without his beloved. He never returned to the island and left behind the structure as a monument to his love. For 73 years, the castle and various stone structures were left to the mercy of the wind, rain, ice, snow and vandals.*

My father submits a proposal to Tom Moore, the president of ABC, with the following opening:

> *A helicopter shot of Heart Island with slow dissolves to a closer angle of Boldt Castle. The latter is the "haunted house" of the world. It is a vast multispired stone mausoleum with hundreds of bare rooms. The camera moves closer to the Castle in a series of shots until finally we're inside its gigantic echoey front hall. Lining the long stairway is a row of shrouded figures that extend into the darkness. Down the steps walks Serling past these figures and ultimately past the lens of the camera to a vantage point (now we are on a studio set) where stands another shrouded figure. Serling removes the wrapping and we are looking at a wax figure of that week's particular episode's leading character.*

Tom Moore and my father cannot reach an agreement, though, and so the concept goes no further. *The Twilight Zone* is officially done. The crew holds a "wake" on the MGM soundstage, complete with a tombstone and epitaph: "Twilight Zone RIP."

At eight years old I am not aware of any remorse on my dad's part at the series' end. I believe he has no regrets. I have vague, fragmented recollections of his telling my mother that he is tired, ready to move on, and wants to try something new.

The Twilight Zone ran for five years and aired 156 episodes, of which my dad wrote 92. He is, for the most part, pleased with the show. "We had some real turkeys, some fair ones, and some shows I'm really proud to be a part of. I can walk away from this series unbowed." He is thirty-nine years old.

In what may be the worst mistake of his life, my father sells the episodes to CBS. He makes the decision not just because he is tired and wants to move on but also because he really doesn't think *The Twilight Zone* series will ever generate more money than what CBS is offering.

He could not have been more wrong; it has, by the hundreds of millions.

In April of that year—1964, my dad is elected president of the American Academy of Television Arts and Sciences, the younger counterpart to the Motion Picture Academy, taking over from universally respected CBS News correspondent and anchorman Walter Cronkite. Some people suggest that both Cronkite and my dad have been installed to lend an air of prestige and respectability to the shaky industry group, which does not enjoy the same status as its movie counterpart and its glitzy Oscar presentation. Their expectation is that my dad will make inspiring speeches, lend his celebrity to various occasions.

He is pleased and honored with the position and almost

immediately plunges himself into substantive changes. He travels around the country giving speeches on his ideas of what television is, and could become, and is highly critical of the medium and stirring up some resentment. He wants to eliminate any traces or vestiges of the notorious blacklist that denied work to anyone even suspected of being a Communist. He is quietly advised not to open up old wounds and cause new trouble.

He also jumps into a controversy between the networks over how the Academy's Emmy Awards are to be given out. There seem to be about a zillion categories, and no one is happy with the way they are judged. My dad feels that making an award in each category, regardless of quality, would cheapen the awards and cause the public to lose interest. With Cronkite's help and backing, my dad proposes that awards should be given by craft—writing, directing, acting, for example—and that if no individual or program deserves an award for merit for the past year's work, none will be presented. On the other hand, if two or even three works deserve recognition, then three awards will be made in one category.

When my dad leaves the presidency two years later, the new administration restores the Emmys to just the way they were before he became involved.

"Television has left me tired, frustrated," he tells a reporter from *The New York Times* during a 1964 interview.

What he doesn't realize is that the frustration is just beginning.

Chapter 19

SPRING, 1964. I am knocking on the glass doors of my father's study. He spins around in his desk chair, motioning for me to come in. He is on the phone.

I slide the door open and he holds up his hand again, signaling for me to wait while he finishes his call.

It is pouring rain and the water has pooled by the door. I sit down by his fireplace and notice I have left wet footprints across the flagstone-tiled floor. My dad won't mind.

Above me, on the fireplace mantel there are six Emmys, including one that he recently won in the category, Outstanding Writing Achievement in Drama, for his adaptation of a John O'Hara short story called "It's Mental Work," for the *Chrysler Theatre*. But I do not know these details then; I know only that where there were once five Emmys, there are now six.

Our dog, Michael, has been missing for two and a half weeks, and every afternoon at this time I come out to talk to my dad to see if he's heard anything.

He finishes his call and shakes his head. "Still no news, honey." It isn't unusual for our dog to wander, but until now he has always come back.

I have heard my parents talking, their voices low murmurs in the hall. Sitting on the stairs, my elbows on my knees, I listen. My father says, "I don't think we'll find him," and I hear my mother quietly agree. But I don't think my dad truly believes that, because he will frequently open the front door, step out, look left then right, call for the dog, and then close the door behind him. Often he walks down the road, searching. In the ensuing weeks he will do this a lot, and I go with him. We take turns cupping our hands around our mouths to project our voices. The streets are fairly quiet in the neighborhood in the evening. Not many sounds; an occasional car, a bouncing ball, someone yelling "dinner's ready," and our two voices, alternating calls of *"Michael!"* echoing down the darkening road.

Michael is gone for almost three months. Finally some stranger calls and our dog is returned, very sickly and thin. We never learn the details of his absence, but there is speculation that he was sold and perhaps sold again and somehow, finally, an honest person has read his dog tag and called us to return him. My dad picks him up and we are all at the door waiting when we hear his car. "Michael!" "Michael!" we shout, running out to greet him. We cover him with hugs and kisses and tears. "Mikey, you're home! You're home! We're so glad to see you!" At first we are shocked when we see how sickly and bone thin he is, wagging his tail feebly when he sees us. But we are all so relieved that at last he is home. My parents are hugging him, too, all of us calling him by his puppy name, "Mikey, Mikey." After a few weeks Michael is better, stronger, and we all give him constant attention and my sister and I sneak him food under the table and take turns letting him sleep in our beds.

The end of that year, 1964, brings with it an incident, I will one day learn, that rivals "Noon on Doomsday" for its vehemence against my father and his "liberalism."

At the time, the United Nations, approaching its twenty-fifth anniversary, is attacked by right-wing organizations. The John Birch Society, prominent among them, accuses the organization of being a front for the spread of Communism or an instrument for creating a single worldwide government. The previous year, UN ambassador Adlai Stevenson was roughed up in Dallas by protesters objecting to the United States' membership in the UN. Appalled, Paul Hoffman, managing director of the UN Special Fund, approaches a public relations specialist he knows named Edgar Rosenberg (who a little more than a year later would marry comedienne Joan Rivers). Rosenberg comes up with the idea of a series of six special television dramas, preferably commercial-free, that will commemorate the anniversary, provoke thought, and highlight the real mission, values, and goals of the UN. All talent will agree to work for scale minimum, so no one will get rich off the project. Joseph Mankiewicz, the distinguished producer who worked for Paramount, MGM, and Twentieth Century-Fox during the golden years of the Hollywood studio system, signs on. Rosenberg gets Xerox, a company with a reputation for having a strong social conscience and a forward-thinking corporate culture, to underwrite the series, without commercials, except for a mention of their name at the beginning. When several conservative stockholders complain about the $4,000,000 price tag, Xerox CEO Joseph Wilson bravely declares, "You can sell your stock or try to throw us out, but we are not going to change."

CBS and NBC decline to air the UN specials in prime time but third-place ABC agrees.

My dad is hired to write the first of these programs, scheduled to be broadcast on December 28. In keeping with the season, the script is called "Carol for Another Christmas." Patterned after Charles Dickens's *A Christmas Carol,* it tells the story of Daniel (Benjamin in my dad's original script) Grudge, played by Sterling Hayden, a powerful but misanthropic industrialist who is still mourning the loss of his son Marley in World War II, fighting in the Philippines, just as my dad had. In part as a result of his beloved son's loss, Grudge becomes a confirmed isolationist, opposed to anything that smacks of international cooperation or sacrifice on behalf of another people.

Grudge tells his nephew Fred, a teacher, played by Ben Gazzara:

> *I am not in the mood for the Brotherhood of Man. Do you mind? I've heard that speech. And heard it. Oh, I've had it with you, Fred, with all of you. Up to here, I've had it. With crusades—with one-worldism, foreign and domestic—with this mania for involvement, for meddling with the problems and concerns of strange people and strange countries—this compulsion to trespass on the private thoughts and private likes and dislikes of other people! Mind your own business—and let everybody else mind theirs! Your responsibility is your classroom, not those of Cracow, Poland—Butte, Montana—or Johannesburg, South Africa! And do you insist upon making it a better world—won't you die happy until you do? Do you insist upon helping the needy and oppressed—is that an itch you can't stop scratching? Then tell them to help themselves!*

Before long, Grudge, lonely and embittered, receives a visit from Marley's Ghost, accompanied by spirits representing the past, the present, and the future. The ghost tells him, "Tonight, Father, you will be shown what you call the rest of the world." An American soldier (played by Steve Lawrence) takes him back in time to Hiroshima. Pat Hingle represents the selfishness of the current times, and Robert Shaw takes Grudge to a post-apocalyptic future where a self-styled dictator (played by Peter Sellers) preaches the gospel of individuality at the expense of society.

At the end of ninety commercial-free minutes, Grudge wakes up on Christmas morning and proclaims, "It seems the conclusion is inevitable that—there must be involvement. That every man's death does diminish me."

My dad is sometimes criticized for being "preachy," but he's also lauded for being one of the few always willing to take a stand.

A firestorm of protest breaks out as soon as the show ends. ABC and Xerox are both flooded with telegrams and letters insisting that they and my father are furthering the Communist conspiracy and naively ignoring the true purpose of the United Nations in establishing a single world government to which the United States would be forced to cede its sovereignty. The boycott threats from the "Noon on Doomsday" response return with equal vehemence.

Shocked by the response but not willing to give up the fight, my dad answers many of the hate-filled letters with long, thoughtful observations, trying to get through to these people. From one example to an irate woman:

> *I note in a letter forwarded to me by the Famous Writers School that I have "aided the Communist conspiracy." If this is indeed true, and I mean this with sincerity and respect, I should turn myself in to any local F.B.I. office. It was not my intention to aid and conspire, when I wrote the TV script, "Carol for Another Christmas," nor was I remotely interested in propagandizing for the United Nations or for any organization. I was deeply interested in conveying what is a deeply felt conviction of my own. This is simply to suggest that human beings must involve themselves in the anguish of other human beings. This, I submit to you, is not a political thesis at all. It is simply an expression of what I would hope might be ultimately a simple humanity for humanity's sake.*

While allowing for genuine political differences, he goes on to say, "Philosophically we stand at opposite ends of the pole, because you choose to believe that anyone who disagrees with you must, of necessity, be subversive," and "But because I'm an American, I suggest this is your right. I suppose the major difference in our philosophies is that I recognize your right. The unfortunate thing is that you don't recognize mine."

Eventually, he concludes that his letter-writing effort is futile and confides to a friend that he is tempted to send back a form letter stating:

> *Dear Friend,*
> *I just thought you ought to know that someone is sending out*
> *crank mail under your name.*

Years later, my dad will give a speech in the Library of Congress auditorium. He will declare: "From experience, I can tell you that drama, at least in television, must walk tiptoe and in agony lest it offend some cereal buyer from a given state below the Mason-Dixon."

By the fall of 1965, life is back to normal and my father is writing a series called *The Loner,* starring Lloyd Bridges. Tony Albarella, the editor of *As Timeless As Infinity*, the book series that compiles my dad's *Twilight Zone* scripts, analyzes how *The Loner* revisits many of the themes prevalent in my dad's earlier writing: ". . . the horrors of war, moral ambiguity, bigotry, and the pressures of command and responsibility."

The Loner opens with the following narration:

> *In the aftermath of the bloodletting called the Civil War,*
> *thousands of rootless, restless, searching men traveled west. Such a*
> *man was William Colton. Like the others, he carried a blanket*
> *roll, a proficient gun, and a dedication to a new chapter in*
> *American history . . . the opening of the West.*

This is my dad's second attempt at a Western. In the 1950s he wrote a screenplay called *Saddle the Wind*. About it he said, "I gave better dialogue to the horses than the actors."

The reaction of CBS to *The Loner* is not positive. The studio wants more action and violence and less character study. My dad says, "What CBS bought was a series of 24-minute weekly shows—all legitimate, human, dramatic vignettes—set against a Western background. What they now want is a show with violence and killing attendant on a routine Western." The show is ultimately canceled halfway through its first season.

We have an album featuring the theme music from *The Loner.* I love it and for a while I play it in my room constantly. Now I wonder how difficult it must have been for my dad, passing by my room, hearing this music (replete with a full orchestra and the sound of horses' hooves) wafting out from under my doorway over and over, a constant reminder to him of this unsuccessful show. I am certain, though, that, being the consummate professional who took the bad with the good, he had moved on.

It isn't long, in fact, before he writes a script that he will regret on a much more fundamental level.

For years, when we fly to our cottage, my mother has my sister and I wear matching outfits. I don't recall this bothering us, but I know I begged, to no avail, to wear a dress matching my mother's.

The flights are long, and if Jodi and I are sitting together, sometimes we'll play, pretending we are our animals and we'll talk to each other in their "voices." If we start arguing, and kicking each other, this elicits stern reprimands from both our parents and then separation.

It is the days before ID checks, security lines, and metal detectors. Stewardesses let children pass out candy to the passengers while flights await departure and meals are still served. It is the days before terrorists made airplanes head straight for buildings. It is the days when air travel was fun. It is still, though, a world with its share of blemishes, a world not devoid of hatred and prejudice and people with serious mental illness and distorted agendas.

In 1966, my dad writes a made-for-television screenplay titled *The Doomsday Flight*. It is based on a real incident: Someone tries to blackmail an airline claiming that he had placed a bomb supposedly keyed to explode when a jetliner already in the air descended below a mile in altitude. In my dad's script, the bomb is planted by a disgruntled and mentally-ill former plane mechanic (Edmund O'Brien), who knew where to plant the device so that the crew could not disable it in flight. The plane eventually lands safely, and the movie, at first, is deemed a huge success. But on the very night that the show first airs, there is a bomb threat, and airlines around the world receive similar threats for the next eight days. My dad takes this all very seriously and personally. He says, "A writer can't be responsible for the pathology of idiots," but he is crushed and tells a reporter, "I wish to Christ I had written a stage coach drama starring John Wayne."

On each occasion that he is asked about the fallout of this script, he is conciliatory, and as his friend Mark Olshaker told me, "Your dad felt he had paid his penance for all the lunatics out there and his thinking was, 'let's keep the whole thing in perspective.'"

When Mark asked my dad how he answered the press, Dad told him that after having been inundated with reporters' questions, he had come up with two stock answers. One he gave, the other he wanted to. "I tell them, 'I am responsible *to* the public but not *for* the public.'" Mark replied, "That's a good answer; what's your other one?" My father responded, without missing a beat, "I tell them—'Fuck off.'"

After this incident, though, he is cautious and acutely aware of the inferno a few words from his imagination can ignite. Fortunately, in his subsequent years of writing, nothing like this happens again.

By the time he delivers the Library of Congress speech in which he took *Hogan's Heroes* to task, he has his perspective back again. It is January 15, 1968, the winter before that terrible spring when Martin Luther King and Bobby Kennedy are assassinated. He calls his presentation, "The Challenge of the Mass Media to the 20th Century Writer." He concludes:

> *Despite everything, despite our controversies and despite what is apparently and tragically a sense of divisiveness that permeates our land, and despite riots and rebellions that go hand-in-hand, mind you, with repression and brutality, one major and fundamental guarantee of protracted freedom is the unfettered right of the man to write as he sees fit, as his conscience indicates, as his mood dictates, as his cause cries out for. The moment you begin to censor the writer—and history bears this out in the ugliest of fashions—so begins a process of decay in the body politic that ultimately leads to disaster. What begins with a blue pencil—for whatever reason—very often ends in a concentration camp.*
>
> *It has forever been thus: So long as men write what they think, then all of the other freedoms—all of them—may remain intact. And it is then that writing becomes a weapon of truth, an article of faith, an act of courage.*

Mark Olshaker, who was there, remembers loud and sustained applause.

Chapter 20

IT WOULD PROBABLY BE accurate to say that my dad had a love/hate relationship with Hollywood and writing for television. In 1959's "The Velvet Alley," one of the last scripts he did for *Playhouse 90*, he describes a television writer from New York, played by Art Carney, who one night "wallops a literary homerun on a network television show" and moves to Hollywood. My dad wrote, "I left strips of flesh and blood all over the studio. The externals of the play are definitely autobiographical—the pressures involved, the assault on values, the blandishments that run in competition to a man's work and creativity, a preoccupation with status, with the symbols of status..."

He also repeats the quote, "Hollywood's a great place to live... if you're a grapefruit." He does love the weather, though; he is an avid sun worshipper. On Saturdays, in the late morning, I often join him after his paddle tennis game. We have some of our best conversations when we are lying on the blue lawn chairs behind our sun reflectors. My dad has written "Rod's" on his reflector. Apparently I, or Jodi, have "borrowed" it a few too many times.

I remember him asking me once, "What does a cow sound like when it goes to the bathroom?" I tell him I don't know. He positions his hands over his mouth and makes some grotesque sound, and we both laugh. Sometimes, taking a large sip of soda, he'll belch—louder than anyone I know.

He'll always follow one with, "Who stepped on that frog?" which never fails to send us both into another fit of giggles. (My mother is always telling me not to laugh at him. "It just encourages him," she will say. But I know he often gets the best of her, and I sometimes hear her calling him by his nick-name "Elyan" and then see them hugging on the stairs, much to my sister's and my embarrassment.)

My dad and I lean back, quiet for a while, in our sun-warmed chairs, petting the dogs beside us.

Unfortunately, this ideal climate does not come without peril, nor does paradise come without a dose of reality. California residents frequently have to contend with updates on the location of wildfires. We can see the smoke and hear the sirens in the distance, but we never actually have to leave.

In the late 1960s, though, it is not the raging fires that almost send us packing. The country is being torn apart by social and racial tension, and the one who comes to represent all of this to my dad is George Wallace. The governor of Alabama, who vehemently opposes the Civil Rights Movement, is running for president. He is quoted as saying, "I draw the line in the dust and toss the gauntlet before the feet of tyranny, and I say, segregation now, segregation tomorrow, segregation forever."

My father is outraged. He tells us that if "that racist son-of-a-bitch" prevails, we are moving out of the country. (He felt the same about Goldwater.) In a speech at the newly opened Moorpark College just north of us, near Simi Valley, California, my dad refers to Wallace as, "that political stalwart who made a public quote that he would never be out-niggered again. This from the man running for the highest office in the land."

When I tell this story to Mark Olshaker, he plays for me a recording from near the beginning of the speech my dad gave at the Library of Congress in 1968:

> In the immortal words of Groucho Marx, it's really not such a phenomenon in Washington, D.C. and Los Angeles, California, that we do have a former song and dance man [George Murphy] as our United States junior senator, and a kind of an actor-type fella [Ronald Reagan] serving as our governor. Groucho goes on to say that, indeed, this is uniquely a part of the American phenomenon. In New York State, ostensibly the financial capital of the world, you have a millionaire—a multimillionaire— serving as governor. In the State of Michigan you have a former automobile executive [George Romney] serving as governor. And in the State of Alabama, world-renowned for its very meaty and sizable pecans, you have a nut!

The speech is just an example of my dad's many outbursts against bigotry. In 1966, *Playboy* magazine runs a lengthy interview with George Lincoln Rockwell, founder and "Commander" of the American Nazi Party, at his headquarters in Arlington, Virginia. The interviewer is Alex Haley, the writer who had just finished collaborating with Malcolm X on his autobiography and who would go on to author the blockbuster, *Roots*. The interview, ignited by the fact that Rockwell did not know ahead of time that Haley was African American, is full of hate, Holocaust denying, and diatribes against Blacks, Jews, and anyone else who does not meet the commander's standards. He goes so far as to suggest that the well-documented bodies of concentration camp victims were actually casualties of the Allied bombing of Dresden. As soon as the interview is published, *Playboy* receives a firestorm of protest and complaint over giving this thuggish hatemonger a public forum.

While my dad is sympathetic to the public sentiment, he feels it is misguided, and that the best way to combat hate is to confront it. In response, he writes a letter that *Playboy* publishes two months later:

> *There is a breed of lay and social scientist who will forever cling to a concept of "defeating by ignoring." Hence, when out of the muck of their own neuroses rise these self-proclaimed Fuhrers, there is this well-meaning body who tell us that if we turn both eyes and cheeks, the nutsies will disappear simply by lack of exposure.*
>
> *My guess is that, in this case, exposure is tantamount to education; and education here, is a most salutary instruction into the mentalities, the motives and the modus operandi of an animal pack that is discounted by the aged maxim that "it can't happen here." So might have said the Goethes and the Einsteins of a pre-war Germany, who thought then, as we do now, that civilization by itself protects against a public acceptance of the uncivilized.*
>
> *What is desperately needed to combat any ism is precisely what "Playboy" has given us—an interview in-depth that shows us the facets of the enemy. Yes, gentlemen, you may be knocked for supposedly lending some kind of credence to a brand of lunacy. But my guess is that you should be given a commendation for a public service of infinite value.*

He signs the letter, "Rod Serling, Pacific Palisades, California."

At the beginning of the 1960s, my dad is a huge supporter of John Kennedy. We have bumper stickers and Kennedy buttons and my parents talk a lot about the Kennedys. My mother, reading that the Kennedy children all brought interesting current events to the dinner table, wants us to do that, too. It doesn't work out as well as she hoped. Our conversations remain silly.

When President Kennedy is shot, I am eight years old. Like

almost everyone old enough to remember, I revisit that Friday, November 22, 1963. I became ill at school and was sent home. I don't know if there was a correlation between hearing the news on the school's intercom broadcast into suddenly silent classrooms and then my abrupt illness, but I distinctly remember my mother's stricken face later that day and that my dad was away in New York on business. I remember, too, the television on, the curtains drawn, and my mother on the couch, silent, watching, or occasionally lingering about the doorway. Even when the room was empty the television remained on, repeating the same shattering footage and the same impossibility: "President John Kennedy has been shot."

My sister and I even stop arguing for a few days. It is as if our house has lost its inhabitants; the only sounds are the distraught voices of the news commentators' over a rapid succession of images and the low drone of people weeping.

My dad, still in New York, has to go on another trip in the midst of this national tragedy, before coming home. Jodi and I do not know why. Later, we learn he has been asked, on the Q.T., to go to Washington. Three days later, as we are watching the funeral on television—Jackie Kennedy in a black dress and black veil, holding her two children's small hands and John-John saluting—my dad is in a hotel room in D.C. He is writing a script for a film commissioned by the United States Information Agency to introduce our new president, Lyndon Johnson, to the world. As he writes, he can hear President Kennedy's funeral procession passing below his hotel window.

At some point during these terrible days my father also writes something perhaps intended as a letter to a newspaper or magazine editor. It is written on his letterhead and clearly typed by him, not his secretary. I read it for the first time

forty-six years after it was written. I can hear my father's anguish:

> More than a man has died. More than a gallant young President
> has been put to death. More than a high office of a land has been
> assaulted. What is to be mourned now is an ideal. What has
> been assassinated is a faith in ourselves. What has been murdered
> is a belief in our own decency, our capacity to love, our sense of
> order and logic and civilized decorum . . .
> . . . To the Leftists and the Rightists, to the Absolutists, to the
> men of little faith but strong hate, and to all of us who have
> helped plant this ugly and loathsome seed that blossomed forth
> on a street in Dallas on last Friday—this is the only dictum we
> can heed now. For civilization to survive it must remain
> civilized. And if there is to be any hope for our children and
> theirs—we must never again allow violence to offer itself as an
> excuse for our own insecurities, our weaknesses and our own
> fears. This is not an arguable doctrine for simply a better life. It is
> a condition for our continued existence.

My father is outspoken and passionate about his political
views. Although I am still young during several pivotal historic events, I readily adopt many of his ideals although I will
never be as vocal, articulate, or eloquent.

I have quotes pasted all over my walls from songs by
Crosby, Stills & Nash, Joan Baez, Dylan, and Joni Mitchell,
and slogans about love. I have peace signs and posters and orange and pink flower stickers. Once, after my dad and I have
argued about something that I can't recall—but do remember
that I held my resolve—instead of yelling, he concludes the
heated discussion by quietly telling me, "You need to go read
the sentiments on your wall about empathy and acceptance."

I hear my dad describe the Vietnam War as "A tragic bleeding mess—dishonest, immoral and self-defeating." This is

what leads him to support the anti-war campaign of Minnesota Democratic senator Eugene McCarthy, and actively campaign for him in the 1968 New Hampshire primary.

My dad is neither a pacifist nor a knee-jerk dove. He is proud of his own army service and willing to consider that force must often be met with force. During the early days of the Kennedy administration, he is also willing to accept the argument that counter-insurgency in Vietnam could halt the spread of Communism throughout Asia, but he quickly becomes disillusioned with the war and its unattainable goals.

He thinks we should immediately stop bombing and find "some kind of honorable pullout." I see the horrific photographs in *Life* magazine, the children burned and torn apart. In ninth grade, my history teacher has us write down our birth dates on a piece of paper. He uses these to replicate the draft's lottery system. He talks about how kids barely older than we are will be selected. My number would have sent me to Vietnam almost immediately. This brings the war excruciatingly close to home.

At school one day, in my homeroom class, I refuse to say the "Pledge of Allegiance." It isn't an original idea, but I think of it as a statement in protest over our involvement in Vietnam. My homeroom teacher, whom I particularly dislike, stands at the front of the classroom and reprimands me. I vividly recall her red lipstick, red dress, and shoes as she gives me a ridiculous assignment: I am to write one hundred times, "I will say the Pledge of Allegiance." It must be signed by a parent.

When I get home that afternoon, I take the paper out to my dad in his office. He looks at it, grabs his pen, and immediately signs it. There is little discussion. In the slight shake of his head I know he finds the assignment to be absurd and punitive, and I know how he feels about the war.

When I am sliding his door closed again, he says, "Nanny?"

I look over at him. He smiles at me and then turns back to his work.

What I don't know that day is the impact my father is having on others, not much older than I am, who are suddenly next in line to be deported into this monstrous war.

Steve Trimm, whose name I will not learn until four decades later, is one of these boys.

Rather than compromise his values and inherent beliefs and be drafted into a war he could not condone, Steve says, "I went underground and became a fugitive for five and a half years."

In the spring of 1975, Steve learns my dad is in the hospital. He decides: "Writing to Mr. Serling could not be put off. I had a lot I wanted to tell him. To begin with, I wanted to tell him why I was in a church basement in Schenectady, New York writing to him."

As he says, "I was there to help poor people but I was also there to earn a presidential pardon."

In a piece posted on the website of the Rod Serling Memorial Foundation, under the subtitle: *Lessons Rod Serling Taught Me,* Steve writes:

It was during those fear-filled years that I sometimes thought about Rod Serling . . . His stories, taught important lessons about ethics and taking personal responsibility for humanity's condition . . . The power of kindness, forgiveness and compassion . . . how each and every one of us, whether religious or irreligious, can triumph over the seeming inevitability of personal moral failure. What it takes is the capacity, despite the seeming omnipotence of the Powers Of Darkness, to keep believing in our own decency. If we can be generous and forgiving to ourselves, if we can hang on to a belief in our essential self-worth and goodness, simple charity will compel us to recognize the worth and goodness of others. This awareness will prevent us from becoming consumed by hatred. Unwilling to hate, we will behave morally. In the chaos of a frightened, angry society, holding tight to such beliefs will save us—and will ultimately save the world.

Mr. Trimm acknowledges other writers who also helped him—Thoreau, Twain, and Vonnegut—but says it was my dad who kept him going. "He taught us to persevere, to look for the hope running beneath the surface of terrible events... even when hope seems preposterous, never to give up on ourselves and never to give up on our fellow man...I was writing to Rod Serling from that church basement in Schenectady to thank him for helping save my life."

I don't think my father ever received Mr. Trimm's letter. There was much chaos and confusion in those months before he died. But this letter would have touched him deeply, and I know unequivocally that as soon as he read it he would have responded.

There were other Steve Trimms back then, other young kids whose spirits were broken, whose ideals and beliefs were conflicted and doubted and challenged, who felt they were living in a world of madness—a world that seemed to have lost all reason. What my dad never knew, and what I have learned, is that he made an enormous difference in their lives. In some dreadfully dark hours, my father's words made it through and helped them.

Chapter 21

IN 1967, MY FATHER writes a screenplay adaptation of a novel by Pierre Boulle, the author of *The Bridge Over the River Kwai*. *Planet of the Apes* is about astronauts who crash-land on a planet dominated by talking (and fully clothed) gorillas and chimpanzees. After my father does several drafts and makes numerous attempts to stay true to the original story, the producers decide it is too intellectual and will be too expensive to produce, and they bring in another writer, Michael Wilson. I remember some contention surrounding the project, and I know my dad was ultimately disappointed with the overall result, but the superb ending—discovering the head of the Statue of Liberty buried on the beach, signifying the planet is a nuclear-ravaged earth of the future—is the one my father conceived, wrote, and was credited for.

My close friend Jencie and I go to see the movie one sunny spring day in 1968. We love it. Emerging from the Santa Monica Theater, blinking our eyes to adjust to the sudden afternoon light (and our return to "old" earth), we talk about the movie all the way home. I feel enormously proud.

Jencie lives down the street. Our birthdays are three months apart. We have known each other since we were little more than toddlers. I am the complete opposite of her. Brunette to her blond, brown-eyed to her blue, and short to her tall. Her father, John Gay, is a screenwriter whose credits include *No Way to Treat a Lady* and *The Burden of Proof.*

We are always at one or the other's house, pedaling frantically on our purple bicycles to get there. Even in soaking rains, our windbreakers whipping behind us, we always manage to wind up at her front door or mine.

Throughout the years, we sit cross-legged on the floor of our bedrooms, talking about music, school, books, movies, and boys. We braid each other's hair and beg our mothers to have an overnight (once we tell her mother that we will clean the *entire* house if she will just say yes). We plan our weekends together and rearrange each other's rooms, helping the other decorate.

One year, when I am about thirteen, my parents buy me a new desk, wallpaper, a bedspread, and carpet. On the day my room is being redone, I watch the clock at school, willing it to rush ahead. Jencie and I make plans for her to come over that night. When I finally get home, I race up the stairs and look around at my "new" room. Everything is perfect until I notice that something is in the corner. On closer inspection, I discover that one of the dogs has pooped on the carpet and I jump back in disgust. Just then, my dad knocks on the door and I point to the spot. He feigns surprise, walks over to it, and picks it up *in his hands.* I stare from him to his hand in disbelief. He breaks out into laughter. "I got you, Nanny!" It is plastic dog poop that he found on a novelty rack and waited, all day, to spring it on me when I got home.

After a few days, I hide it in his office. A week later it appears in my closet, then on the floor at his side of the bed, under my desk, his, on his chair, on mine, and on and on. This continues for months, and Jencie and I laugh, planning places where I should hide it.

For years Jencie and I are an integral part of each other's life, doing our homework together, piecing back one or the other's shattered heart, and navigating our way through adolescence. We talk about boyfriends, and I ask her one afternoon, "Can you believe Mr. Kagan found our note and read it in front of the whole class?!" We roll on her bed laughing, grateful that although we had revealed each other's latest love interests we'd only drawn pictures of the boys and hadn't signed our names to our note.

There is a relative tranquility in our lives. Our talks are the typical conversations of two young girls becoming teenagers whispering in the dark at bedtime.

One Friday night Jencie is doing something with her family, my parents are at a dinner party, and I am curled up on their bed watching *Get Smart*.

My sister suddenly shouts my nickname up the stairs, "Caldie, I'm going." She has started jogging over the past month or so. This is before it has become popular, before everyone is doing it. For some reason, when she goes, she wears our dad's old boots. I don't think he ever knows this. She always leaves them exactly where she found them. Years later we talk about this, why she didn't wear her sneakers, why she wore his shoes. I don't remember if she had an answer, even then, but I remember us laughing for a long time.

That night she is back about a half hour later, standing by the bedroom door. Her face sweaty, and her brown hair pulled back in a messy ponytail. Silently, she points down to her leg and I see that she has fallen, ripped her pants, and that her knee is bleeding. "What happened?!" I nearly shout at her but she only responds with the obvious, "I fell."

This little accident doesn't deter her. She's out again the very next night, beneath the lights, down the neighborhood streets, and still running in our father's shoes.

Chapter 22

The tools of conquest do not necessarily come with bombs and explosions and fallout. There are weapons that are simply thoughts, attitudes, prejudices—to be found only in the minds of men. For the record, prejudices can kill and suspicion can destroy, and a thoughtless, frightened search for a scapegoat has a fallout all its own—for the children and the children yet unborn. And the pity of it is that these things cannot be confined to The Twilight Zone.

—Closing narration, "The Monsters Are Due on Maple Street," *Twilight Zone* episode, March 4, 1960

IT SEEMS WE HAVE been driving forever and I don't recognize where we are; the sky has a dull, colorless hue, and there are unfamiliar hills and signs. "Mrs. Robinson" is playing on the radio. My sister, sitting in the front seat, keeps changing the station, and I shout, "Jodi, change it back!" Finally my mother reaches forward and turns it off entirely.

It is April 4, 1968. My mother has picked us up early at school. Deedie, my mother's half sister, is getting married in the summer in Missouri, where she lives. We are going to have dresses altered for the wedding, since we are to be "candle lighters" in the ceremony.

The alterations seem to take forever, but finally we are done and back in the car. My mother turns the radio back on and slows for a yellow light. Suddenly the song we are listen-

ing to stops and a voice breaks in with those ominous opening words—"We interrupt this program...Martin Luther
King Jr., leader of the American Civil Rights Movement, has
been shot."

While we were trying on these stupid pink dresses, standing there in our matching pink shoes, the world, once again,
was falling apart.

Riots break out in over a hundred American cities. Many
students are involved, and the police respond with mace and
clubs. A few months later, my father gives a speech at Moorpark College in which he states:

> *I would rather have a son or daughter of mine march through the*
> *streets of Chicago protesting injustice—than I would siring a*
> *Chicago policeman who'll club anyone who'll get in his way, and*
> *that includes sixteen-year-olds, newspaper photographers, and*
> *senior citizens. And if anyone wants to raise the specter of*
> *"provocation"—I say this categorically—there is no provocation*
> *extant short of a motive of self-defense to excuse a representative*
> *of law and order wading in with a billy-club under the pretense*
> *of saving the sovereign city of Chicago. Of the four hundred*
> *young people currently held under arraignment for so-called*
> *assault and battery, half of them are under eighteen and half of*
> *those under a hundred and twenty pounds.*

He writes a letter that appears in *The Los Angeles Times* on
April 8:

> *There is a bitter sadness and special irony that attends the*
> *passing of Martin Luther King. Quickly and with ease, we offer*
> *up a chorus of posthumous praise—the ritual dirge so time-*
> *honored and comfortable and undemanding of anything but*
> *rhetoric. In death, we offer the acknowledgement of the man and*
> *his dream that we denied him in life.*
>
> *In his grave, we praise him for his decency—but when he*
> *walked amongst us, we responded with no decency of our own.*

When he suggested that all men should have a place in the
sun—we put a special sanctity on the right of ownership and the
privilege of prejudice by maintaining that to deny homes to
Negroes was a democratic right.

Now we acknowledge his compassion—but we exercised no
compassion of our own. When he asked us to understand that
men take to the streets out of anguish and hopelessness and a
vision of that dream dying, we bought guns and speculated about
roving agitators and subversive conspiracies and demanded law
and order.

We felt anger at the effects, but did little to acknowledge the
causes. We extol all the virtues of the man—but we chose not to
call them virtues before his death.

And now, belatedly, we talk of this man's worth— but the
judgment comes late in the day as part of a eulogy when it
should have been made a matter of record while he existed as a
living force. If we are to lend credence to our mourning, there are
acknowledgements that must be made now, albeit belatedly. We
must act on the altogether proper assumption that Martin Luther
King asked for nothing but that which was his due. He
demanded no special concessions, no favored leg up the ladder for
his people, despite our impatience with his lifelong prodding of
our collective conscience. He asked only for equality, and it is that
which we denied him.

We must look beyond riots in the streets to the essential
righteousness of what he asked of us. To do less would make his
dying as senseless as our own living would be inconsequential.

Two months after Martin Luther King's assassination, a
sleepover is planned for my thirteenth birthday. Eight friends
are invited. We'll have pizza and soda, a birthday cake, and
chocolate ice cream. We'll lie in our colorful sleeping bags, all
lined up on the living room carpet, and giggle and tease and
whisper and share the secrets that thirteen-year-olds share.
Just as we did the year before—when we were twelve.

The morning of the party, I get up early and can hear the
television in my parents' room. Walking down the hall, our

dog Michael beside me, I peek in through their open bedroom door and ask them what they are watching. Without
looking back at me, they tell me Robert Kennedy has been
assassinated just hours before and this is a replay of him ad-
dressing his supporters at the ballroom of the Ambassador
Hotel in Los Angeles. [It is nearing the end of the 1968
Democratic presidential primary campaign, and Kennedy
appeared to be a serious challenge to President Lyndon Johnson.]

I look at my parents sitting on their bed, and then at the
TV listening as the crowd chants "We want Bobby, we want
Bobby!" Instantly this image is replaced with the sudden
mayhem of motion and noise and chaos. My father leans forward, my mother beside him, and they stare straight ahead.
There is yelling and screaming. People wearing Kennedy
campaign hats have their hands to their faces, the continuing
footage captured through a wobbly camera's lens. Someone is
lying on the ground. Another person leans over him, waving
a magazine or newspaper. I walk closer and stand beside my
father. I see that the man on the ground is Robert Kennedy.

Although I remember some discussion about it, we don't
cancel my party. My friends arrive as planned, and we have
pizza and cake and lie in our sea of multicolored sleeping
bags. The television in the family room is replaying the news
footage of Robert Kennedy, and although almost muted, we
all know what has happened and the commotion and the
sadness hangs in the air silencing us.

In the corner of the living room, a Beatles' album plays
over and over. No one seems to notice or care. The HAPPY
BIRTHDAY banner hangs by one piece of tape, most of it pud-
dled on the floor. When the record ends and the needle lifts
to begin it again, we hear, in that brief space, the television
and my parents talking softly; we hear, too, that inaudible
sound of all reason evaporating.

Chapter 23

FOR WEEKS FOLLOWING ROBERT Kennedy's assassination, coming as it does practically on the heels of Martin Luther King's, my father seems quiet, preoccupied. I think perhaps he is particularly glad to be leaving LA this June and looking forward to another summer spent thousands of miles away, back at our old red cottage, sitting by the water.

Jodi and I are away at camp for several weeks through these summers in the sixties, and at first I am often homesick. I save the letters from home in my camp cabin, in a shoebox under my cot, beside my copy of *A Tree Grows in Brooklyn*.

Sometimes I wonder what made me keep them. Was it the years of hearing the screen door close at the cottage and watching my dad carry his own collection of letters to the chair across the yard, all of the words he held on to from his past? Was it seeing his eyes well up and knowing, on some prophetic level, that I, too, might need these someday; that like him, I'd have to go backward to find him, too?

His letters to me are often reflective of what is going on in the world at the time. Sometimes they are typed, sometimes handwritten. Sometimes they are brief, often funny; always, even now, they make me feel better.

August 8, 1969
My Dear Miss Grumple,
There's really not much newsworthy quality to write to you. We're all well—Mom, Jodi the dogs, cats and me—We really miss you, Popsy. It just occurs to me in less than three weeks we'll be picking you up. We'll take a leisurely drive back— museum, ferry boat, etc. I've decided not to do the sequel of "Planet of the Apes." They wanted the script much too soon for me to handle it. I've got too much to do anyway.

He closes with, "Not much else. Please forgive this brief— too brief letter. Nixon got nominated last night and that's depressed me all by itself..."

After camp that summer, my friend I met there—another Jency—Jency Pelley, visits me for a few days at the cottage from her home in Ridgewood, New Jersey. She remembers: "Your parents took us out on the boat overnight, you and I were in the front berth. Late that night, we overheard them talking about you, so you went to press your ear against the door, which one of them opened suddenly and you literally fell into their room, or whatever you call it on a boat. Anyway, it was *hilarious*. Just like a cartoon in real life." She can't remember, nor can I, whether it was my dad or my mother who opened the door, but she does recall "what a sweet, goofy-funny, loveable man" my dad was and that he and I teased each other a lot.

In November of that same year, three months after Charles Manson inspires two nights of unbelievable carnage not too far from us, information leaks into the news about a target list, a hit list that he and his followers maintain. Seeing these shaven-headed, smiling, dancing monsters on the news, and knowing what they have done and that they have been in the

Pacific Palisades near where we live is frightening. For some reason my California friend Jencie and I, in one of our whispered sleepover conversations, share our panic that our dads might be on the list, and for a long while our conversations revolve around that fear, exacerbated by our escalating imaginations.

I don't remember if we voice this to our fathers, but it seems, for a long while, we pedal our bikes a little faster. Each shadow a potential peril, every sound a stranger with outstretched hands.

My dad, though, does not seem fazed by what keeps Jencie and me up late at night. He is certainly not looking over his shoulder.

The cancellation of *The Twilight Zone* has not slowed him at all. Producer Aaron Spelling wants him to write a pilot for a series called *The New People* (the show, some think, is the inspiration for J.J. Abrams's *Lost*). The story is about a group of college students who are returning from a goodwill tour to South East Asia. Their plane crashes near a deserted island, and they are forced to create their own society in order to survive. My dad sends over his script but later comments that while its "sub-*Lord of the Flies* theme" may work for television, it doesn't work for him.

In June of 1969, my dad shifts gears to host a game show called *Liar's Club*, in which celebrity guests are given esoteric objects and have to produce plausible explanations of what the object is or what it is used for. Only one of the celebrities knows the actual use, and my dad, as host, is not told so that his reactions are spontaneous and genuine. Regulars like Betty White and Jonathan Harris—who had appeared in two *Twilight Zone* episodes and became well-known for his role in *Lost in Space*—then bet on which celebrity guest is telling the truth. My dad lets me go on the show on my fourteenth birthday. The format has changed a little, and again, as it was in the other show a decade before, the panel has to guess who I am.

Although I begged for this opportunity, I am stricken with severe stage fright, and standing there in my new orange dress, I shift from one foot to the other, play with my hair, the hem of my dress, and probably look right at him throughout the entire show. I truly don't remember the outcome, but I suspect everyone guessed me right away.

Though at the time I don't question anything professional that my dad does, I've since wondered why he agreed to do a show like this that had so little to do with his image as a serious television writer or his goals for the medium in general. I have heard some suggest that he did it for the obvious reason—easy money—just as he agreed to do commercials. But from what I now understand, he was paid relatively little, even by the standards of the time.

Although it was a silly game show, I think he did it because, despite his reputation as the "Angry Young (and not so young)" man, he did have a strong silly streak. He would let me draw striped socks on his ankles with bright red and yellow markers. On one occasion, he forgot, and went to have a suit tailored, only to return laughing so hard he could barely tell the story.

He was the greatest (as well as only) gorilla impersonator I have ever encountered. He was addicted to practical jokes and genuinely loved to laugh. I think, quite simply, he did *Liar's Club* because he thought it would be *fun*, a change of pace. And it was.

Chapter 24

DURING SCHOOL VACATIONS WE often drive to Palm Springs and stay at a place called The White Sun Guest Ranch. Jodi loves it because she likes riding and because she has an enormous crush on Ed, the stable manager—never mind that he's almost seventy-five years old. My riding days end abruptly there after "Cochise" runs away with me, charging down some very steep dunes to get back to the stables. After this happens twice, I am too afraid to go again. Instead, I sit by the pool with my dad.

We talk or read out there, and he gives me change to buy him Cokes and myself chocolate drinks. My sister is off riding all afternoon, and my mother, golfing.

Sometimes we go with family friends, the Arlens. Liz Arlen and I are good friends, and her older brother Mike is a year younger than Jodi. Hal is a psychiatrist, but we don't know him in that capacity. Hal and Mary and my parents spend a lot of time together. They play cards, go to social events, movies, dinners, and parties. Knowing my dad's fixation with the weather, Hal buys him a small weather radio that does nothing but give updated forecasts. This is years before there is such a thing as a weather channel. My dad lies out in the sun, listening, as this tiny, tinny radio announces the temperature, the wind speed, and makes promises of sunlight or storms.

On one trip to the desert, we pass the Arlens on the freeway and Mary Arlen throws dozens of candy bars into our car. I remember our hands reaching out the windows and catching all but a few that scatter on the road behind.

It is not, though, the actual vacations that I recall as vividly as the time spent getting there and back. It is the hours in the car, sitting behind my father and watching as he drives. His arm stretched out across the seat, my mother beside him, and my sister and I in the back, as far away from each other as possible, like typical siblings. The breeze from the half-open window blows through my father's hair. I notice there are a few streaks of gray, but I don't tell him that.

He always listens to the radio, mostly to baseball games, and he slaps his open palm on the steering wheel when some exciting play is announced. It startles my mother, and she jumps a little and shakes her head. She is not a big sports fan. That's an expression my dad uses a lot. He calls people "sports fan." "Hello, sports fan!" "Good morning, sports fan." "How you doing there, sports fan?" This does not amuse my mother, but it does me. I am a good audience for my father. Even in my teens I think he is a riot.

Almost without fail, when we drive through the desert, a strong wind kicks up the sand. My dad has a thing about cars, so I know this disturbs him; he worries about the car's finish.

There are three items on which my dad splurges: (1) the paddle tennis court, (2) two boats, and (3) cars. The first boat he purchases, unbeknownst to my mother, is a thirty-foot Chris-Craft he names *The Carolyn I,* after her. He also has mats, pillows, and a boat bag initialed with her name. After that, how can she resist? *The Carolyn I* is eventually replaced with a thirty-six-foot Chris-Craft, *The Carolyn II.* My mother loves the boat trips they take every summer through the Finger Lakes to the Thousand Islands, my dad at the helm, shirtless and tan, my mother in a hat and huge Jackie Onassis sunglasses.

One year the boat is damaged while going through the locks and is taken to Hibiscus Harbor for repairs. After my parents pick it up, my dad shifts into reverse and instead it goes forward onto the shore. The mechanic had inadvertently put the props on backward.

My dad loves cars. He has a rebuilt Auburn Speedster. After that, a black Excalibur. Every time the horn is pushed, it blares "The Colonel Bogey March." My mother refuses to ride in it. She thinks it's garish and hideous with its exhaust pipes hanging out on either side. She prefers "sensible" practical cars.

Sometimes my dad picks me up at school in this car, and one Saturday morning he drives my friends and me, all piled in the back, around the neighborhood.

Once, driving home from the studio with the top down, my dad is listening to big band music. He tells me that when he stops at a light, he is completely immersed in the music, "playing" select instruments, holding midair his imaginary horn and trombone and tapping the "drum" on the seat beside him. He looks over at the car beside him where a woman sits very still, watching him, unsmiling, like he has clearly lost his mind.

My dad smokes constantly, even on these relatively short drives back from the desert. His smoking, combined with my mother's, arouses ardent complaints from my sister and me as we madly wave away the smoke in the backseat, shouting in unison, "Put the cigarettes out! It stinks back here! We can't breathe!" and often we launch into some dramatic coughing spell.

They open their windows wider, but it doesn't really help.

The noise drowns out the radio, and my dad has to turn it up louder to hear the sports announcer. Whoever is on third has made a run for it; my father bangs his hand on the steering wheel again, my mother jumps, and the four of us head home on the Santa Monica Freeway.

Chapter 25

My dad's office phone is also our home phone, but there are two lines, so if one is busy, the incoming call rings through to the other. A few months before the premier of his show *Night Gallery* on NBC, the phone is ringing constantly, in his office and throughout our house.

The pilot for *Night Gallery* includes three stories, two that he wrote for a collection of three novellas called *The Season to Be Wary,* published by Little, Brown in 1967. He dedicated the book to Sammy Davis Jr., who he says, came up with the idea for one of the stories when they were having a beer together. He and Sammy had considered doing a fantasy film for television consisting of three separate stories. The one by Sammy Davis involved a Southern racist who gets his comeuppance in a highly appropriate fashion when he is transformed into a black man and dies at the hands of a fanatical mob. When the film project fell through, my dad redirected the ideas into the book. Then, in a roundabout way, two of the three stories made it back to television for the *Night Gallery* pilot.

Though my dad is known for his scriptwriting, *Season to be Wary* was not his first foray into narrative fiction. In 1960, Bantam Books published *Stories from the Twilight Zone*, which includes six of my dad's scripts that he had turned into short stories, including "Walking Distance," "Where is Everybody?" and "The Monsters Are Due on Maple Street." It sold well, went through multiple printings, which led to the publication of *More Stories from the Twilight Zone* in 1961 and *New Stories from the Twilight Zone* in 1962. In that same year, he rewrote "Requiem for a Heavyweight" into a short novel published by Bantam to tie in to the release of the movie version, starring Anthony Quinn, Jackie Gleason, and Mickey Rooney. So that by the time he began writing *Season to Be Wary*, he was ready to stretch his wings by writing novels. He intended this collection as the lead-up to this new phase of his career.

The lead story in *Seasons*, "The Escape Route," returns thematically to "Death's-Head Revisited":

"Gruppenfuehrer Joseph Strobe, former deputy assistant commander of Auschwitz, former confidant of one Heinrich Himmler, former wearer of black shiny boots, crisply pressed black uniforms; and former frequent maker of love in the back seat of his personal, chauffeur-driven Mercedes-Benz" . . . is now relegated to a sweat-logged rat hole of a flat in Buenos Aires, reminiscing about the good times back in Germany. But when Adolf Eichmann is captured by Israeli agents, Strobe's tawdry existence is in jeopardy. While evading the agents, he escapes into an art museum where he realizes he has the uncanny ability to lose himself in a tranquil painting of a fisherman on a lake. He develops this power until he can actually will himself in and out of the painting.

With the Israelis in hot pursuit, Strobe rushes into the art museum and up to the painting. He wills himself back into the painting, not realizing that the fisherman canvas has been loaned out. In its place is a painting of a concentration camp, its central image a cross on which now hangs Joseph Strobe.

It is clear to me that among my father's moral and philosophical outrages are the Holocaust and the American civil
rights struggle, so it is not surprising that he deals with both
in his first serious go at fiction.

This is the origin of his next attempt at series television.
The premise of *Night Gallery*, similar to the one my dad de-
veloped in his proposal for *Rod Serling's Wax Museum*, has him
in a dark and eerie sort of art gallery, where he uses a creepy-
looking painting to introduce each episode. The pilot begins
with my dad walking into the gallery, and as he approaches
one of the paintings, he says:

> *Good evening, and welcome to a private showing of three*
> *paintings, displayed here for the first time. Each is a collector's*
> *item in its own way—not because of any special artistic quality,*
> *but because each captures on a canvas, suspends in time and*
> *space, a frozen moment of a nightmare.*
>
> *Our initial offering: a small gothic item in blacks and grays. A*
> *piece of the past known as the family crypt. This one we call*
> *simply "The Cemetery." Offered to you now, six feet of earth*
> *and all that it contains. Ladies and gentlemen, this is the Night*
> *Gallery.*

One of the pilot's stories, "Eyes," stars movie legend Joan
Crawford in one of her final performances. She plays a ruth-
less, wealthy blind woman who will do anything to have her
sight restored, including buying the eyes of a healthy, sighted
person who desperately needs money. At the time, I know
Strait-Jacket, but I know nothing about her earlier career, so
my perception of her is of a scary old woman in a rather
chilling film.

Ms. Crawford, apparently a perfectionist, calls my dad incessantly, which accounts for many of the pre-premier phone
calls. Perhaps she was like this on every project she was involved in, but eventually it begins to wear on my dad, and
often, when the phone rings and he is in the house, not his

office, he will hesitate a moment and say something under his breath before picking it up.

Nevertheless, her performance, which is directed by a then unknown young Steven Spielberg, pays off, and *Night Gallery* is the highest rated show that night.

I am babysitting on the evening it airs. I know my dad hopes that *Night Gallery* will be successful, but he is also apprehensive that it may appear as an attempt to replicate *The Twilight Zone*. I feel very protective of him and concerned about the show. When the kids I am babysitting go to bed, after a few moments of deliberation, I pick up the phone, dial a random number, pretend I am someone from the Nielsen Ratings, and when a woman answers, I say, "Good evening. We are taking a survey and wondered if you or a member of your family watched the *Night Gallery* this evening?" If they say they did, I get excited and my voice rises, sounding younger and less professional. I slam the phone down when the woman asks, "Who is this?"

Prank calls like this are nothing new in my family. I call my dad all the time from the home phone, pretending I am his agent Roberta Pryor or someone he knows. "Rod?" I'll begin. "How are you?" I must be fairly good as he always replies, followed by a hesitation, recognition, and then "God damn it, honey!" He cannot get angry though. After all, I'd learned from the best!

It seems at the start that *Night Gallery* may be successful. My dad wins an Edgar Allan Poe Award from the Mystery Writers of America, and *Night Gallery* is given a one-hour time slot on NBC. Within that time frame, stories can be any length and so the number of stories varies. Not having a time limit is supposed to open up my dad's and the other writers' creative possibilities, as if they were writing for the stage or the movies.

The fundamental difference between *Twilight Zone* and *Night Gallery* is that my dad does not have creative control of *Night Gallery*. He soon recognizes this to be a grave error, and that his assumption that he would still be included on some level in any production discussion is false. Despite the fact that the show is presented as his, my dad explains, "It is not mine at all. It's another species of a formula series drama."

Jack Laird is the producer of the show. His name is frequently mentioned in our house—through my father's gritted teeth. In a letter my dad subsequently writes to Universal Studios, he says, "I wanted a series with distinction, with episodes that said something; I have no interest in a series which is purely and uniquely suspenseful but totally uncommentative on anything."

Years later, my dad is asked in an interview with Linda Brevelle for *Writer's Digest* magazine if he ever removed his name from the credits because of changes to a script that he didn't approve of. He said he hadn't; there were a few times he wanted to, but he found out too late. One of those shows, he said, was *Night Gallery.*

In that same interview, though, when asked which of his scripts he has special feelings for, he mentions "Requiem for a Heavyweight" and an episode of *Night Gallery* called "They're Tearing Down Tim Riley's Bar," for which he received an Emmy nomination.

"Tim Riley" is similar to *The Twilight Zone's* "Walking Distance." Both truly represent my father's writing at its absolute best, and both evoke the theme of going backward and going home again.

Randolph Lane, the main character in the story, lives on Bennett Avenue, just like my dad. Lane was also a paratrooper in World War II. And, like my dad, he has a preoccupation with the past and a particular sense of nostalgia and infinite longing.

Although I would never characterize my dad as a dark person, he is glaringly aware of his own mortality due to a genetic predisposition that, given his own health habits, could conceivably lead to an early death. Because of this biological time bomb, he never forgets where he is chronologically in relation to his own father and how little time may be left. He doesn't say this to me in so many words, but he sometimes talks about feeling old. In the opening narration of "They're Tearing Down Tim Riley's Bar," he describes this foreboding as: "the quiet desperation of men over 40 who keep hearing heavy footsteps behind them and are torn between a fear and compulsion to look over their shoulders."

In the story, Randolph Lane is forty-six years old, like my dad. "I'm six years younger," Lane tells a policeman, "than my father was when he died. And I keep getting beckoned to by ghosts. Every now and then it's 1945 . . . and if you think that sounds nuts—try this one. I wish to God those ghosts would stick around."

In the introduction to their 1999 book, *Rod Serling's Night Gallery: An After-Hours Tour*, Scott Skelton and Jim Benson write:

> In a fresh examination of the series, we have also noted some past inaccurate impressions from some of Serling's earlier biographers, the primary myth being that Serling's dramatic skills had waned in his last creative years. An overwhelming number of his scripts for *Night Gallery* show a high degree of quality, on a par with his earlier work and often better.

Certainly, one of these scripts is "The Messiah on Mott Street," which aired December 15, 1971, as part of the second season and a year later was printed by Bantam Books.

The story takes place on Christmas Eve in Manhattan's Lower East Side and takes my dad back to his immigrant Jewish roots more directly than anything else he has written.

In the show, Edward G. Robinson, nearing the end of his illustrious career, plays Abraham Goldman, a sick old man who refuses to go to a hospital for fear of losing his orphaned nine-year-old grandson Mikey. Though Goldman senses the presence of the Angel of Death, he is also hopeful of the appearance of the long-awaited Messiah, who will deliver both of them from their troubles.

When I watch this show, I am struck by how much it captures my dad's love of the Christmas season, yearning for perfect justice, the power of belief, common cause between races and religions, and the ambiguity of what has actually happened. It reminds me of *Twilight Zone's* "Night of the Meek," and the adoration between an adult and a child of "A Big Tall Wish."

Because he is contractually obligated, my father stays with *Night Gallery* until it is canceled in 1973. I am at MacDuffie School, a private girls' boarding school in Massachusetts. Again, worried about class sizes in the LA schools, my parents and I make the joint decision that I will go away for eleventh and twelfth grade to the same school my mother attended. The first year I am there the headmaster is, astonishingly, the same one she had. For the first months I am desperately homesick, thousands of miles away from home, missing Jencie and Liz and a few other friends, and trying to adjust to the rules. During the second month of school, my friends Joan, Susie, and I are caught smoking cigarettes in the basement. "Have you been smoking, girls?" the dorm mother asks. Although we are sitting in a cloud of smoke, we tell her no. Finally Joan, the most honest one among us, confesses, and Susie and I follow suit. We are suspended for a week. My mother flies from California to get me, and we stay at the cottage. It is unusually warm that week in October, a late Indian summer, and we sit on the dock talking. Despite the circumstances, we actually have a nice time together. I tell her how the headmaster told my friends and me, "I'll be the first to welcome you girls back." My mother and I smile about that. Although we may disagree with him, his values are in the right place and he's nothing if not enormously kind.

The lake is quiet, empty of its summer people that time of year, and we stay there a long time talking. "You know you have to obey the rules" my mother says, "despite how you feel about them." I remember being incredibly relieved that she understands how archaic they are and that she is not angry. We forge an understanding, a friendship.

And, in fact, a year later, when I graduate and announce to my parents that I have been offered a position as female vocalist in a band that is forming, it is my mother, not my dad, who is more tolerant of this idea, probably suspecting that what would happen did—the band never took flight.

When I return to school, growing friendships and letters from home make the stay bearable. Sometimes my dad visits me on his trips to New York City or arranges for us to meet there. In a letter written just as *Night Gallery* is renewed for another year, he writes:

January 17, 1972
Dear Miss Grumple,
As promised—this letter. I've pondered the possibility of visiting you the week after next but it is simply impossible. I have to record in New York on the 27th, and leave the same night. I even thought of possibly going a day earlier but with Night Gallery being renewed I am going to be deep in the throes of writing the next several weeks. Then, of course, there's the novel I'm finishing now (and which I think you'll like).

So here's a promise. Either in February or March, I'll go into New York expressly to see you. I think it would even work out better because your semester break will get you out of there and let you recharge batteries and you really won't need my presence then. Later on I think you'll be more in need of a distraction (My God, Pops, here I am at forty-seven years of age, and suddenly I'm a "distraction").

He is not a distraction, of course. We have fun together. For all the times my dad may have indeed been looking in reverse, accompanied by ghosts, he also lives in the present; he knows how to laugh, he knows how to have a good time, and no matter who you are, he knows how to make you shine.

I never did see the novel to which he referred, and I'm not sure what it was about. Mark Olshaker, who visited him at our house in California during his Christmas vacation from college in 1971, remembers my dad showing him a manuscript for a novel version of *A Storm in Summer* and mentioning that he had an idea for another novel he wanted to write.

Though I have not seen the first manuscript and don't know what happened to it, and have no idea if the second even got under way, I do know that, as he got older, my dad became more and more interested in seriously pursuing both fiction and playwriting. Both of these would have given him greater freedom and allowed him to be independent and away from the Hollywood scene he was finding increasingly frustrating and empty. Had he lived, I am convinced that this shift in focus would have filled the next phase of his career.

He said as much in one of his college lectures:

> *The greener grass syndrome is as applicable to writers as to anyone else. The poet wants to write a novel. The novelist yearns to do a screenplay. And very frequently the television playwright has a special vaulting itch for the free and unsullied air of the theater piece. Sometimes it's simply the obligatory exercise in changing pace. But for the guy who has written under the watchful eyes and ham-fisted stewardship of network executives, ad agencies and television censors, writing and watching the production of his own play in a theater is a little like getting a pardon from a chain gang, along with a train ticket to a happier place.*

Chapter 26

He heard the sound of voices . . . and laughter—and hellos and goodbyes—and all the jumbled language of the past—so sweet, so unbearably sweet.

—ROD SERLING, "They're Tearing Down Tim Riley's Bar"

I KNOW MY DAD knew how I felt about him, but I sometimes wonder, did I say the right things? Use the right words? Say enough? I found the answer in a letter written on February 3, 1972.

My Dear Miss Grumple—
You know the very nicest thing I've received in a long time? It was your altogether sweet and gentle note. It's a funny thing, Nanny—part of this "Generation Gap"—and the part so different than my recollection of growing up—is the apparent mutual disinclination to admit affection. Oh we say it—we write it on occasion—but it's ritual and it seems to come from embarrassment. That's why when you mentioned the funny little remembrances of things we did and said when you were little—I felt warmed by it. Not only that you remembered— but that you felt at ease enough to broach them. And do I remember them? (Nannie—whattie) (Too hot to hold paddles) (Daddy is my best boy he kisses me and loves me. Daddy is my worst boy he never kisses me or loves me.) Nannie—I cherish them. They're like a treasured photo album inside my consciousness—or like baby shoes in bronze. Oh yes—I'll remember them!

*I'm sorry I couldn't get there this month. My trip to New
York was one hectic day with no free time at all. And since
returning, it's been the same. Night Gallery (ugh!) the novel, and
myriad recordings and stuff. I'm hoping that in March I can
make the trip and we can eat and talk and reminisce—but no
paddle holding if it's too hot!*

*Mom's birthday today. I didn't do too well. Four items-two
returned. But she seemed pleased with what was left. (Blouse
and slacks.) Your gift will no doubt come tomorrow or over the
weekend and she will write you herself.*

*What else. My son and my grandchildren [note: he is talking
about our animals] are all fine. Mom and I leave for Mexico on
the 11th. We're sending you addressed envelopes so you can write
to us during the two weeks. And you'd better!*

*Stop the long distance telephoning—you hear? I don't mean
to us—I mean to your far-flung social circle around the
continent.*

*Now I am going to take a nap. I'm just about recovering from
my cold and laryngitis. (For a week I sounded like Augie
Doggie—remember?)*

*Hey Pops—you're loved, missed, cared for and really
cherished.*

Yo te amo-

Rodman E.

I am so fortunate to have kept many of my dad's other letters as well. Like touchstones, they offer comfort even after all
of these years.

3/12
Dear Miss Grumple,
*I was sorry to have missed your call today. I was out buying clam
chowder. To think—to get aced out of talking to my young bunny
by a bunch of clams in water! Anyway the days grow short until*

you're back with us. We're looking forward to your trip probably
as much as you are!

Study . . . work . . . persevere . . . Hang in tough!

> Much, much Love
> Dad
> Rodman Rabbit

October 27th, 1972:

Dear Pops-Grumple,

As usual I was out meandering in the academic (teaching at
Auburn Community College) when your phone call came. I was
disappointed that I wasn't here.

Now what follows isn't necessarily meaningful—it may be
one of the less memorable letters you get from anyone—but I
wanted you to hear from me, if only to make partial amends for
my silence during your stay at MacDuffie.

You're getting pretty damned grownup . . . and very lovely.
Here's how I peg you, Anne C. Serling: you care for human
beings. And I suppose in the final analysis, that's how you
ultimately judge the nature of a person. Does he love or does he
scar—and I don't think you'd knowingly scar anyone . . .

Stick it out there. I can't support that exhortation with
Socratic logic, the awful statistics of what happens to drop outs or
much of anything supportive—except this: it's helping you. It's
giving you a more one-to-one education and a helluva lot better
one than an oversized, deeply impersonal public high school. It's
also providing you with friendships which you, as an expert on
friends, must realize are close and special.

Please for God's sake—no cigarettes, wine, drugs or any of the
other myriad no-no's that you may feel are stifling remnants of
Victorian discipline. Maybe I share your questioning as to their
relevance and validity. But they're the rules and you're honor
bound to obey them. Get the word, Pops? HONOR. It means
a helluva lot—not the least of which is keeping faith with
yourself.

And as to you—despite my rages, impatiences,

inconsistencies—I have a great deal of it when it comes to you.
And there's a maximum of love attendant as well.
  Stay in touch, enjoy, study, see you Thanksgiving.

          LOVELOVELOVE
          Dad

October 30th, 1972
Dear Miss Grumple,
Just a few early-morning thoughts. (It's 7:30 and I've despaired
doing cops and robbers on this NBC thing I'm doing—and
failing.)
  Weather cold, rainy, overcast, miserable. Not the Autumn we
anticipated and looked forward to. And yet, the trip back to the
coast offers no particular joy. I really love it here in the east.
There's such a freshness, Nanny—such an aliveness.
  I've been reading about college catalogues. I like the look of
Beloit. I'm especially taken with the "Beloit plan"—the off
campus work idea. I remember my salvation at Antioch was the
change of pace offered by the co-op plan—the chance to go off
and recharge batteries and sort of replenish. Beloit's system is
similar in that you're not anchored to the sameness of a campus
the entire year . . .
  No more now . . . except I wonder if you know how proud I
am of you? Talking to the teachers during Parents Day was a
special joy; hearing them tell us of your efforts . . . your work . . .
We drove back that Sunday feeling you've come of age. And the
slides you showed of the photographs of children granted a certain
fatherly bias—that showed a glowing sensitivity that made me
proud.
  Bye for now Pops. I'll write from the coast and we'll talk
weekly on the phone . . . and then there's Christmas—which is
actually right around the corner. After all, this is practically
November . . . which leads to December and you can eliminate
the first fifteen days which brings to . . . (Remember the game?)

          Much Love . . . muchmuchmuch

My dad knows of my terrible propensity to laugh when I am nervous or during inappropriate situations (classes, weddings, etc.). I have exploded into uncontainable laughter at the worst or most serious moments, trying desperately to suppress it behind my hand cupped to my mouth. My father, seeing this vulnerability, takes advantage of it. Often when we are just about to walk into a room full of company, he will do one of his dozens of impersonations, replete with distinct facial expressions of someone we are about to see. Or he will tell me a joke when we are about to be seated in a restaurant. Or the worst: when we are riding in an elevator together, he will whisper something funny to me, sometimes an off-color limerick, just before we step on; the elevator doors close on all of those silent people and our faint giggles grow increasingly louder. Once I get going, my dad also has trouble containing himself, and it becomes very embarrassing.

My dad and I meet in New York City during my senior year in boarding school. We go out to dinner, climbing the stairs to one of his favorite restaurants, Frankie & Johnnie's Steak House, and he tells me about the time he and my mother and some friends went to the musical *Hair*. He says he fell asleep, and when he woke up, one of the actors was sitting on his lap.

Later, back at the hotel, we have one of our elevator moments as he begins one of those limericks: "There once was a laddie from Boston . . ."

After the trip, he writes me:

January 1973
Dear Pops, I thought New York was a delight. One of the major problems of you growing up and my growing old is the fact that distance and time separates us much too much. You are really a dear kid and despite elevator giggles, mutually obscene finger

*gestures and mutual dirty name-calling—I think we have fun
together.*

>*Much Love, honey, and keep in touch.*
>*Dad*

*P.S. (1) Dentist. (2) Pay attention in typing class and (3) Take
Mr. Allen's class in Study Habits.*

Chapter 27

My father loves animals. There is even a time he wants a chimpanzee. I don't know how serious he actually is but do recall discussions on the practicality of the adoption of a chimp. I remember my mother saying they smell, are a lot of work, and they both had many questions revolving around ethics—is it really fair to the animal?

Although our menagerie grows—caged birds on a bathroom counter, two rat cages on the floor, two dogs scratching at the door, and two cats asleep on beds and couches—our home never includes a monkey.

My dad particularly loves the dogs. Sometimes, when we have guests and it is getting late, he gets down on all fours, like their littermate. We know he is playing but this could also be an indicator that he is tired and hoping the company will go home.

Perhaps because he's frequently there on the floor, children are naturally drawn to him. Or maybe it is the way he speaks to them; there is a gentle respect, a kindness in his tone.

My father's voice has many different intonations and pitches. There is the tight, clipped *Twilight Zone* or *Night Gallery* host voice introducing that week's episode. There is his regular Dad-speaking voice. There's the voice he uses for his *PBS* narrations or commercial spots, all of his different and funny dialects and accents, and, finally, his playful voice. It is the latter that pulls even the shyest child to his side.

The daughter of a producer we know once said she remembers my father at parties and how he seemed to prefer to be in the room with the children rather than with the adults. I am certain that on more than one occasion my dad did find the children more interesting and often more genuine, preferring their conversations over the ones wafting out in strident tones from the adult room.

I don't know how many of the child actors who were in *The Twilight Zone*s my dad actually got to know, but I clearly remember how thrilled he was with the performance of N'Gai Dixon, the young boy who plays Herman Washington in my dad's script for the 1970 *Hallmark Hall of Fame* production of *A Storm in Summer*. It is about the friendship between an African American fresh-air kid and a cantankerous delicatessen owner in upstate New York.

Initially, I remember, there is great concern with the casting of the very British Peter Ustinov. My dad is worried about his credibility as a Jewish delicatessen owner, but he needn't be. What results is a tremendously moving and poignant story and one of my dad's eventual favorites. And at Emmy time, Ustinov won the award for Best Lead Actor in a Dramatic Presentation.

A few months after *A Storm in Summer* airs, my father hurts his back during a game of paddle tennis. It is more serious than originally thought; he has torn all of the ligaments on one side. Although in a great deal of pain, he is determined not to delay our trip back east to our cottage for summer vacation.

June. Warm. Sunny. We pull up to the loading area at LAX; waiting forever for a break in the stream of traffic, hearing over and over, "The white line is for loading and unloading passengers only . . . The white line is for loading and unloading passengers only." We finally get my dad into a wheelchair. I push him through the airport, following my mother's quick steps to the gate as we maneuver our way through crowds of baggage-burdened people. My father is wearing dark sunglasses, and I pretend I am pushing a movie star. I am a little nervous, though; he is on pain medication and is clearly a little loopy. He acts funny, saying silly things, and suddenly he tells me, "Pops. I have to have a chocolate malt right now!" We have an hour until our plane leaves, and realizing he is serious, I am determined to find this for him. My mother is pretty certain I won't. "Okay, go look, Anne, but listen for our flight announcement and get back quickly."

I look in every restaurant, every coffee stand, and every gift shop.

Breathless, I run back to the gate. I can see my mother looking at her watch and waving frantically for me to hurry. I am about to deliver the bad news to my dad, having to tell him that nowhere in the airport can one buy a chocolate malt. But before I have a chance to explain, he looks up at me and asks, "Where were you?" Thanks to the medication, he had completely forgotten his request for a malt.

I can only respond with a phrase he often used and might have said had he not been so out of it: "Oy vey."

Chapter 28

My dad and I often draw cartoon pictures of each other. I have stacks of these caricatures that we did on paper plates. The ones I draw of him are usually in profile, often with a cigarette dangling from his mouth and featuring whatever nickname I am calling him at the time. "Rodman Raisin" reads one; he calls me "Young Raisin" because we both like to sit in the sun. We do these drawings after dinner at the cottage, teasing, exaggerating each other's features more and more. I copy his signature below the ones I do of him.

During these years of the 1970s my dad is teaching Writing for Television at Ithaca College in the summer. He genuinely likes college students and thoroughly enjoys teaching. Often he holds these classes at the cottage, out on the lawn. Sometimes, though, he gets up very early to drive the forty minutes to the college to open the recording studio, recognizing that the students need a faculty member there and that recording time is at a premium.

One summer he records a voice-over for each of their in-

```
                        ROD SERLING
                INTERLAKEN, NEW YORK, 14847


                        July 17th


Dear Pops,

As of this date still no word from you. But we're
not unfamiliar with the vagaries of the mail. We're
nonetheless looking forward to some word.

So what else can I tell you? The weather's improved;
today was 85 degrees and simply beautful. The dock's
being repaired and I hope Jo-Nan will be here the
end of the week.

Now what about your trip? We're frustrated as hell not
knowing what you're doing or anything. If you don't write
I'll never take you to Portnoy's Complaint again!
(Mom still won't let me forget that)

This is brief, bunny - just shot out to let you know
that all was well and we're thinking of you.


            LOVEWRITELOVEWRITELOVE
```

dividual projects. The head of the department is impressed by his generosity with his time.

I would love to have had my dad as a teacher. For the most part, we have the same tastes. We like similar stories and movies and generally have the same criticisms and the same reactions. There are two occasions, though, that I remember reality falling short of our expectations of one another. He takes me to see the play *Our Town*, and tells me, "This is right up your alley. You are going to love it." I like it, but I don't love it, and I know he is a little disappointed. Today this would have been a completely different conversation; I would have agreed with him it was great, but at the time I was too young to appreciate Wilder.

The other time . . . when we go to see Paul Zindel's movie, *The Effect of Gamma Rays on Man-in-the-Moon Marigolds*, my dad laughs at the line, "My heart is full." I am shocked and furious that he has missed the poignancy of the moment. Later, when we are discussing the movie in the car I tell him, "I can't believe you laughed at that line. It was a critical, important, heartbreaking moment! I thought you, of all people, would 'get' it!"

"It was funny—out of place, over the top. A little corny. Admit it," he says.

I sit sullenly beside him and don't speak to him until, almost home, he says, "C'mon, who's your best friend, Pops?" and despite myself, I have to smile and I answer, "You are."

From a distance, on the cottage porch, I sometimes watch my dad out on the lawn surrounded by his students, laughing, writing, critiquing films, and all having a good time.

When I see the videos, now, of his lectures from classes held at the college, and I hear the questions the students ask and see the expressions on their faces when they look at him, filled with reverence, I imagine they would probably be amused if they knew his nickname was "Roddy Rabbit."

As a teaching tool, my dad talks about his writing, what makes some scripts succeed and others fail.

One of his screenplays that he uses to represent what doesn't work is a script called *The Man*, based on the novel by Irving Wallace and starring James Earl Jones. It is a story about the first African American president. My father must feel the movie doesn't live up to its promise or the depth the characters deserve; that Jones's character comes across as a cipher, a noble symbol rather than a flesh-and-blood human being. Mark Olshaker told me, "Your dad said, 'That script taught me never to write about someone who doesn't go to the bathroom.' "

In the seventies, a black president seems very much in the range of "science fiction." The only way Wallace could "realistically" get an African American into the Oval Office was to make him interim president of the Senate and then stage a catastrophe in which all those ahead of him in line of succession are killed. How thrilled my dad would have been to see Barack Obama inaugurated as president thirty-seven years later.

My father also teaches Creativity Seminars at Ithaca College. In some of his notes he writes:

All writers are born; they're never made . . . I take off and write, out of a sense of desperate compulsion.

I always write as if I'd gotten my X-ray back from the doctor on Monday, and I'd best check with the insurance man to see whether or not the house is free and clear.

Who was it that said 'Writing is the easiest thing on earth.' I simply walk into my study, I sit down, I put the paper in the typewriter, and I fix the margins, and then I turn the paper up— and I bleed.

Often he is asked to speak at high school and college graduations. Most of his talks have a common theme. He writes a letter to the woman organizing one of his speeches at Bergenfield High School in New Jersey:

Dear Ms. Jaeger,
I usually make it a practice to send along no ostensible words of wisdom to high school or college students. This is simply because most of them are so much brighter than I am that comments of mine sound pompous and a little unrealistic. But since I've been invited to speak my peace, the following is a brief philosophy that I believe in, and which may be of help to someone:
If you write, fix pipes, grade papers, lay bricks or drive a

taxi—do it with a sense of pride. And do it the best you know
how. Be cognizant and sympathetic to the guy alongside, because
he wants a place in the sun, too. And always . . . always look past
his color, his creed, his religion and the shape of his ears. Look for
the whole person. Judge him as the whole person.

In a commencement address on March 17, 1970, at the
University of Southern California (the sentiments are relevant even today, decades later) he says:

. . . It's simply a national acknowledgement that in any kind of
priority, the needs of human beings must come first. Poverty is
here and now. Hunger is here and now. Racial tension is here
and now. Pollution is here and now. These are the things that
scream for a response. And if we don't listen to that scream—and
if we don't respond to it—we may well wind up sitting amidst
our own rubble, looking for the truck that hit us—or the bomb
that pulverized us. Get the license number of whatever it was
that destroyed the dream. And I think we will find that the
vehicle was registered in our own name.

Chapter 29

IN 1973, THE SUMMER I turn eighteen, I begin working at Camp Iroquois, a camp in Ithaca for children with special needs. I become good friends with the director, Rochelle Mike, who hired me. At the end of the session, we have a staff party at Johnny's Big Red Grill, a well-known place near Cornell University. I still don't have my driver's license, despite those early lessons from my dad when I was four, so he picks me up. One of the counselors, someone who I don't know and who doesn't know me, begins talking about a *Twilight Zone* episode he watched late the night before. He says, "I fell asleep right before it ended. Did anyone see it? Can anyone tell me what happened?"

He doesn't see my dad come in and take the empty seat beside him, and he is still asking around the table if anyone knows about last night's episode. Someone begins laughing, and he finally turns and sees my dad sitting beside him. The expression on his face is priceless.

My dad stays for a while. He orders a Coke and fills in the

curious counselor on missing information. Before long, he has engaged the attention of everyone at that table.

That same summer, Jodi, now twenty-one, is married in a production rivaling *Father of the Bride*. Three hundred guests, mostly friends of my parents' from California, are invited to the ceremony, held in the Unitarian Church in Ithaca, New York.

In the months and weeks prior to the wedding, my mother and sister begin to unravel with all of the preparation: the planning and arranging, the invitations and flowers, the dresses, the cake, the photographer and music, the parking, reception, the food, and on and on.

For the most part my dad and I stand on the sidelines, afraid to get too close. But with only a few nervous faux pas (my sister introduces her maid of honor, as her "best man," and her new mother-in-law as her "grandmother") the ceremony goes off without a glitch. Jodi is a beautiful bride, and my dad is smiling as he walks her down the aisle.

The reception is held in an inn overlooking Cayuga Lake. I remember dancing with my father, the towering cake on a table in the corner, my aunt drinking far too much, and my sister and her new husband, Steve, looking happy, running to their car, leaving for their honeymoon in the rain.

Anyone who knows my dad says he is nothing like the image on screen. What initially surprises many is that he is only five-foot-five, or, as he sometimes says, "Five-four and three-quarters." People are constantly saying, "Hey, Rod; Hey, Mr. Serling, we thought you were SO much taller!" If it fazes my dad, he never lets on. He just smiles and shrugs.

One of his favorite stories, in fact, and one he tells frequently, is about when he was in the audience of a show hosted by the comedian Don Rickles. Rickles yelled out to my dad, "Hey, Rod! Stand up. Oh! You are standing!"

About his appearance, my dad is quoted as saying,

Apparently, on the screen, I look tall, dark, and close to omniscient, issuing jeopardy-laden warnings through gritted teeth. And then they look at me [in person] and say, "Why, God, this kid is five-foot-five, he's got a broken nose, and looks about as foreboding as a bank teller on a lunch break."

Once past the initial surprise at my father's small stature, all it takes is moments in his presence to experience his genuine warmth, humor, and his innate ability to put everyone at ease.

My friends adore him. Having him around is like having a playmate who can drive and take you wherever you want to go. It isn't like having a normal parent, one you can't wait to flee. With my dad, you want him to stick around; you want him to stay, to play.

My friend, Joan Barnes Flynn, remembers meeting him in 1973 when he visited the boarding school we both attended:

Anne's dad was coming to take her to dinner, and I was invited. I admit that underneath my excitement, I was a bit unsettled. Rod Serling in person? What would I say? How would I act? What if something strange happened? Should I call my parents one last time, just in case we got caught in another dimension and couldn't get back?

The evening arrived, and I kept trying to quell my nervousness. Anne told me over and over that her dad was great and I believed her. I also believed that he was deep, dark and scary, and maybe I should let them go by themselves. But, no, my curiosity, friendship with Anne and need to escape the institutional setting all convinced me that I could make it through no matter what happened. I took a deep breath, squared my shoulders and went down the stairs. Anne and her dad were standing in the front hall as I approached. I suddenly felt great relief. He wasn't much taller than I was, and when he turned toward me he had the warmest smile on his face—no weird music, no sinister aura. I smiled back and shook his hand.

We went to the only decent restaurant in town—a steak house across the river. Rod told us funny stories and treated us like adults. There was such a close rapport between the two of them, but he made sure to include me in that warmth. I felt deeply flattered and very glad I had come. I was happy I hadn't called my parents to say goodbye.

After dinner, we went to see the movie "Nicolas and Alexandra"—very Russian, very romantic and very long. During the intermission, we went out to the lobby for sodas and popcorn, and a young guy approached Rod as we were standing in line. He held out a pen and said that he didn't have a piece of paper, but was wondering if Rod would autograph his girlfriend's chest. With a wry grin, Rod politely refused and turned his attention back to us. He had such style, and I was captivated!

One Christmas vacation, I flew out to their home in California and spent four days with Anne and her family, getting the full tour of Disneyland, Universal Studios and all the special out-of-the-way places that only the locals had access to. I fell in love with the palm trees and the weather, but I especially fell in love with the private Rod Serling—the family man who got down on the floor and rolled around with the Irish Setter; the man who ferried his daughter and her wide-eyed friend around because it was fun for him, too; the man who wasn't afraid to be silly and laugh at himself.

Over time, Rochelle Mike, the camp director, becomes my close friend. At first she, too, seemed somewhat apprehensive to meet my dad.

Meeting Rod Serling for the first time was all you expected a television star to be in person—handsome, deeply tanned and extraordinarily memorable. But, it was what you least expected from the creator and host of The Twilight Zone that endures—his brilliant humor and his ability to play any willing audience for all it was worth.

My introduction to him took place at the family home on Cayuga Lake; I had given Anne a ride home from the summer day camp where we both worked. He was tending his roses, a scene as far from The Twilight Zone as one could imagine. I vividly recall how genuinely pleased he was to see his daughter home safe and sound, as if she'd returned from a lengthy journey, rather than just a day at a summer job.

Chapter 30

When I start looking into colleges, my parents think Beloit College in Wisconsin would be the perfect place for me. My sister, by then, is at Ithaca College graduating in a year. I, like her, want to stay on the East Coast. I don't want to be in the middle of the country where I know no one, but my parents are hoping I will choose Beloit and when I get accepted my dad writes to me at MacDuffie: "Listen Bunny, we were proud about Beloit but are not rushing you. It's your decision." Shortly after, he and I visit the campus together. We run through the rain and the puddles and the mud to get to the admissions building. Our guide, a junior, is pleasant and bright and says all of the right things, but I cannot get past the dismal gray or the explanation that it has just been a particularly rainy spring and that is why the campus (stuck in the middle of the country) looks colorless and dreary.

Around this time my father receives an honorary degree from Alfred University and tells me about the school. It is in upstate New York, a few hours from our cottage.

My dad understands my decision not to go to Beloit and thinks I'll like Alfred's campus and the fact that it is small. The day we visit is sunny and warm, the grass an almost emerald green. For this reason, and this reason alone, I select Alfred as the college I will attend my freshman year.

As I arrive for orientation, my regrets about this decision begin to escalate in direct proportion to the endless flights of stairs I climb to reach my new dorm room.

When touring the campus I had not noticed how remote the school was, how the town looked abandoned, like something out of the *Twilight Zone* episode "Where Is Everybody?"

It takes a while to meet people and to make friends. I remember entering the school cafeteria and hearing a kid in a yellow shirt at a distant table laugh and say something like, "Yeah, her father is Rod Serling. She better go get her teeth sharpened." It's as if I'm back on the elementary school playground all over again.

I call home a lot that fall. Often my dad is preoccupied, sometimes distant. I can hear him exhaling his cigarette smoke and flipping through papers on his desk. I know he is busy, and he often quickly passes the phone over to my mother. He is hosting a radio anthology show titled *The Zero Hour*, a dramatic series that features many of the actors and actresses from *The Twilight Zone.* He is also doing the narrations for *The Undersea World of Jacques Cousteau*, a series that excites him because he is fascinated by the subject matter and by Cousteau himself.

He does some Public Service Announcements—Forest fire prevention and Environmental PSA's—and continues to do commercial spots (Anacin, the bug spray called 6-12, a car wax, and beer). The irony of this is never lost on him; he is profiting from the sponsors he battled for so long in his early days of writing. I remember my parents discussing this, even arguing. I remember my mother telling him he needs to investigate the things that he is trying to sell to the public, and his acknowledging this, but commenting on how ludicrous it is that by recording a sixty-second television spot he can make more money than he can writing. Or, as he told his media class at Antioch, "I get $3,000 to make beer commercials and the same amount to teach for six months." Regardless of this logic, I know he is conflicted, and one day says, "My crime has been committed, and there's very little defense for it. I was not conned into doing the beer commercial. Rather, a sizable check was thrust in front of me and I plowed in with no thought to its effect or ramifications."

Al Rosen, who took a class of my father's in the sixties, told me he enjoyed my dad's commentaries as they screened old *Twilight Zone* shows after dinner in a lecture hall. Al said,

When the commercials interrupted the shows your dad was screening he'd belittle all the actors appearing in the spots as "whores" and sometimes worse.

After graduation I became program director of radio station WTKO which was an Ithaca pop music station back in the day. You can imagine how surprised I was when I played a new commercial and heard your dad doing the commercial! Soon I saw him doing a commercial on television. I mentioned to one of the guys at the station how surprised I was because of how he used to talk about anyone involved in advertising. I said that if I ever saw Rod again, I'd ask him about it. I could be brave because I had graduated and didn't think I would ever see him again. Well, just a couple of weeks later I was shopping at the Co-Op food supermarket in Ithaca one Saturday morning and saw your dad pushing a cart there. I took a deep breath. Should I really say anything to him? (After all, I knew he had been a boxer.) He was approaching the checkout and I decided to do it. I introduced myself to him again and said I hoped he wouldn't be upset with my question about what changed his mind. Your dad was gracious as always and smiled. He said something like "I deserve this." He went on to explain that one day he had a meeting with someone from an advertising agency and the guy handed your dad a piece of paper. He said, "Listen Rod, if you just read what's on that piece of paper into a microphone, I'll give you enough money to put one of your kids through college." He said he read the paper, it looked innocent enough and he decided to do it.

And the rest, as they say, is history.

David Brenner (whose humor my dad became a huge fan of) told me a similar story. He said that when he was a Communications major at Temple University, hoping to have a career as a TV playwright, he noticed that my father was doing a commercial for a cigarette company.

It upset me that such a great writer was doing that, so, being the outspoken person I was since I could talk, I got out my semi-broken typewriter and with the elevated trains roaring by my bedroom window in the rank apartment in which I lived in a Philly slum, I wrote my protest letter, never expecting a reply, of course, but glad I voiced what I thought, including that I might have to change my goal, because I couldn't "sell out." A couple weeks later, I received a reply from your dad, explaining that sometimes one had to do such things because of pressure placed on creative talent by the networks and he ended by telling me to stay in the business, because, maybe I would be one of the young men to change that. Needless to say, I was blown away that he answered, and, better, I decided to pursue my writing.

Sometimes when I call home in these early fall months and my dad answers, our conversations are brief. In November 1973, he writes me:

Dear Miss Grumple,
As must be obvious by the neatness of the typing, Margie is taking this via dictation. It's being typed on Thursday the 15th—the day before sailing, and I've asked her to include it in the care package that she'll mail to you after Thanksgiving.
All is well here and even a little exciting, what with the boat trip and you coming out here for Christmas. I'm phoning White Sun before I leave tomorrow to arrange rooms for us there so you

can go back to Alfred in dead winter looking like Raisin's
daughter!

   I'm conscious, honey, of kind of short shrifting you during our
phone conversations. You do have an uncanny knack for phoning
either in the middle of a vital scene or at a game-winning
juncture of a pro football game that I bet on. But just because I
quickly turn you over to Mom, my interest, love, concern is
nonetheless real.

If I feel temporarily dismissed by my dad, or, as he says, "short-shrifted," I do not remember this. I know, unequivocally, that in the long run and for the long haul, my dad is there. And so, three months later, while experiencing an abrupt and profound bout of depression that seems to come out of nowhere, I turn to him. I attempt to rein in these derailing emotions, capture them with words, and send them to him. I tell him how isolated I feel, that although I have friends and a boyfriend—a nice Jewish boy who is an extraordinarily gifted artist—something just feels wrong. I don't believe I fit in here; the school is too much of a party school. I end my letter by saying I don't know what I really want to do with my life, and feel afraid that what I am feeling seems beyond the angst typical of my age.

   In response, my father writes:

February 14, 1974
My Darling Little Raisin,
I've just received your note (or shall we call it blank verse?) and
in part I was moved, and in equal part, I was a little disturbed.
As must be obvious, I'm dictating this—not through laziness but
as so often is the case with me, my mind works faster than my
typing fingers, and this seemed sufficiently important to get it
down properly and accurately to you . . .

   It's your depression that concerns me most. Your sense of
sadness. Again, how does one refurbish the feelings of another to
remind them of their beauty, their worth, their warmth and their

simple humanity. All of which you have in abundance. Of course
I'm prejudiced and biased and desperately one-sided in my
analysis of you. I'm your father, and flesh not only builds up
virtue and extols it—it also distorts it out of love and caring. But
in truth, in examining you—Anne, the person—I know deep
down that you are a very special girl. Sometimes the merit of
your own sensitivity works against you, like welcoming a bright
day that is so bright that it hurts the eyes.

That's all I have to tell you. That you're being thought of
constantly . . . and worried about, as well . . . We want you to be
happy more than anything on God's earth.

I fold his letter and put it in the top drawer of my desk. I
will glance at it again and again throughout the school year.

There isn't much involved in becoming a transfer student. I
fill in the necessary paperwork to apply to Elmira College in
Elmira, New York, for the following fall, majoring in elementary education. And on a June day, much like the one when
my father and I first visited Alfred, I pack up my things, return
the room key, and my dad lugs my suitcases back down all
those flights of stairs.

Thirty-four years later, in a different desk and in a different
city, I still have the letter he wrote me, his words comforting
me even now.

Chapter 31

ON THE LATE SUMMER evening of August 8, 1974, my friend Rochelle and I are in the new house my parents built in 1970 beside the old red cottage (where I am staying). It is very different from the cottage and with all of the openness and conveniences of a modern home. The kitchen and living room are separated by a stone fireplace, and each room has an abundance of light pouring through numerous glass doors and windows.

Rochelle and I are sitting on the floor of my dad's study, a room much larger than the little shed that he once used near the cottage. The sliding glass doors are partially closed and we can see a portion of my father's reflection behind us. We are all turned toward the small television on his desk.

Richard Milhous Nixon is just beginning his resignation speech:

"Good evening. This is the thirty-seventh time I have spoken to you from this office, where so many decisions have been made that shaped the history of this nation. Each time I have done so to discuss with you some matter that I believe affected the national interest..."

Nixon goes on and on and finally my dad, walking closer to the television, says, "They ought to hang the bastard by his balls." He looks back at us and adds, "Sorry, girls."

In a speech my father later gives in Binghamton, he puts it a little more eloquently:

> The use of illegal wiretaps to spy on reporters and political opponents, the secret and illegal bombing of Cambodia, the authorization of "plumbers" to burglarize and spy upon political opponents, the withholding of evidence in criminal cases, the defying of court orders, the obstruction of justice—this is the province of President Nixon and all the rest of that shabby crew who have written indelible chapters in the threadbare saga of the most corrupt, incompetent and downright immoral administration in the history of the American Republic.

The final few weeks of the summer following Nixon's resignation, my dad is working on an adaptation of a political thriller. It's a book by Morris West called *The Salamander*. He is doing the screenplay for Carlo Ponti and later describes it in an interview as "a very difficult, ball-breaking script [that is] beginning to destroy me piecemeal."

Although I am generally three thousand miles away (with the exception of summers and vacations) and not home to witness my dad's day-to-day life, his professional struggles, or the inordinate time I know he puts into his work, writing, rewriting, perfecting, I sense the level of distress and difficulty that he is having with this project. And it seems so uncharacteristic. Writing always appears to come so naturally, spontaneously, almost instinctively for him. But not this time.

I think he's tired, maybe feeling old. One night at dinner he talks about having grandchildren and how he looks forward to sitting on the porch and playing with them. He wants to rest awhile but, immersed in this difficult project, he doesn't know how to step away.

A few days before I leave for school, I pass by his partially open office door and see him working. He is leaning back, holding the Dictaphone microphone in his right hand. The room is silent and smoky. He does not look up. He seems to not even be moving. The cigarette glows orange in a jam-packed ashtray on the desk before him. I raise my hand to knock. I start to call, "Dad?" but change my mind and walk away. I decide not to disturb him after all.

Three months later my parents finally take a vacation. My father, still entrenched in this screenplay, has also completed twenty-seven of the twenty-eight narrations he will do for *The Undersea World of Jacques Cousteau*. He writes me at school on the night before he and my mother leave:

> *Nov 14 1974*
> *Dear Nanny,*
> *I was disappointed not to be able to talk to you tonight when you called. I'd hoped to say goodbye before our trip tomorrow night. As usual, I'm counting the hours for the boat whistle to blow. Mom, on the other hand, has some misgivings about the journey—not nearly as content as I am to just sit in the sun, staring at the waves. I think she's taking this trip for my benefit more than anything else.*
> *She said that you sounded much more content on the phone tonight and much more with it—and for this I'm thankful.*
>
> > *Much love, small raisin—*
> > *Dad*

At school, walking through fresh snow to class, I think of something my father once wrote before *The Twilight Zone* aired its final show: "In these last few years, I've written so much I'm woozy. If only I could take off about six months and replenish the well."

I remove his letter, still in my pocket, unfold it, and read it again. He indisputably needs the rest but the "well," I am convinced, will never run dry. He just needs to get away, and this cruise they are taking to Mexico is the perfect salve. The minute he and my mother step onto the boat, he will not have access to a phone, an agent, a director, producer, or anything connected with work. He cannot reach back even if he wants to.

When they return, following a quick phone call, my dad sends a note:

My Dear Miss Grumple.
I know I promised you a long letter—(not a rose garden—a long letter) and this itsy bitsy one doesn't nearly satisfy that description. But at least you know I'm thinking of you and missing you.
  Is the cold improved? Are the studies coming along? Quick! Answer!

Love, Daddy-Boy

I write him back. Things are better. I have met a new boyfriend. Although not Jewish (I think my dad would have liked it if he were), Ken is a great guy, an artist who does phenomenal political cartoons. I quickly add that, yes, of course he is a Democrat. I don't tell him how one night Ken crawled up the drainpipe to my dorm room to see me past curfew and appeared at my window, but I should have. He would have loved that, so adventurous, ballsy, so like something he would have done . . . or very likely may have.

Chapter 32

SHORTLY AFTER IT GOES off the air, *The Twilight Zone* begins its seemingly eternal life in syndication. My father sees what syndication does to each episode and says in a newspaper interview, "You wouldn't recognize what series it was. Full scenes were deleted. It looked like a long, protracted commercial separated by fragmentary moments of indistinct drama."

It is tremendously frustrating for him to watch the dissection of his stories, and it is equally disturbing for him to see some of his other ideas hijacked.

One afternoon, Rochelle and I are again watching television with him at the lake. It's a movie where an atomic bomb or another catastrophe has wiped out the human race. Throughout the entire movie, my dad is grumbling and making comments. "They stole my God damn script!"

In one of the final scenes, a man stumbles out of the debris and the camera pans to a horse standing near a dust-covered car. The man is clearly trying to find a way out of this apocalypse. The camera pans back and forth from the man to the horse to the car.

Finally, my dad has had enough and can no longer contain himself. Unselfconsciously he yells, "Oh, just shove the battery up the horse's ass!"

Suddenly remembering his audience—my friend—he immediately apologizes. But Rochelle is rolling on the floor, laughing, tears streaming down her cheeks.

That spring, on a warm evening in late April 1975, my dad gives a speech at Elmira College, where I am a student. I have never heard him speak in public before. I am excited and enormously proud. He is not feeling well, though, and has to sit down in a room off the auditorium while people are filing in. Someone brings him a cup of water. He accepts it graciously. My mother and I are thinking he must be getting a cold. Or the flu. We are all in denial. Even though my sister told us that when he visited her the night before she was concerned; he looked ashen she'd said.

After a few minutes, his color starts to look a little better, and he announces he is fine. I hug him and tell him, "See ya soon, baboon."

The auditorium is packed. Every seat is full and there are people standing in the back. Rochelle and I and some friends are told we can sit on the floor in the front.

The 1970s are not an easy time for an adult to connect with young people. Many students are angry about the Vietnam War, the Watergate cover-up, and the general state of world affairs, so they are distrustful of adults. The "Generation Gap" is in full bloom. But in that hour or so my father captivates the audience. He nails it. They love him. The clapping and the laughter are deafening. I am so filled with pride, just watching him, that I am not even following his words.

At one point he comments, "My daughter is out there, somewhere, where are you, honey?" I see him scanning the audience, but I know he'll never find me. Just in case, though, I shadow the person in front of me. I will *not* let him embarrass me in front of all of these people. He finishes his speech, walks from the lectern, crosses the stage, and exits to thunderous applause.

It is not until many months later, when I look at the photographs taken of him around this time, that I see it. I look at a series of black-and-white prints: in one my dad is looking up from his desk, a script in his hand. Another shows him sitting outside in a lawn chair. Others capture him standing by the grill, by the lake, on the dock, by the porch. There is something alarming in my father's eyes. It is the unmistakable weariness that we have all, unwittingly, failed to see.

It isn't difficult, though, to understand how we could overlook these signs. As Rochelle remembers:

> *I had become a great fan of Rod's at-home humor. This particular summer he had come east to their lake house a couple of days ahead of Carol. (She arrived a few days before his speech at the college.) Rather than spend time alone at the lake, he had convinced Anne to come home from her nearby college to spend the night, and I gladly joined them. The following morning, for no particular reason, he launched into a reenactment of a favorite scene from, of all things, "Gone with the Wind." He played several parts, male, female, it really did not matter. Each one was more hilarious than the last, and each brilliant, I might add. The dialogue was flawless and props and costumes were whatever happened to be handy, from housecoats to bandanas, anything he could snatch. The whole performance could not have lasted more than two minutes, but years later, the mere thought of it can still transport Anne and me into fits of hysterical laughter all over again. I later learned that he had been known to stage this little vignette for other appreciative audiences; I was flattered to join their ranks.*

Chapter 33

THAT MAY NIGHT, I stay at Rochelle's instead of the cottage. If not for this last-minute decision, I would have been there when, at dawn, my dad decides to start the rototiller. I would have been there and could have helped him, or I could have pushed the bloody thing up the slope with him. Or I could have set it on fire, or, perhaps, I could have changed his mind.

As it happens, though, I am not there. And my father cannot get it started. He is determined; he wants to prepare the soil for the corn he wants to plant. He tries and tries, and finally it starts but gets stuck in the damp grass, and he can move it no farther and there, right there on the summer lawn, my dad collapses.

What is he thinking in that instant? Does he know what is happening to him? Does he think of his father, dead at fifty-two? Does my mother see him when she stands by the window, stretching, unaware, opening the curtain?

Does time go in fast motion or slow?

And all the while, as my father falls, I am fast asleep at my friend's house. Confused when she wakes me, when she tells me we need to leave right away, when she looks so alarmed, when she says, "Your father has had a heart attack. Hurry."

Chapter 34

CHAOS. Disorder. A waiting room, all of us, there, waiting.

How long until we can see my dad?

There is a doctor. "Dr. Goodfriend." I would have thought my father had made that up had I not heard it myself.

Dr. Goodfriend explains about the heart attack, about the obstruction, about something called angioplasty.

Days pass. A week. My dad, still in the hospital, is sleeping a lot or sometimes staring out the window, quiet and restless. He is gradually getting a little better, though; his humor is returning, and on the eighth day, I notice daffodils in bloom all the way down the road to the entrance of that old, stone hospital. Paths of blazing gold, signs of life and hope.

I sneak in the puppy my boyfriend, Ken, has given me, past the nurses and into my father's room. My dad sits up, smiles, and begins to play with her. I can see the cardiac monitors pasted to his chest. He swears into them, pretending the nurses can hear his words. And then he looks up, and in that instant I see something happen, pain suddenly sweeps across his face.

The crash cart tears into the room, pushed by two or three nurses. I am told to step aside as an oxygen mask is placed over my father's face. Just before they attach it, he looks at me and says, "I'm all right, honey. Don't be afraid."

But I am clutching my new dog and trying to reach for my father's hand through all of the people and the machinery and the noise, and I am terrified.

May 19, 1975
Ms. Anne. Bunny: the following: in my 50 years, I'd conjured up an illusion of permanence. Other, overweight, overdrinking middle-aged bastards got carted off in screaming ambulances to intensive care units. But not your old man! Not wiry, tough old Rod. Well, my darling something did die last week. My infallibility. And a sizeable portion of an irreplaceable youth. It's not to be mourned or wept over. But Bunny—it's a loss of something quite irreplaceable.

Bear with it with me.
You are loved.

Dad

We don't know, we could not possibly know, that my father will have only about a month more. One more month. Seven hundred and twenty hours left. If he knew, what would he want to say? Where would he want to go? What would I tell him, whisper to him? How many words fill a moment?

Chapter 35

THERE IS DISCUSSION ABOUT open-heart bypass surgery. Dr. Goodfriend is against it, but my dad's doctor in California says it is a viable option. They cannot do it in Ithaca. There are alternative hospitals; the procedure is still so new. Should he go back to California? Or Rochester? He can go to Strong Memorial in Rochester, an hour and a half away.

But first he will come home to the cottage for a while. Decisions will be made, but not then, not in that moment in the hospital.

He is told, of course, no cigarettes, no this, no that, and is given a long list of dietary and physical restrictions and suggestions.

My father is not the same. He loathes being an invalid or being treated even remotely like one. Understandably, his moods are mercurial. He says he needs to be by himself. He takes short walks. He hides matches in his shoes, in planters, in bowls. The cigarettes we will find months and months later behind the file cabinet, behind the wall, tucked into drawers.

He is going stir-crazy. We plan a night out, dinner and a movie. I watch my dad closely, but I cannot begin to know what he is feeling emotionally or physically. He jokes and laughs. But we don't make it through the movie. He says he'll be fine, he's just tired, he just needs to get home.

Later my father is in pain. The nitroglycerin is not working, and in the middle of the night we leave for the hospital. My mother drives, my father beside her, and I am in the backseat pulling the bobby pins out of my mother's hair for her.

There are few cars on the road at that hour. Occasional bright lights in the distance that quickly dim. The trees go by in a blur of shadowed darkness, quick shots of the whitest most iridescent moon between them.

I want to lean forward and touch my dad. Reach for his hand. Squeeze his shoulder. But I don't want him to know I am afraid for him.

Sometime at dawn, or later, or before, the doctor in California is urging the open-heart surgery.

My father goes by ambulance to Rochester, an hour or so away. He wants to stop at the cottage. He wants to stand on the porch one last time before he goes, but there are, I guess, schedules to follow, appointments that must be kept, and so, he can't go back.

Halfway to Rochester, though, he does ask the paramedics to stop so that he can smoke. Astonishingly, they pull over. Because of the oxygen in the ambulance, my dad has to get out. There they are, all of them, smoking on the side of the road like something out of a *Saturday Night Live* skit. When we hear this we are not entirely surprised. At the hospital in Ithaca, he had convinced an orderly to sneak him cigarettes. My dad kept them in the battery compartment of his radio. It heated up, and the cigarettes caught fire.

My dad is hopelessly, helplessly addicted.

At Strong Memorial Hospital, I have to show an ID to see him. I bring him his mail (he insists on this), and I also bring an audiotape I have made for him for Father's Day. On it I pretend I am several different relatives. I make the phone ring each time before I answer, and then, in the voices of the relatives, ask for him—"Is Roddy there? It's..." From his hospital bed, my father laughs. He asks me repeatedly how I got the phone to ring.

His days in the hospital are long. He walks to the bathroom or to the chair by the window, and then back to the bed. His steps are careful and slow. This is hard on him. The man he meets in the mirror looks tired and old, like someone he doesn't know.

I'm not certain he believes us when the doctors, my mother, sister, and I tell him he's okay. He says, "I listened to the radio to see what my condition *really* is." He laughs a little when he says this.

One morning, just as I am about to tap on the door of his hospital room, I hear him talking to the doctor. "I think my survival chances may have been better in the war," I hear him say, and I wait until the doctor comes out. When I see my dad, I don't admit that I have overheard him. For just a moment, we are quiet, the brown of his eyes reflecting my own. Deep down, in a place I don't want to glimpse, is a fear as immeasurable as his.

I pull up a chair beside his bed and together we watch television or talk a little. Despite what I have overheard, he looks at me and says, "You know, Pops, for the most part, I am feeling confident about this surgery."

He has, apparently, shared the same sentiment with Dick Berg who will later recount: "The fact is those last weeks were affirmative ones for him. And he was moving more and more toward the conviction that the prescribed surgery would revitalize his condition..."

Nurses draw his blood repeatedly. His levels are checked, his blood pressure monitored. At one point, there is something wrong; his blood is not clotting correctly. The surgeon thinks they may have to postpone the surgery, but this anomaly soon corrects itself.

Several days before the surgery, we check into a nearby residence for patients' families where my mother has been staying. Prior to that, the rest of us had been driving back and forth from the cottage.

I walk to the hospital, show my ID at the entrance desk, push the elevator button for the eighth floor, and step out into that sea of bright walls.

My dad is asleep. For a moment I watch him, sitting beside him, leaning, waiting, and thinking of another time when he was ill and I was little. In a white skirt, a hat I'd made myself, and teetering in my mother's heels, I'd knocked on his door.

"Mr. Serling?" I said, in my six-year-old voice. "I'm your nurse. I have candy for your flu, candy for your throat, and candy for your stomachache."

I took his pulse, wiped his forehead dry, and sat with him for hours.

Now, watching him so still, just days before surgery, the recollection feels so long ago and I barely know the girl and her dad looking back at me in that memory.

Down the hall, outside his room, people passing by speak in whispers. Despite the hushed tones, my dad wakes and sees me. He says he is so sorry. He says I should have woken him.

As if he should not have been sleeping, as if he should not have been gone, and afraid for him, I want to weep.

He doesn't belong in that bed in the hospital. This is all a mistake.

The next day the surgery prep begins, and his chest is shaved, making it look like a boy's. A team of doctors tells him what he can expect post-op. They say he may not recognize people right away.

"Don't worry," he tells us. "I'll know who you are." He smiles and winks and says again that he is feeling positive, confident that this surgery will fix things and he will soon get on with all of the things he wants to do.

The moon that night is full, a white-yellow glow pouring through the hospital window. It shines on my dad, illuminating him. In the shadows beside the colored wall, we kiss him good night and tell him we'll see him tomorrow.

The next day, the "four- to five-hour procedure" stretches to six, to seven, to eight and a half.

My mother, my sister, and I sit in the waiting room and stare at the walls. Ken, Rochelle, my sister's husband Steve, and my uncle, my father's brother, are there now, too. Few words are exchanged. Hours pass when we say nothing at all.

The sky is black when, at last, the doctor squeezes into the small room and tells us my father is on a heart-lung machine and dialysis.

"The surgery went well," he says, "but he had another heart attack after we closed him up."

"After we closed him up." I do not want to think of my father in those terms. Opened, sewn shut. I just want him there.

The doctor has a diagram of a heart. He holds it up and points. He indicates the area where something has gone wrong. But of course they can fix this, or more surgery will, and certainly my dad will get well and isn't that just what the doctor is saying?

Chapter 36

THREE DAYS PASS. The sun rises like an inferno, orange and enormous. A sign, I am sure, my dad will be better.

My mother, my sister, and I have been sleeping in shifts on the foam green couch in the waiting room. Three soldiers on duty. Three soldiers keeping guard. And when the nurse comes in, carrying a stack of new magazines, she tells us he is better. She says, "He is responding to pain."

This is, apparently, a good sign, a positive sign.

But my father is hurting.

In these final hours, as the day moves forward, people, faceless forms, drift in and out. Seats are filled and then emptied, like a child's game of musical chairs. Doctors and nurses hurry down halls, white coats flowing behind them, their soft-soled shoes silent against the tiled floor. Elevator doors open and close, telephones ring, announcements echo paging doctors, and we pace, keeping step with strangers' ankles.

I am in the hospital hall leaning over the drinking fountain when I see them coming forward like a firestorm.

Something is different in their step, something ominous, and there are too many of them walking toward me. I back into the waiting room and tell my mother and my sister, "The doctors are coming."

And suddenly, there they are, looking at us. White forms leaning against a pastel wall. The air conditioner, the only sound for moments, strains against the late June sun pouring through the expansive glass. Magazines on the window ledge flutter open. One doctor sits down. Another stands beside him, near a nurse. They are watching us—the waiting people—the patient's wife and daughters.

The sitting doctor clears his throat. I hate him instantly. I want to throw my hands up and press them over his moving mouth, mute his words.

He crosses his leg and looks at us.

He explains what happened, making certain not to leave a space where some errant hope might erroneously crash through and challenge what he has to say. He has to speak quickly, all in one breath. He says something again about the surgery and other words I cannot hear. There is no diagram now, nowhere to divert our eyes, no chance to look away.

The doctor clears his throat again. "We are so sorry. He's gone."

Gone? Gone where?

That's the thing about euphemisms. They never speak the truth. They leave all sorts of questions and dangling expectations. "Gone" would imply he'll return, or he's just momentarily slipped away. Around the corner. Off to the nearest store. Gone might mean there would be footsteps to follow, tracks in the snow, a place to set at the table for later.

Gone would not necessarily mean "never coming back."

Chapter 37

WE GO IN REVERSE; we walk to the nurses' station where a nurse with dark hair and a sad, trembling smile hands us my father's black shaving kit and a small paper sack no larger than a lunch bag. In it, his wedding ring, watch, and his paratrooper bracelet. A life reduced to ounces. We move on, past the painted walls, past people in wheelchairs, and past doctors and nurses—a whirl of faces and colors, voices and sounds.

Silently, mechanically, we step into an elevator, descend, then walk across the echoing lobby floor. When the exit doors blow open, we walk out into a backdrop of summer, a day so brilliant that my father's death feels even more implausible. The loss, even in its immediacy, is so blinding that, like the day, we cannot look at it.

I don't know if, across the steaming parking lot, we walk in step, my mother, my sister, and I, or if we scatter, one or more of us staggering behind through the colored maze of cars in the lot. Finally, finding ours, climbing into the backseat, I turn as we drive away; looking out the rear window, at the light changing, at the groups of people walking by in slow motion, and the hospital growing smaller and smaller until it is an unrecognizable silhouette on a distant hill. I watch as the summer day goes by and birds flock together in a sky that looks so extraordinarily ordinary. We drive by the cottages on Route 89 and see a blur of people standing on docks. Finally, turning right, we drive down the gravel road to our summer cottage. In the late afternoon shadows it looks like any other day there. Why hasn't it been blown to smithereens?

News of my father's death has already reached the press. I remember hearing a bulletin on the car radio just as we drive in. A sentence, a string of words so inconceivable, no more comprehensible than if the words had been spoken in a foreign language. A purported fact: "Rod Serling died today at two twenty p.m." There is more. Something about the open-heart surgery. Something about how he had another heart attack, and then . . . a flash of a hand as someone in the front seat—my mother?—clicks off the radio mid-sentence.

As if we can stop it if we don't hear it, turn back time. Make it not be true.

Don't let the words into the house. Hurry! Slam the doors! Lock the windows, shut the curtains! Stand guard!

I find that what is left behind, what remains initially, defies the reality of my father's death and perpetuates false hope. His shoes by the door, his comb by the sink still holding a few strands of his hair, papers on his desk, mail just that day addressed to him; all concrete acknowledgments of his presence, possibilities of his return, challenged only by the sudden, insidious silence of the house, the low murmur of voices in the living room, the sea of dark, crushed faces.

That first night, Rochelle stays in one of the bedrooms, some friends in the other. Jodi and her husband are in the cottage and so I sleep in my parents' bed beside my mother. Something I haven't done since I was a little girl. I listen to the voices in the hall, the toilet flushing, someone whispering for the dog, and doors almost soundlessly closing. I look at my mother in the darkness; I can just make her out in the moonlight. She is curled on my father's side, her brown hair spread across the sheet, a pillow in her arms. Is it my father's? For a moment I watch her and listen to her breathe until, somehow, I am asleep, too. When I wake in the early morning light, I am confused, startled to find my mother beside me and for a nanosecond, I have forgotten where I am and what has happened and that my father is dead and that I am not in my room at all, but theirs, and in that instant, I realize that I have wet the bed.

Sometimes, evenings, I seek refuge in my father's closet. Closing the bedroom door, I hide in there, surrounded by him, his ties, his shirts, his Mr. Rogers sweater, his soft, camel-colored sports coat that still smells of his aftershave. On the floor his blue slippers, worn at the heel just like the ones he has in California. As if he has walked in the same pair from coast to coast.

Someone asks me—was it the minister or my mother?—if I want to say anything at the memorial service.

In the late afternoon, I sit at my father's desk and write several pages. I later give them to the minister. He asks if I want to read what I have written at the service at Cornell's Sage chapel but I cannot. He will read it for me:

> *The winter was so cold and endless. I couldn't wait until the season would take on a warmer color and when it finally changed and the sun bent down offering us the summer's warmth, my father had a heart attack and I wished that the season would retrace its steps. And I wished with all my heart that it would be winter once again, seizing us with her bitterly cold and endless days.*

Never have I known this depth of pain and loneliness. Never had I realized how insignificant so many things were until now—emotions that cannot be turned on and off with a change of colors.

It's hardest at night when all the sounds of the day have ceased, most of the people have gone home and thoughts of him fill me. I'll remember something he's done . . . and smile and laugh out loud. And I'll remember him kissing me on the forehead or the way he said, "I love you." . . . Mostly I remember his eyes. My father had very intense, yet soft and gentle eyes.

Sitting in his office, he surrounds me. All the things he's collected through the years—pictures of himself as a child in his Boy Scout uniform smiling the same smile. A little boy—he never really did grow up. He had that rare quality of being able to hold on to the things one usually leaves behind. Most people can never envision their father as a child—can only hear stories and see pictures that are only moments of their many moments. But I feel that I almost grew up with him because he shared so much of himself with me. He was the kind of person who when he told you a story, no matter how many times you heard it—he made you laugh.

He gave so much of himself and touched so many people's lives. So many loved him. So many will remember.

If there had been some way that I could have slammed that door shut so that the doctors couldn't have gotten in, that final time to empty us—I would have. I would have locked it forever because it will never seem right to me that a man who loved life so much—so very much—had to leave it. I thank God, only, for never allowing him to know that he was going. I feel bitter and filled with a pain that goes beyond words. My first thoughts, my last thoughts—even most of my in between thoughts are all of him.

My father . . . my friend . . . who passed through my life for a very short time . . . and loved . . . and then had to go, still loving.

Another color will come. Leaves will fall and summer will be done; but my father will remain in every color, every season. He will never really be gone and I will continue to speak to him each day and hope that someday he will be able to show me he can hear me.

Though small of stature, he was a giant . . . and I love him.

I have to believe what I have written. How my father will never be gone. The notion that he will not be back is too shattering to consider, as if to suddenly comprehend the distance to the sky.

Chapter 38

I HAVE NO RECOLLECTION of the planning, implementation, or the scheduling of the service in Ithaca. Only the memory that there will be one held simultaneously in California for his friends there and that a few days before, his close friend, Dick Berg, flies in from Los Angeles. A guardian angel with sad, dark eyes, arriving in the middle of the night and appearing suddenly the next morning at the kitchen table, just as the sun began to beat against the shimmering, green lake. Dick is there, and he is taking care of things. Screening calls. Telling someone, "No, the family doesn't have anything to say. No, they don't want to be interviewed outside the church." He becomes our voice when we can attach no thought to words.

But then he has to go, leaving behind what he will say at the West Coast memorial service:

That was the essence of our friend. Wisdom tempered with fallibility, sweet enduring love and its corollary fear of loss, feisty courage laced with wit.

It's been said that he worked hard and played hard. That isn't so. He played with the enthusiasm of an innocent. And the work, in fact, came naturally. Relatively speaking, of course. For the dramatist's craft is a highly sophisticated one, and surely he was one of its most gifted and innovative practitioners.

But where his peers may have anguished over the creative process, Rod woke up each day saying, "Let me tell you a story." This was his badge, his thrust, his passkey into our lives. He was eternally the new boy on the block trying to join our games. And he penetrated the circle by regaling us with those many fragments of his Jewish imagination . . . intellectual stories, fantastic stories, hilarious stories, stories of social content, even one-liners about man's lunacy.

However they were always seen through his prism, becoming never less than his stories. And because he came to us with love . . . seeking our love . . . we invariably let him tell us a story. And how much richer we are for it.

He ends with: "And that's it. No literary critiques or biographical footnotes are required. They are a matter of public record. But just for the personal record . . . please believe this, Rod. That wasn't the sound of a rototiller back in May. It was the peel of thunder. And we all heard it loud and clear."

For a while there is a steady stream of people coming and going. My friend Ken is there. I remember him hugging me, his eyes red and his cheek wet against mine, and then suddenly Julie and Rhoda Golden arrive. Did they stay a day? Longer? Time has no meaning. Like living on the moon. We are floating through space where there is no logic, no gravity, just these days of people passing in and out, passing by, the trampled faces of my father's friends.

And then they have to go, too, get on with their own lives, leaving behind the almost deafening silence of the house, doors quietly opened, closed, locked. The dogs' nails clicking across the kitchen floor, clocks ticking, moving forward. All of the stillness so incongruous to what it should be, what it was, with my father there. It isn't merely his physical presence that has vanished; it is the sounds that he takes with him. His cards slapping the kitchen table, his bellowing laughter, his voice on the phone, his calls to us from the porch when we are outside on summer nights. "Who wants to go get ice cream?" "Who wants to play miniature golf?" "Who wants to go swimming?" "Who wants to go for a boat ride?" His voice talking to the dogs, his snore from the hammock that suddenly, unimaginably, now swings empty in the yard.

Nothing, not even the memorial service—a blur of faces and voices and a daring blue sky—or the silent, dead house, is as unassailable as the day when my father's clothes are removed, his closet emptied in a slow progression, up and down the stairs. Someone—who—their arms filled with stacks piled high, a myriad of colors: shirts, pants, slippers, sweaters, jackets, belts, coats, robe, and a red tie that slips from the pile and floats to the ground.

When everything has been taken, when the screen door closes a final time, I look at my uncle rocking on the porch, rocking in my father's shoes, and I wonder, with everything tangible gone, what can I touch now?

Days later? Weeks? Final arrangements must be made. It had apparently been decided that my dad would be buried in the cemetery near the cottage. Years before he and my mother had discussed it and planned it as part of some insurance, so that when the time came it would all be taken care of. But where, exactly? That hadn't been decided. They could not have anticipated this day actually happening—and happening so soon—that day years ago when they signed the necessary papers. After they'd passed them back across the table to the attorney, then stood, pushed back their chairs, and left.

They could not have imagined what would follow: my father falling to his knees, the surgery, the madness when his heart finally gives up, just stops, and the doctors cover him. They must have covered him, then backed away, their footsteps silent down the hall, like thieves, to find us, their eyes searching the room, their mouths moving, speaking, two words, it takes only two words: "He's gone." And then the crash landing.

We walk on the gravel road of the cemetery. The tree branches rub in the wind, creating an eerie whine, a kind of orchestra for ghosts. It is frightening there, even with the sunlight pouring through the trees. Shadows pass across the tombstones. Some are ancient, crumbled, fallen. Clearly no one has been here recently. There has been no thought, no prayer, no one to remember or to tend. It is as if for decades no hand has brushed away a leaf. No one has knelt, weeping, dampening a name with life.

We walk quietly, deferentially, looking for a place to bury my father's urn.

It is warm in the cemetery. Isn't it warm? It is summer. Why am I freezing? Is anyone saying anything? Is my sister there? Or just my mother? I remember only my mother—mother duck, me the obedient duckling, following.

And then her asking, "Here? Should we bury him here? He'd like this tree. Wouldn't he like this tree?"

There is a mutual, unspoken recognition of the absurdity of the question. A nervous laugh. My father would have diffused that moment. He would have made some slightly off-color remark or a joke.

We would have laughed, and our laughter would have temporarily stalled that lacerating grief.

It is agreed. Someone speaks, someone decides. We will bury him by the tree.

Eventually the flood of cards and calls slows, and my mother begins to take long walks at dusk. Sometimes Jodi and I panic, calling out for her through the darkness. "Mom? Mom?!" And no answer. We never learn where she goes those nights, alone, walking in the dark.

Sometimes my sister goes up to the field by herself, and I can hear her crying in the distance. When I meet her at the door, her face is wet with despair.

We grieve separately. We still do, but I understand now why the wounded set off alone. Survival after such loss is an uncertain prospect, and grief and grieving, ultimately autonomous. There can be no set, appropriate measure of time, no prescribed formula to follow. Initially anesthetizing, this is, at last, an agonizing process.

As these first days of my father's absence grow impossibly to weeks, then months with different names, the hammock fills with autumn leaves, piles of brilliant colors, shriveling, scattering, finally blowing away. Suddenly, then, snow is falling, and the ultimate question remains: How, when, does this happen, seasons changing, and life moving on?

Chapter 39

My mother is in California. At some point there had been discussion about my taking time off from college and going with her, but a decision is made; hers—not the one I chose. "You need to go back to school," she had said, sitting very close to me. I was crying. She was insistent. So pragmatic. So convincing. "You need to get on with your life . . . staying with me won't help either of us right now." And so a few weeks later, I am back at school and she is there, in California, alone.

I don't know how my mother manages in that big empty house, memories of my father, his empty office in the backyard, the stunning realization of his absence assaulting her at every turn. She takes classes on stock investment and finance, educating herself in areas my dad usually took care of. She sees friends, stays busy, and seems to keep her sadness at bay.

Jodi, too, is moving on. She goes to nursing school; a decision motivated in part, by watching and being impressed by all the nurses in the hospital taking care of our father. Like my mother, she, too, seems to be coping. Why can't I?

Sometime during that year, I take a class called "Death and Dying." We learn how different cultures and religions deal with death. We learn the different rituals, burial procedures, and beliefs, and we see how occupation, religion, and social class all affect mourning. We talk about suicide and the terminally ill and the death penalty. We read a book by Elizabeth Kubler Ross and learn the various stages of grief: denial, anger, bargaining, depression, and finally, acceptance.

At the end of the class I receive an "A."

Proof positive I am healed, prepared to move on. I have accepted my dad's passing. Only I still can't say "death." I say "passing." I am extremely anxious and experiencing what the textbooks call "complicated grief" or "prolonged grief." I am having panic attacks, moments where I feel I can't breathe. I am becoming agoraphobic, but I don't think this is even a word back then or if so, rarely used. I don't know what is happening to me. I am prescribed Valium. Here's what it does: Takes the edge off. Here's what it doesn't do: Bring my father back.

I go home to LA on a school vacation, but it doesn't feel like home. I want to sleep all day and stay awake at night. In the darkness I can pretend my father is just upstairs, and there is no light to challenge that.

Lying in my twin bed I think about when I was little, spending hours playing hide-and-seek with the dogs. I would tell them to stay and I'd run off and hide, sometimes flying by my dad in the hall. Then I'd call them, trying not to giggle when I heard them bounding up the stairs to find me. I wonder if my dad is just hiding. Behind the door or crouched behind the living room chair. Maybe behind the tree in the yard. I think about that possibility, or the alternative one: that I may be losing my mind.

Dick Berg and another close friend of my dad's and the family's, Hal, call and take me to lunch on separate occasions.

What do we talk about? How do we fill that enormous empty space at the table?

I see the sadness in their eyes, the strain in their smiles as their hands rest on the table, folding and unfolding.

On television I sometimes see or hear about my dad when I least expect to. One night Johnny Carson suddenly is talking about *The Twilight Zone*. Referring to my father, Johnny says, "God bless him."

Back at school, I do just what I need to do to pass. I go to my classes, eat meals in the cafeteria, and meet with friends, and Ken, though less and less. I inadvertently exile myself into a stunned silence. A month turns to another, nothing defining one day from the next except the cold, and then, suddenly it would seem, the green of summer.

A year has passed since I have seen my father, and we are back at the cottage. It is the eve of the anniversary of his death. I need to find a Yahrzeit candle by sundown and haven't found one in any of the grocery stores. I am desperate. Finally Rochelle remembers that her cousin knows the son of the owners, the Geldwerts, who own a Mom and Pop grocery store on Plain Street in Ithaca. We race to the store and I ask the woman if she has Yahrzeit candles, and she walks me over to the shelf. I feel tremendously relieved, and then speechless when I see the numbers tattooed on her arm. The Geldwerts had been at Auschwitz.

At sundown I light the candle. It burns on a shelf in the corner of the room. I stare at the photograph I have placed beside it. There, my father looking at whoever took the picture. My father smiling, alive. I check the candle throughout the next day. It continues to burn long past the hour my dad died, long into the dark night. There is some comfort in that as we all pass by it.

John Palmer, a friend and one-time agent of my father who I met with my dad in Chicago, sends a rose bush with small, red buds. It arrives in a floral delivery truck driving

slowly down the cottage road. Rochelle helps me place it beside the others my dad planted.

Although she lives in Ithaca, my sister and her husband
spend time at the cottage while she studies for her nursing
degree. I often see her sitting cross-legged on the couch, a
stack of books by her side. Sometimes I see her just staring,
and I'll wonder if she's thinking about Dad. Occasionally I
will sit beside her and will start to say something about how
she's doing. I want to ask her, "Do you miss Dad? Do you
think about him all the time?" but the words never come and
I sit, for the most part, silent, watching as she highlights pages
in her book and then looks back at me with a sad, empty
smile.

Another slow passage of days, weeks, and months, and again I
am back at school. My mother encourages me to push myself
through. I try. I try to stay focused on my classes.

One day a friend introduces me to someone she had dated
and who later became a friend of hers. He graduated from
another college two years before. We begin to go out.

I knew he was bright. I thought he was kind. Within
months he asks me to marry him. Despite the drastically lim-
ited knowledge we have of one another, and the fact that he
tells me if I say no, we can't see each other, I don't want him
to vanish, and so I agree.

I don't know what either of us was thinking.

Hal, now in psychiatrist mode, calls me one night from
California. He does not mince words. He says, "I'm not sure
you realize what you're doing. You are trying to replace your
father."

On some level I am certain I already see this. I must realize
that, for my part, I am completely absent in this relationship.
It eventually collapses. Not, though, without the inevitable
ending: the anger, the rush to pack things, shirts, pants, every-

thing pulled from drawers, then shoved into bags; the irate words, his, mine, slicing at one another, the car rushing away, and all the drama and sadness and misery you're quite certain will never fade away. And it doesn't fade for me, not for a long time. But this is a grief I can touch, I can deal with and manage. This is a tangible grief. I almost welcome this loss because it is a surface sadness that seals up the much greater loss. It distracts me from grieving for my father.

I move back into my dorm room and at some point call Hal. After an hour or so, he calls me back with a name of someone to talk to. The person he recommends for me attended the same medical school as Hal. Dr. Feinstein practices out of his home, here in New York, and as it turns out, not more than a few miles away.

It takes me a while to make the appointment—months in fact.

I sit quietly in Dr. Feinstein's office every other week or so. I offer virtually nothing. Dr. Feinstein nods a lot and doesn't say much, either. Silence pervades in those early sessions; expectations feel minimal, manageable. It's a steep price to pay, though, to just show up, and the panic is increasing, the agoraphobia escalating, too. I am becoming more and more incapacitated. I don't want to go out, don't want to be with friends, don't want to be in social situations where I'll have to come up with some explanation as to why I am suddenly fleeing. One day Dr. Feinstein asks, "Why do you think this is happening?" Initially I am frustrated with him, hate him even. "I don't know," I spit back. "Why do you think it is?" He stares back, offering nothing. My heart is pounding, my hands sweating. I want to leave. I start to. "Sit down, Anne. Put words to what you're feeling." What he is saying feels so stupid and clichéd, but I am afraid enough that I try. I look at the books on the shelf just past him and say, "Because I miss my dad? Because I hate every morning that I wake up and realize he's not there, that I'm not going to see him ever again and because I don't know if I can accept that, live with that, move on." I know that my face is bright red, I'm shaking, but I'm talking, I'm finally talking, and Dr. Feinstein is, too. "I think that's exactly right," he says, and if nothing else, it's a start.

My appointments are switched from every other week to three times a week. Months on end. Things seem to move in slow motion, I feel water-logged, deadened. Still, in June 1977 I graduate from college with a degree in Elementary Education and a minor in English. On graduation day, Ken pulls me into the pond with him, a tradition at the college. We are soaked and shivering and ridiculous, yet, for a moment, I am laughing. There's a photograph: me looking like a normal girl.

This is what I remember from that day: my dad is absent in those rows of applauding parents; I have a diploma; the water is freezing; I am already numb; the cap and gown need to be returned; I need to do what Dr. Feinstein is suggesting. I need to go to my father's grave. Yet still, I can't.

Sometimes I hear one of my dad's commercials. I am not focused on the product or the message, only his voice. "Stopping pollution is a people thing. It means cooperation and understanding. It means getting together and working..." Hearing him is surreal in the solitude of those months. Initially jarring, it becomes comforting. I close my eyes. My father is there.

Chapter 40

A YEAR PASSES, TWO? I am anxious and scared, and Dr. Feinstein offers, "Maybe you don't want to get better? Maybe staying like this helps you hold on to your father?" I'm certain of two things: (1) he's wrong and (2) he's an ass. I tell him, "I would never choose to be like this."

I manage, somehow, a flight home, back to California. My mother has prepared me, somewhat. "There's something you should know." Already I'd wanted to hold the phone away. I didn't want to hear these words. "I'm seeing someone," she had said. "A man named Norman." He lives perhaps an hour's drive away.

Norman is nice enough, but he's not my father, and I make certain to grab my dad's chair at the dinner table, just in case he, unwittingly, does. Funny, the idea of Norman in my mother's bed seems more manageable than him taking my father's place at the table.

My mother is careful, sensitive. She doesn't want me to know that they're sleeping together, and to punctuate the point, the bed in the guest room is left unmade, as if he had slept in it. She doesn't have to go to these measures; I'm hardly a kid, but I appreciate her gesture.

One night she and Norman arrange for me to go out with Norman's nephew and for the four of us to go to a place called The Magic Castle in Hollywood. I'm not certain why I agree to this or why I think I'll be able to manage, but, armed with two Valium, I decide, for my mother's sake, I'll give it a try. I remember almost nothing of the evening. Not Norman's nephew's name, not what he looked like, not whether it was raining or clear, not what we talked about, not if we all went together or drove separately. Only that I had a panic attack before we'd even sat down to dinner. That I'd tried to fight it, tried to reason with myself, tried to remember the words and techniques Dr. Feinstein had taught me: "Breathe in deeply and slowly, tighten and relax your muscles." I tried everything. Even the Valium in my purse. But nothing was working. Nothing. And I was sweating, my heart was pounding. I was dizzy, terrified; I had to get out of there. I finally found my way to the entrance, started to push open the enormous doors, and this I remember clearly: I was told by someone who worked there, someone sitting in a chair in the dark, someone who did not smile when he said, "You will need to say, 'Open Sesame' before the doors will open."

The years have softened the memory of that night, but at the time I was quite certain I was dying. I felt badly for my mother, devastated that I couldn't get it together for her, for me. I was so consumed by my sadness, in what I thought was merely self-pity. I had no understanding, no grasp of this grief.

The only thing I knew for certain was that I was drowning and something needed to change.

When I returned back east a few days later, I told Dr. Feinstein about the evening. "I can't control my thoughts, my panic. I can't relax. Nothing I try stops this." I was desperate, and after a few more sessions he prescribed an antidepressant, Elavil. He explained, "It will take several weeks before you will feel any effects." I hated to be taking medication. I'd only taken the Valium in emergency situations, but those emergencies were beginning to run together, and were defining the days.

One night Rochelle convinces me to go to some movie starring Peter Falk. It's a terrible movie, and I am not paying much attention until suddenly Peter Falk turns in profile and for an instant it isn't Peter Falk at all but my father. The black wavy hair, certain features projected on the large screen, they all blur together and I find myself weeping, trying to muffle my sobs. Rochelle looks at me. "What is it?! What's the matter?!" But I can't tell her. Not in this crowded theater with this stupid movie blaring, not in a whispered response. It's all suddenly too much and we leave, making our way out the doors and into the night. We stand beneath the lights of the parking lot until the cold becomes evident and my crying subsides, all the while Rochelle trying to comfort me and me stupidly telling her, "I'm sorry you're missing the movie."

Later that week, another appointment with Dr. Feinstein, and I tell him what happened. He is quiet for a moment, folds his hands on his lap, and tells me, "As the antidepressants reduce the anxiety, it is normal to feel the grief more acutely."

I guess this is the good news?

More weeks, more months, more appointments with Dr. Feinstein.

Memories of my father are palpable, but for so long I haven't been able to face them. I haven't been able to let them in. I begin to watch his show *A Storm in Summer*. I get a cassette version from the archives at Ithaca College. I watch it over and over and listen to the lines. He talks about the impact of death on those left behind: "You feel like your life has

ended. That some vital part of your body has been stripped
away. That you'll never heal, never smile, never laugh. That the
sorrow is just unbearable and that the tears will never end.
But they do. Somehow, someway, the crying does come to an
end."

I try to memorize those words. I take them as a message
from my father, a sign. I finally, gradually, let go. And when I
do, when I allow myself to go back, to grieve, I begin to understand that I can find him again.

Eventually it becomes clear the medication is also working; the panic begins to dissipate. I am looking at Dr. Feinstein, not away, and talking more and more. But grieving is
not tidy. Not organized or easy. And still, I cannot go to my
father's grave.

Chapter 41

ROCHELLE AND I ARE both working at BOCES—a school for children with special needs. Three years have passed since that day I walked, numb, from the pond after graduation. And five years since I last spoke to my father.

I am an assistant teacher working primarily with a little girl named Christine who has been diagnosed as emotionally disturbed. She also has mild cerebral palsy. I love our time together and think she is brilliant. Every afternoon I wait for her in the school library. She has a limp, and I can hear her foot dragging and her talking to herself from down the hall far away. She always smiles when she sees me—her face lighting up, perfection, despite her imperfect world.

I have found that exercising has helped curb the anxiety, and so I swim at the Y in the afternoons after work.

One Friday night, Rochelle and I go to a restaurant/bar owned by her cousin in downtown Ithaca. Across the room in one of those movie moments I see a man with dark hair and a beard. He quite literally takes my breath away. He is sitting in a corner with some people.

We don't speak, but I find myself thinking about him the next several days, and a week later I go back to the same bar.

It's Halloween night. Complete mayhem. Through a maze of people I get a fleeting glimpse of him sitting in the corner. Somehow the crowd pushes us closer, and we start talking, shouting really, through all the noise and music. We see each other again the next week, and the next, and finally I agree to go with him for coffee.

His name is Doug and he tells me he has lived in Ithaca for fifteen years, graduated from Cornell, and is an architect with his own design/build business. He says he is divorced and is a father. I am a little wary when I hear the last part and learn he is thirty-four, nine years older than I. Quick calculation reveals that when I was playing school with my Irish setters, leading them out to recess, clacking in my mother's blue high heels, Doug was about to begin college.

He takes me to his house, and standing in his living room, he explains it used to be the garage. I am impressed, struck as much by his talent as by those sky blue eyes. But I am also cautious, familiar with the magnetism of a new relationship; the perfection of those first stilled moments. I understand well that surreal light of distortion that comes from not really knowing someone. The initial politeness, graciousness, that certain reserved kindness. I know how a person might initially look flawless in unfamiliarity, and I also know how quickly the simplest word can cut through that illusion, shred that picture. Someone you think you know can be entirely different, and when the mask slips, someone you really never knew at all.

At first I am a little cautious when I think of Hal's words about my last relationship—"You are trying to replace your dad"—and I wonder how my dad would feel about my dating someone nine years older than I am, but the more Doug and I are together, the more that fear begins to dissipate.

When we're not working, we are almost always together, and there is a lightness, an easiness. Even something else, something I haven't felt in a long time—joy.

One day I take him swimming with me at the YMCA (having no idea that sliding into the pool is the last thing he really wants to do). He tells me, "I had to buy this suit today." He pauses with a little embarrassment and then adds, "It's the only one I could find."

It's a silly suit with sailboats on it, like one a child might wear. Neither of us realizes that he has put it on backward until he starts to get into the water and we both notice at the same time and start laughing. He quickly swims over to me, and by now we are both laughing so hard that he swallows a large gulp of water and has to make his way to the side of the pool. He is coughing and sputtering intensely, and when the lifeguard leans down beside him and asks, "Are you okay?" we become even more hysterical.

Things feel easy with Doug. We like the same movies and some of the same books. We share similar values and tastes, and our politics are the same. And perhaps what I am most touched by—what I love especially is that when he watches a really good play or a sad one or sees someone with extreme talent, or even if he's just tremendously moved, he's not embarrassed by the tears rolling down his cheeks.

The fact that he adopted a three-year-old African American child, Michael, is something that would have impressed my dad enormously.

After several months, I move in with Doug. One morning I make breakfast for him and two of his kids, Nicole, eleven and Michael, twelve. I am a little nervous and want them to like me. I decide, for some reason I can't fathom now, to add a little vanilla to the scrambled eggs. After all, it tastes so good in chocolate chip cookies is my early morning reasoning.

When his kids wake up, walking sleepily into the kitchen, I tell them in a cheery voice, "Breakfast!"

They sit down yawning and stretching and finally begin to eat the eggs I have placed before them. Delighted smiles are what I'm hoping for, but instead when I look at them, they are expressionless. I then take a bite, mumble "Oh, God, that's awful" with my mouth full, and immediately spit the eggs out. They are such troopers to be so nice to their dad's girl-friend. By then we are all laughing, noisily clearing away the plates and Doug is already stirring a new batch of normal scrambled eggs, looking at me over his shoulder and smiling.

In the summer of 1983, when I am twenty-seven, Doug and I marry on the cottage porch. It has been eight years since my father's death. The progression of our wedding day is a blur in my memory, but I remember my sister couldn't find her shoes and had to borrow someone's. They were too large, and I re-member her clomping down the stairs. I know that I forgot my flowers and that my mother, who walked me across the grass, whispered, "Where are your roses?" and after a fleeting instant of deliberation, I raised my hand to the minister mouthing what he couldn't possibly understand, "I'll be right back!" and raced into the house to grab them. Everyone laughed and applauded when I returned. I held the flowers up and pointed at them. Still there must have been some who wondered if I had just changed my mind.

I barely remember the minister reading the vows we chose, but I know he made reference to the children we might one day have and what we wished for them. I remember imagin-ing these barefooted, faceless, nameless children running through sprinklers across that sunlit, green summer lawn. And I remember, too, someone toasting my father: "To Rod in ab-sentia."

Chapter 42

ONE NOVEMBER WEEKEND AFTERNOON, a few months after the wedding, Doug and I are talking in the kitchen. I don't remember the conversation, how it segues back to my father. But I do remember him asking, asking again the second time in a month, "Do you think you're ready to visit the grave?"

I don't recall, either, what finally convinces me to go. Only that we are suddenly in the car driving the thirty some minutes to get there and that the day is cold and gray and colorless and, instantly, it seems, we are pulling into the cemetery, past the black iron gate, past benches and the small dark chapel, and Doug has turned the motor off and we are sitting in a pale blue Honda; the car, the seats, the dashboard the only color for miles. Even our coats, our gloves, our hats are gray. There is no one around. Not even a caretaker. Doug looks at me. I don't look back at him. I know what he's going to say, and I don't want to hear it.

"Go on," he says, gently touching my shoulder, leaning

over me and opening the car door. A gust of wind blows, and the last of fall's leaves brush against the door.

"You can do this," he says.

I turn my body to step out of the car. My legs feel numb, like they may not work, like I've been in a wheelchair for years and am suddenly miraculously told "You can walk."

"Go on," he says again. I start walking in the direction I think I need to. My hands are in my coat pockets as I walk quickly, stumbling. I am looking for the tree I remembered my mother saying eight years before, "He'd like that tree. Wouldn't he like that tree?" Was it a maple? An oak? How tall would it be now?

It's cold, so cold. I pull my coat around me and look at gravestone after gravestone after gravestone. Name after name. None of them his.

Where was that stupid tree? If I don't find it, can it not be true? After a few moments, I run back to Doug. He has taken his gloves off and is blowing on his hands. It's so cold. I am about to tell him, "We should leave," but he looks up at me and says again, "Go on, it's okay, hon," urging me with a nod of his head and those clear blue eyes.

I turn around. And again pass more gravestones. Not his. None of them his.

And then.

My father's name, his birth date, the date of his death. WWII paratrooper. A small American flag.

And something else; someone has written something on a piece of masking tape attached to the flag. Three words.

"He left friends."

In that instant comes the finality and inconsolability I'd feared; a sorrow so forceful that it pulls me to my knees. It is only moments before Doug comes running. He picks me up from where I have collapsed sobbing.

We stay what seems like a long time. The only sounds

when I stop crying are some birds in the distance and an occasional car from far away. I see a tree nearby, presumably *the* tree, but I don't recognize it. It's been so many years. It must be taller now, wider; it's a different season, colors change. Everything does.

It is clear that I have stumbled here without a map. And so these perfectly etched letters beside me are even more startling as they spell out my father's name. As I kneel, trying to take it all in, trying to maintain balance in the unreality of it all, I think about his parents, and how if my dad's friend hadn't been there that day when the Japanese soldier took aim at him, it might very well have been them kneeling where I do now. That thought, that fleeting image in my mind of my grandparents receiving the news from some officer—who hadn't kept walking to another house after all—but stopped at theirs, up the steps, to tell them that their son had died in battle, fills me with almost as much anguish as I feel all these years later being the one to wipe the leaves away from my father's name. And I wonder, could his parents have survived that loss?

Some papers blow around in the wind, and as Doug and I sit down, I can't help thinking if maybe I thought I would never find my father's grave, that maybe I had never meant to, that I could just go on pushing against this loss. But as we sit there together, the light slowly leaking from the sky, I realize that each time I look at my father's stone, my gaze stays a little longer until very lightly, very tentatively, I trace his name.

The sky grows darker and the chill in the air is relentless. I look again at the message on the masking tape, in the faded blue letters, and then we get up and turn to go.

Maybe I find some comfort in this message left behind. Perhaps there is some element of peace, at last, not only in the realization that I have finally done this, but also in the quiet and the recognition that I don't need to be here to find my father.

The following summer, I begin to watch *The Twilight Zone*—surprised by the number I haven't seen. I am sure I am doing this more to see my father than the actual show. I start with the first season episode, "Walking Distance," the one about the need yet the impossibility of going home. It is the one that is the most biographical, the one my dad symbolically reenacted every summer when he drove from the cottage back to his hometown.

I randomly select another episode—this one titled "In Praise of Pip." It is another of my dad's stories on the theme of returning to the past, but this one has an achingly sad twist poignantly acted by Jack Klugman.

Klugman plays Max Phillips, a small-time bookie who knows he has been deficient as both a father and a man:

> *Submitted for your approval, one Max Phillips, a slightly-the-worse-for-wear maker of book, whose life has been as drab and undistinguished as a bundle of dirty clothes. And, though it is very late in his day, he has an errant wish that the rest of his life might be sent out to a laundry to come back shiny and clean, this to be a gift of love to a son named Pip . . .*

In a spasm of remorse for his wasted life, Max gives money back to one of his unlucky clients. While facing the music with his boss for this act of kindness, he gets a call that his soldier son, Pip, has been wounded in Vietnam and is dying.

In true *Twilight Zone* fashion, Pip and his father get another chance together. Max, who has been shot by the crime boss, finds himself in a closed amusement park, the same one he and Pip always visited. There he sees his son as a little boy. Suddenly the lights of the park come on and the two of them relive simple pleasures, running through the park until Pip tells him, "The hour is up and . . . and I'm dying." Once again, in real time Max offers God a trade; his life for Pip's. In the final scene, Pip, in uniform and walking with a cane from his injury, is back at the amusement park, recalling with fondness how he used to come here with his late father.

The episode is filmed at the Pacific Ocean Park, the same amusement park on the Santa Monica Pier that my dad took my sister and me to.

What is so striking, so personal, and so moving about this particular story is some of the dialogue. In this episode, Jack Klugman says to his son, "Who's your best buddy, Pip?"

"You are, Pop."

Just like the words of my dad's and my routine.

I watch this episode on a rented projector in a darkened room of our lake house one hot July afternoon and remain there a long while after the film has ended. Through the screen door I can hear the boats on the lake below. An occasional shout rises as a water skier falls and in response, a motor quickly shuts down. I hear the gulls' cries in the ensuing silence and then someone shouting, "Okay, ready," and a boat speeding away, transforming the water, reviving the waves slapping thunderously at the shoreline.

I am cognizant of all of the summer sounds in those moments and of this life that moves forward despite my absent father. I am still haunted by the void, by the reality of this empty space, and yet, these past thirty minutes spent watching this *Twilight Zone* have brought a reconnection with him in a most unexpected way.

In the episode's closing narration, I watch my dad saying, "The ties of flesh are deep and strong, the capacity to love is a vital, rich, and all-consuming function of the human animal, and you can find nobility and sacrifice and love wherever you might seek it out; down the block, in the heart, or in The Twilight Zone."

I find it in a darkened room on a summer afternoon. Something invisible, inaudible, and until now, quite mistakenly presumed gone.

Epilogue

WHEN MY DAD WAS in the hospital, he asked for his tape recorder. A year or so after going to his grave, I removed the tape from my desk drawer, closed myself away in my bedroom, took a deep breath, and finally pushed PLAY and listened for the first time. There was background noise—people talking in the hall, doors closing. His voice was not the strong, dramatic, resolute one the public has come to know, and for a moment, so overwhelmed, I had to stop the tape, saddened by the weakness of his voice. I thought of him making this recording, and for an instant could see him so clearly, his black wavy hair against that white pillow. I could see him sitting up wearing a hospital gown pushing the buttons on his recorder that I pushed now.

There were long, painful pauses between his thoughts, and he turned the machine on and off several times before he began:

I thought I might jot down certain reflections that relate to what a man feels like following a heart attack. The first thing I notice,

as I speak into this thing, is I feel seriously devoid of energy,
something I have never lacked for . . .

He pauses and then,

The days are infinitely longer in the hospital, not only in
chronology and in time passing but also in the actuality of the
event. They start early and last a long time. And there is so little
during the course of the day's activity to punctuate the regimen,
that you get more of a sense of the prolongation of the day.
*   Another item: I discovered that I don't nearly have the fear of*
death that I once had. What I do have is the terrible awareness of
how little time there is to accomplish so many of the things that
you want to accomplish.
*   The other thing that seems accentuated, almost to a point of*
distortion, is the need, the desperate need you have of family, of
loved ones. When it appeared possible I might not make it, I
didn't feel so much the awful awareness of, Jesus Christ, it's
going to be me ending the earth. What seemed to me the most
predominant in my fears was that it would be the relationships
that would end.

My father makes note, too, of the humorous aspects of hospital living, and here, he laughs.

The fact that, like all good dramatists, one always, I suppose,
thinks subconsciously or at least if not preoccupiedly with the way
that it happens, the moment of the death. Whether it be
Valhallian in some way, semi-heroic, at least with the sense of the
drama . . . And how the hell did I go? Fucking around, trying to
start a rototiller, and I find that is an ignominious way of going.
Lightning maybe should strike me, or I should invent some
incredible new Lutherburbankian plant at that given crashing
moment of incredible pain as I look up and say, "Okay, God,
now you can take me, because I have discovered this new breed of
plant." But no, no. Nothing that heroic. All I was able to

accomplish was to start the engine of the rototiller, nothing more than that. Nothing more contributory.

Thirty-five years after my father's death, four decades after *The Twilight Zone* went off the air, its parables are still relevant today. But he did not believe he would be remembered. "I've pretty much spewed out everything I had to say, none of which has been particularly monumental, nothing that will stand the test of time . . . Good writing, like wine, has to age well, and my stuff is momentarily adequate."

In what was to be my father's final interview, he was asked what he wanted people to say about him a hundred years from then. He responded, "I don't care that they're not able to quote any single line that I've written. But just that they can say, 'Oh, he was a writer.' That's sufficiently an honored position for me."

Each year, the entire fifth grade in the Binghamton, New York, school district is using the episodes as a teaching tool to enlighten students about prejudice, intolerance, and scapegoating. They write my dad letters. Some are addressed, "Dear Rod," others, "Dear Mr. Serling." "We learned that you made your shows to make people better"; "Where did you get your ideas?"; "Do you want to go to Mars?"; "I liked the episode 'People Are Alike All Over' because it was sort of saying, 'Don't judge people by the ways they look'"; "I'm not sure what you would think of the world today because there are wars going on"; "If it wasn't for you, people would not know how to tell the world about what they feel is wrong. You are a great person and a wonderful role model for me and for others. One last thing, thank you." That letter is signed, "Your Fan D.J."

Of all the awards and accolades my dad received throughout his life, I believe he would have considered this program his greatest.

My father lived only fifty years, of which half represented

his professional writing and producing career. Despite the brevity of those years, his accomplishments were vast. Still, there is so much he missed.

In my mind I try to complete his unfinished life, fill in the missing pieces. I imagine him standing in a house my husband Doug designed and hear the amazement in his voice, the praise in his words. I watch my children growing up and think of the relationships that would have been between them and my dad. I see glimpses of him in both of them. As a little girl, my daughter Erica was a voracious reader. Sometimes she would read aloud in her own dramatic voice replete with different accents. When she was twelve she won an award for playwriting. My son, Sam, is named after his great-grandfathers on both my side and my husband's, and his middle name is Rodman. While a sophomore majoring in screenwriting at Ithaca College, he transferred to Emerson College, from which he graduated in Writing, Literature, and Publication, and is now pursuing his own passion for writing and poetry.

Both of my children have my dad's imagination and his quick humor. They have his sensitivity and his compassion. They would have adored my dad and he them.

What a loss that is for all, and I understand, now, the depth of my father's words when he said what I say now: "If only you had known your grandfather."

I don't go back to the cemetery very often. I know, now, he isn't there. But I often think of that message on the masking tape over the paratrooper flag that marks his grave.

The very words he had once told a college audience, that all he wanted on his gravestone was the phrase: "He left friends."

My father left behind countless friends that summer day in 1975 when the sky was too bright and the sun, scalding. He could not have known the sheer devastation so many would feel when they heard the news of his passing. Something was extinguished in us all that June day. Something quite inimitable and irreplaceable vanished.

In those difficult weeks before he went to Strong Memorial, my dad watched a movie titled *I Never Sang for My Father*. He watched it on the small television set on his office desk and when I walked by, looking for him, I saw that he was weeping.

I know, now, a final line in that movie is "Death ends a life. But it does not end a relationship."

The gifts and the lessons my father left me will last forever: Never take yourself too seriously, never miss a chance to laugh long and hard, speak out about political and social issues you believe in, use the written word as often as you can to make yourself and the world a better place, and love your children with all you've got.

My dad's death had a seismic effect on me but so did his life.

And I have to think that although time cannot ameliorate the loss or make up for all of the years we didn't have together, I am so fortunate to have had this most extraordinary man as my father.

"Who's your best friend, Pops?"

"You are, Dad."

The memory is not specific to any particular season or year; it could be a replay of any. Except each year we are a little older and after a while there is a different dog and the car is a different model, a different color, circa fifties, sixties, and then the seventies. But beyond that, nothing really changes.

My father is driving. I am beside him. We are going to look for the dogs; once again they have roamed off. My dad calls them "the friendly travelers."

On this trip, we are driving along the lake road, looking out at the yellowing August grass. One of us begins to sing and the other immediately joins in. It is a well-rehearsed ritual. We jump from song to song, stopping only when we forget the words and can't make up any more. Usually we sing rounds. He begins; I join in. "Michael, Row Your Boat Ashore" is a favorite. The car windows are down, and there is warmth and a breeze. A perfect end to a late summer day.

After a while, we catch sight of them—the setters, Michael and Maggie, lumbering way ahead into a spectacular sunset, a dramatic collage of color.

Suddenly they turn in the opposite direction and don't even glance at us as they pass by.

Even after we see them, we are still singing, my dad and I. Our voices, perhaps just slightly off-key, are nonetheless strong, content, confident, in perfect synchronization, growing slightly softer, slightly fainter, in that car following two red dogs, now within walking distance, home.

Acknowledgments

To quote my father:

On a writer's way up, he meets a lot of people and in some rare cases there's a person along the way, who happens to be around just when they're needed—perhaps just a moment of professional advice, a brief compliment to boost the ego when it's been bent, cracked and pushed into the ground, a pat on the back and… words of encouragement. . . .

In my case, there have been so many I could attribute that quote to, and I am humbled and grateful beyond words.

To Charlotte Gusay and Richard Wexler, who were there way back when.

To Dr. Tony Pane and Lee Moon for the life raft and the oars.

To Robert Gottlieb at The Trident Media Group, who called me back the same day I sent the query and passed me along to my wonderful agent, Erica Spellman Silverman, who then introduced me to Marlene Adelstein, editor extraordinaire.

To Sarah Hepola at Salon.com—Thank You! To Anna Sussman at NPR's *Snap Judgment*—equal thanks to you.

To Michaela Hamilton, I adore you, and the skilled people at Kensington Publishing.

To Robert Redford, Carol Burnett, Alice Hoffman, James Grady, Betty White, Caroline Leavitt, and Dr. Mehmet Oz, for stepping out of their busy lives to touch mine and offer cover quotes.

To Jim Evans, who read the manuscript at its conception and suffered through its many grammatical errors.

To Mark Olshaker, who tirelessly gave me "that other dimension" of my dad. I am so grateful for all your help. We got it right this time.

To Amy Boyle Johnston, for your incredible research and generosity.

To David Powers, for your keen eye.

To Julie and Rhoda Golden, old friends, great friends. Julie—thank you for taking me back to Bennett Ave, and for those wonderful mental snapshots of you and my dad as kids.

For Rochelle Mike, dear friend, who has been there through it all. . . . Thanks, too, for tirelessly reading every single version of this manuscript.

To Russell Schwen, for all of the moments I would have never known from those dark war days in 1944. Steve Trimm, for your unforgettable words; David Brenner, for the laugh about that flight with my dad to LA; Earl Hamner, for your kind memories, and Mike Newman, for giving me that glimpse of my father's passionate social conscience way back at Antioch College.

To Ron Simon, curator at the Paley Center for Media, and Susan Charlotte, producer/founding artistic director, Food for Thought.

To Dick Berg, in absentia, for your encouragement and for filling in. And Hal Arlen, too.

For Jennifer Gay Summers, Joan Barnes Flynn, Jane Powers, Pat Amato, Bob Nevin, Colleen Evans, Carolyn Olshaker, Jon and Mimi Gould, Sarah Pitkin, Dorothy Gish, Caroline Cheshire, and Brian Frey—profound gratitude and love to you all.

I am forever indebted and grateful to my friends on Facebook; the ones rediscovered and the ones newly found, to those who shared memories, and to all of you, too, who supported this book. I am so appreciative of your kindness and your friendship.

To Al Magliochetti, for your help with the photo.

To James Latta, for some great suggestions about marketing.

To Jeff and Michele Serling, forever there.

To Andy Polak, president, and Steve Schlich, webmaster, of the Rod Serling Memorial Foundation, the teachers of the Fifth Dimension Program, and Larry Kassan, director of special events at the Rod Serling School of Fine Arts and Video Festival—you all do so much to keep the legacy alive.

To my mother, for your call of endorsement after you read the manuscript, my sister for your card, and my nephew Ryan.

To Rebekah, Nicole, and Michael, my "first" wonderful kids.

To Erica, Sam, Alyssa, and to my husband, Doug. You are my lights. My life. And Doug: without your encouragement and belief, I would never have reached the end.

Index